Choosing Africa

A Midlife Journey from Mission to Meaning

Portions of this work were originally published in different forms in *The Georgetown Review, The Apalachee Review, Red Wheelbarrow Literary Magazine,* and *A Matter of Choice* (Seal Press).

Library of Congress Control Number: 2009905501

ISBN 978-1-60145-868-1

Booklocker.com, Inc.
Bangor, ME
2009

Front and back cover photos by Louis E. Bauer

See photos and more at www.choosingafrica.com

Printed in the United States of America.

Choosing Africa

A Midlife Journey from Mission to Meaning

B. Susan Bauer

To my dear friend, Joan
With love and best wishes
and continued great
adventures!
～ Susan Bauer

This Book is dedicated

To

My father, Frank S. Bilton (1921-2009)

Dad, you were a true global soul

Author's Note

Telling true stories can be as perilous a journey as the adventures that inspire them. Sugarcoating the truth or omitting the awkward or the unpleasant parts serves no good purpose. Although I affirm the accuracy of the experiences recounted in *Choosing Africa*, it has never been my intent to harm or embarrass anyone in these pages. For that reason, I have chosen to change some of the names.

This book would not be possible without the support and encouragement of many who made the experience possible. Through our years of missionary service, the Evangelical Lutheran Church in America (ELCA) encouraged us, trained us, supported us—and paid us! Special thanks to the Rev. Benyam Kassahun, the Rev. Dan Olson, the Rev. Harold Hanson, and Ms. Tanya Rosland, as well as to the dozens of congregations who sponsored us. You helped us become a bridge between two cultures.

To my students and faculty colleagues of Paulinum Seminary, some of whom have become lifelong friends, my gratitude for your patience, trust and laughter. You welcomed me into your villages, your lives, and your hearts. Your generosity showed me the true meaning of *ubuntu*: a person is only a person through other people.

To my dear friend and writing mentor, Sandra Eisdorfer, who tirelessly and carefully read this manuscript in its early stages and offered her insight and encouragement: I treasure your gifts.

To my children, Jason and Megan, it wasn't always easy having your mom and dad so far away. Thank you for allowing us the freedom to follow our dream and live our vocation.

Finally, to Lou, my soul mate and fellow adventurer, I thank you for your courage, your love, and your *joie de vivre*. Through the years you have inspired me to live a bigger life than I could have ever imagined, and you have been my cherished companion every step of the way. Is there thanks enough?

How hard it is to escape from places. However carefully one goes they hold you—you leave little bits of yourself fluttering on the fence—little rags and shreds of your very life.

Katherine Mansfield

Table of Contents

Chapter 1
A Handful of Leaves

*O*ur overnight Air Afrique flight from New York to Dakar, Senegal, had spilled us out into the transit lounge of the Yoff International Airport for our four-hour layover. My lanky husband struggled to find a comfortable position for a nap on the hard plastic chair next to mine. Despite the sticky heat and the filthy toilets, I was happy to pass those hours watching busy Africans in their colorful clothes. The men sauntered past in their brocade dashikis and elaborately embroidered *boubous*, loose-fitting shirts worn over matching trousers. No less elegant were the women in their vivid blues, greens, and yellows. Most wore tight wrap-around skirts and matching full-sleeved blouses, nipped in at the waist and flared to the hips. These were the well-heeled international African travelers. At the back of the lounge, sitting not sauntering, were tired-looking men in crumpled white shirts and trousers a bit too short for their limbs. Their wives wore Western-styled suits of soft blue and pale pink. Surrounding them was their luggage: huge shopping bags of red, white, and blue woven plastic, the kind of material I recalled seeing on lawn chairs. While I waited, I tried to pick up snatches of French conversation.

When our flight to Niamey, Niger, was announced, a herd of swarthy-looking men in long white robes charged out of the first-class lounge, and started pushing their way to the front of the line. I remembered this was an open-seating flight. Lou grabbed my hand.

"Stand your ground!" he said. "We were here first."

As we hurried across the dusty tarmac to the aircraft, the white-robed ones grumbling in our wake, I remembered the village feasts to which our study group had been invited the previous year. It was always the same. While villagers gathered in the open space outside the chief's hut and stared at our group of thirteen Americans and five drivers, the elaborately garbed village chief would say a few words of welcome. Well, more than a few. After ten minutes, everyone's gaze was fixed upon whole roasted goat on the table in front of us. The poor creature looked as if he had simply fallen asleep in the sun. There were huge bowls of *foufou* (millet porridge), rice, and groundnut stew, and plenty of bottles of Orange

1

Fanta, Coke, and Sprite. I could tell, from the expectant twitching of the crowd, that the chief was winding down. As soon as he finished speaking, the villagers surged forward and attacked the groaning board, yanking greasy hunks of meat from the sacrificial goat and filling their plates with huge spoonfuls of everything else. We had already learned an African lesson about he who hesitates.

Happy to find two seats together, Lou and I settled in for the flight to Niamey with, we had been told, a brief refueling stop in Ouagadougou, Burkina Faso. The pilot announced that we might experience some turbulence from the typical evening thunderstorms. I watched Lou's knuckles turning white on the armrest as the aircraft rocked and rolled its way across West Africa.

We landed in Ouga in dusty twilight. The pilot said we'd only be on the ground a short time, so we would not disembark. We didn't know it then, but "short time" is what Africans say when they want to make sure you don't grow impatient with delays. This particular short time lasted one hour. Then two. Finally, the pilot said a small repair was needed, and we were welcome to disembark—for another short time. As we left the aircraft, we saw the white-robed ones scrambling for empty rows of seats in the middle section.

Only one other plane was sitting on the tarmac, and it didn't seem in a hurry to depart. The two small concession stands in the terminal had closed for the night. My eyes felt gritty and I tried to calculate how many hours I'd been awake. From time to time, Lou would walk out onto the tarmac to check on the progress of the repairs. Several workmen seemed to be holding a conference around the left landing gear. Finally, at 4:00 a.m., one of the flight attendants said we could board the aircraft. The white-robed ones were all sleeping soundly, row after row of them, in the middle section. Thirty minutes passed. Lou got up and walked to the front of the plane. When he returned, his face looked grim.

"I stood at the door with a Peace Corps Volunteer, and we watched this guy in dark trousers and a white shirt. His tie was tucked into his shirt. He kept taking off the wheel, examining it, and putting it back on. Susan, it was the flight attendant!"

Forty minutes later, the pilot announced that the aircraft was ready to depart, and would we please put on our seat belts. Somehow, seat belts seemed inadequate for the crash landing I knew awaited us. I also worried about our friend, John, waiting for us at the Niamey airport. Our flight was already twelve hours overdue.

When we began our descent to Niamey, I looked out the window and saw what appeared to be military vehicles on either side of a runway at the farthest edge of the field.

"Uh oh," said Lou. "Look at those tanks. Remember what we read last week? That there was a bomb threat at this airport?"

All the passengers applauded when we touched down, jostled but safe. The vehicles turned out to be fire engines, and the firefighters were rolling up their hoses while we walked across the tarmac.

I'd never had the slightest interest in traveling to Africa. If I wanted heat, humidity and bugs, I could rent a cottage without air conditioning at the beach. I knew as little about the continent as most other Americans, but a chance encounter in May 1992 changed my thinking. I had accompanied my husband to the annual weekend gathering of Lutheran clergy and laity in North Carolina. I'm still not sure why I had decided to go. Conventions and conferences always made me feel shy, awkward, and uncomfortable, so I tended to avoid this sort of event. I put on my best pastor's wife smile and joined the other clergy spouses gathered for breakfast in the college's dining hall. After we refilled our coffee cups, a vibrant, gray-haired lady stood up and said, "I will be leading a study tour to West Africa in November. If anyone is interested, I have brochures." Edna explained that before she retired she had worked for Lutheran World Relief, an organization dedicated to providing assistance in developing countries. I stuffed a brochure in my handbag.

The following afternoon, during our drive home to Chapel Hill, I found the pamphlet and read it to Lou. "It seems as if there will be about a dozen people in the group, and for three weeks they're going to visit LWR projects in Niger, Mali and Burkina Faso. Things like irrigation and gardening, well drilling, women's empowerment, and literacy. Apparently, LWR has a regional representative who lives in Niger—an American fellow—who will oversee the trip." This was sounding more interesting than I'd thought.

I expected Lou to say that the cost, about $4,000, was much more than we could afford. Instead, he began telling me how we could squeeze the money from several savings accounts and arrange the time away from our jobs. I caught his enthusiasm and tossed it back. We could probably persuade Jason, our 22-year-old son, to move back home from his apartment on the other side of town and take care of his 16-year-old sister during the three weeks we'd be in Africa. We were still chattering when we pulled into our driveway two hours later. Of course, we wanted to see the good work those Lutherans were doing in West Africa but, to be honest, it was the adventure that was reeling us in.

When Lou and I had become engaged in 1967, we wove together dreams of living abroad and raising bilingual children. But dreams had given way to duty, and we had slipped into a more conventional track for a clergy family. For most of the next twenty-five years, Lou had served as a parish pastor in various congregations and I had learned how to be a minister's wife, a role for which I had absolutely no training. My parents had not been churchgoers, and I had taken myself to Sunday services and youth group activities. Halfway through college, I was so young and so head-over-heels in love with my tall, handsome divinity-school graduate, I never once thought about what it might be like to raise a family in a series of church-owned parsonages. Some clergy spouses resented the fishbowl life in which parishioners always seemed to know exactly what was going on in their families. I had not minded that aspect very much because our congregations had almost always treated us kindly. What I did mind, though, were all the nights and weekends my husband was engaged with church meetings and other people's problems. We had so little time together. I had begun to wonder what had become of those two dreamers who had thought their life together would be unique, even adventurous.

When we moved to the university town of Chapel Hill, a physician in the congregation asked me if I'd like to work for him. John was the chairman of one of the medical school's ethics committees, its Institutional Review Board. The board's task, said John, was to review research protocols and clinical trials, many of which were designed for desperately ill patients. Within a year, I was the director of the University of North Carolina's School of Medicine's Office for Human Research Studies. For the first time in my life I felt as if I, like my husband, had a calling, a vocation that mattered. As much as I loved this job, I was asking myself if this was what I still wanted to be doing ten or twenty years from now. When I shared those thoughts with Lou, he confessed that life had begun to feel flat for him, too.

A three-week trip to Africa offered an exciting diversion. We renewed our passports, updated our vaccinations, and read travel books. I learned that West Africans consider it disrespectful for women to wear slacks, so I bought cotton skirts and dresses. We obtained a prescription for anti-malaria pills and went to a camping store to buy their strongest insect repellent. I listened to French-conversation cassette tapes while driving to work to reacquaint myself with the language. Our friends and family considered us brave and adventurous for choosing such an exotic vacation.

Lou and I joined ten other people on the study tour. We were a diverse bunch: from the young professional couple in their twenties to the 79-year-old widow who was fulfilling her life's dream. Excitement ran high, and the complaints were surprisingly few. For three weeks, we traveled the rough roads of West Africa, visiting mud-hut villages and women's empowerment projects. Everywhere we went, the villagers greeted us with dancing and singing and their gentle hospitality. The children giggled, pointed, and sang songs to us. We slept in tiny hotels and freshly-swept huts. We learned to eat *foufou* and chewy pieces of goat.

In Burkina Faso we met a retired government official who said, "We watch your TV shows, like *Dallas*, and we see that you Americans have so much. Why can't you share with the poor who have so little?" Although we tried to assure him that most of America was not like what he saw on *Dallas*, his question wouldn't go away.

West Africa not only saturated my senses, it assaulted my conscience. Against the romantic images of teeming markets and Fulani dancers were the ragged village farmers, the polio victims pushing themselves along the dusty road in their wooden carts, and the children. Always the children.

On our final day in West Africa, Lou and I were sitting at a small table in an outdoor café with John, the Lutheran World Relief tour guide who had been living in West Africa for seven years. We sipped our Cokes and watched the market women peddling bananas and fried pastries. When Lou asked John, "What, exactly, is it like to be an American who lives here?" I knew that he had already begun to wonder, "Is there any way we could do this?"

At the time, the thought was too big for me. I had too many "Yes, but…" thoughts.

Yes, but our children needed us.

Yes, but what about our secure, lucrative jobs?

Yes, but what would we actually *do* in Africa? We weren't exactly trained for development work.

Back home, we gave the expected talks and slide shows. As the months passed, I noticed that my friends' eyes would glaze over when I kept talking about those three weeks. "Do you know that the illiteracy rate for women in Mali is sixty percent?" They nodded politely. "And that literacy is the key to a better life for those women and their children?"

They were grateful when I switched the subject.

Meanwhile, Lou and I bought more books and maps, and as we pored over them, I remembered our premarital scheming and dreaming. We may have missed out on rearing bilingual children, but perhaps it wasn't too late to make something of those dreams after all. Maybe we really could do something worthwhile in Africa. And have an adventure, too.

We were no longer twenty-somethings, and we knew a lot was at stake. Figuring out how to finance such an undertaking was only one of our concerns. If we moved to Africa, we would probably have to sell our house and put our possessions into storage. Could we undertake such a venture with a daughter still in college? Would our children feel abandoned? And what about my elderly parents? What if our yearning was nothing more than the foolishness of two middle-aged warblers who knew they'd soon be sitting on an empty nest? I knew those guided, protected, three weeks in Africa bore little resemblance to real expatriate life, but how could we know what that life would be like unless we could somehow sample it? Somehow, we would need to test our desire and own physical stamina.

We wrote to John in Niger. He said that he could provide us with a Lutheran World Relief vehicle if we wanted to visit West Africa on our own. His assistant, Yacouba, would be honored to be our driver, guide, and translator. Now, almost one year to the day of our previous departure, we had returned to West Africa. Inside the terminal, John and Yacouba were waiting for us. "I had invited a group of my friends to meet you here last night, but I sent them home to bed around midnight." Our sleepy friend chuckled when we told him our tale.

"I guess I never told you my name for this airline. *Air Tragique.*"

By the time we reached John's home in Niamey, I'd lost track of how many hours I'd been awake. When Yacouba finished unloading our luggage from the Land Cruiser, John handed him a few coins and asked him to buy some fresh bread at the *boulangerie* down the road.

"Why don't you both take a shower?" He gestured toward the bathroom. "I'll make some coffee, and we'll have some croissants and fruit. Then we can all have a lie-down." John had been awake all night, too.

Although I'd been yearning for a chance to get horizontal, I was too exhausted, or maybe too excited, to sleep. I listened to bees buzzing on the flowers outside the window of the little guest room, and wondered about the coming weeks. The itinerary John and Yacouba had proposed at breakfast included trips to some remote places with exotic-sounding descriptions. We might even travel to Timbuktu.

Later that evening, I sat in John's kitchen watching him prepare dinner. He was soaking carrots in a mild bleach solution in his sink.

"If you find yourselves living in West Africa, you'll have to do this, too. You don't want to know the sort of water the locals use to water their fruits and veggies."

While the stew simmered on the stove, we sat on John's screened front porch nibbling cheese and crackers. I looked up at the thatched roof.

"What's that crackling noise, John?"

"Oh—those are termites. I have to replace this roof every year or so."

When we awakened the next morning and walked into the living room, John and Yacouba were stashing canned food, plastic plates, cups, and cutlery into a metal footlocker.

"We've loaded the Land Cruiser with two cases of bottled water," said John. "You can always buy more along the way. And we've strapped some chairs, camp beds, and mattresses on the top."

While we sipped John's good, strong French press coffee and spread jam on the baguettes still warm from the bakery, Yacouba proposed a small change in the itinerary.

"I would be honored if you both could come to my village. It is called Sorbon Goungou. It is really an island in the Niger River. We could go there for two or three days, and then continue our trip. It will only take us two hours to get there from here."

Lou and I exchanged quick glances and nodded. This was exactly the sort of encounter we'd been hoping to have, the chance to spend some time with villagers in their own environment.

"The honor would be ours," said Lou.

Yacouba parked the Land Cruiser under a tree near the riverbank and handed some money to a young man who would watch it while we were visiting Sorbon Goungou. He carefully loaded our gear into the pirogue: camp beds, sheets, mosquito nets, two boxes of food, a carton of bottled water, ice chest, and our suitcase and tote bags, an embarrassingly huge array of supplies for our two-day visit to the tiny island village. Holding my sandals in my left hand, I waded out to the boat and reached for Yacouba's outstretched palm. Yacouba exchanged a few quick words in Djerma with the bare-chested young man who would row us across the river, and we began our fifteen-minute trip.

A dozen grinning children in tattered T-shirts were waiting for us on the edge of the island. One little fellow waded into the muddy water and pulled our craft ashore. A young teenaged girl grasped my hand and pulled me up the sandy riverbank. She told me, in the easy-to-understand French of West Africans, that her name was Beba Sumana. The children grabbed our gear, hoisted it to their heads, and marched, single-file, to the village. Disturbing movie memories filled my mind: white men in khaki shorts and knee socks tramping through the jungle followed by a procession of African porters. I wondered what the adults in the village would think of these two Americans with all their gear. When we arrived, Yacouba showed us the mud hut that would be our home for the next two days and hurried away. Perhaps he was going to tell his father that we were here. A young woman smiled at us while she continued vigorously sweeping the dirt floor. Our neighborhood was an assortment of mud-brick huts with pointy, thatched roofs. I heard a rhythmic thunk-thunk and knew that somewhere a woman was pounding millet into meal. A few skinny chickens, displaced by our arrival, resumed their hopeful pecking. A faint, hot breeze bore the pungent-sweet aroma of dust, dung, and woodsmoke, a scent I would forever associate with Africa.

Yacouba returned carrying two tin pots: chicken and sauce in one, rice in the other. We expected him to join us for lunch, but he simply smiled and said, "No, here we honor our guests by allowing them to eat alone."

After lunch, Yacouba enlisted two young men to carry our beds to the large mango tree at the river's edge. Here we would pass the heat of the afternoon, he said. The children gathered around us again, and we showed them postcards of our home in North Carolina. Amadou, a boy of fifteen, was peering at the words on the back of the card when Beba took my hand and indicated that I should follow her. We stopped outside a small hut surrounded by dusty bushes, and a wizened woman with tired eyes emerged from the entrance. Beba introduced me to her mother who gestured for me to sit down on one of the woven blankets on the sand. She ducked her head and disappeared inside her home. I watched a teenaged girl braiding a younger girl's hair. Another young girl of about seven shyly fingered my straight, brown hair and giggled. Who was this *anasara* (white woman) who refused to tuck her hair into a headscarf? Beba's mother returned with a baby on her hip, put a small square of fabric on my skirt, and placed the naked infant on my lap. The baby grasped my finger, looked at me, and cooed. Before Beba walked me back to the mango tree, she gave me a handful of leaves which I tucked into my pocket.

Back at the tree, Lou and Amadou were hunched over a book. Lou was naming the pictures in a coloring book we had brought for the children, and Amadou was busy scribbling the English words into a small notebook. "Teach me!" he kept saying. Although my college English degree hadn't prepared me to teach, I wondered if I could teach English to children like Amadou.

At twilight, after another solitary meal, we slathered ourselves with insect repellent and noticed a small, wavering light coming closer. It was Yacouba, carrying a kerosene lantern. "This is for you," he said. I asked him why we saw no other lanterns in the village, only the flickering glow of cooking fires. "The villagers can no longer use their lamps. They have no money to buy oil. I do worry about my family here. When my father, the chief, passes away, I will be responsible for all of them."

As I was getting ready for bed, I reached into my pocket and found the leaves. I tossed them under a bush. The next day I asked Yacouba why Beba had given me those leaves. "Oh," he said, "those are for tea." I was glad I hadn't told him I had thrown them away.

During the next three weeks, Yacouba became a friend. A good friend. We had driven and walked, laughed and sweated our way through hundreds of dusty miles. On our last evening in West Africa, we sipped cups of tea in a restaurant in Côte d'Ivoire. The crisp white tablecloths and flickering candlelight again offered a movie image: *Casablanca.* We reminisced with Yacouba about the places we had visited, like the animist Dogon villages in the Bandiagara Cliffs and the Great Mosque in Djenni, a holy pilgrimage for Yacouba and many other West African Muslims. Without this trip, he said, he probably would never have seen them.

"Oh, no," said Lou, "We are the ones who are grateful. Very few Americans have had the privilege of traveling where you have taken us. Very few have had the honor of knowing someone like you." Although we had already paid him well for his services, we wanted to give Yacouba a gift. After dinner, Lou handed him a fifty-dollar bill and said he should use it as he wished.

"Could you please write a small note?" asked Yacouba. "I will need a letter when I take this to the bank, so they won't think I have stolen the money."

The following morning we sat on the tarmac of the Abidjan airport, waiting for our Air Afrique flight to depart. My mind was still replaying scenes from our three-week adventure. I had only one regret: I had really wanted to brag to my friends back home I had been to Timbuktu. We had been a mere four or five hours' drive from that exotic city whose very name suggests the end of the earth, but Yacouba had said, "I've been there many times, and I always get two or three flat tires on that bad road. Really, there isn't much to see." We hoped that we would see Yacouba again, but nothing is certain in Africa. As he himself would say, "*Enshallah.*" God willing.

The trip was physically demanding, and it had shown me my limitations. I could not live in a mud hut, pee in bushes, and wash my clothes in the river, but I knew that one day I wanted to eat dinners with the villagers. I wanted to bring oil for their lanterns, and respond to Amadou's urgent plea for English lessons. I wanted to be a woman who knew what to do with a handful of leaves.

Chapter 2
You're Going *Where?*

*O*ne September evening in 1994 Lou came home from church whistling. Lou never whistled. He unhooked his clerical collar from his shirt, poured himself a glass of iced tea and planted himself next to the kitchen sink, where I was peeling potatoes.

"Susan, I think I've figured out a way for us to go back to Africa for longer than just a few weeks." My husband's predisposition to nonconformity had always been, for me, one of his more endearing qualities. Instead of attending a Lutheran seminary as most pastors in our denomination did, Lou had worked three jobs to acquire his four years of theological training at Yale Divinity School. During his third year, when other seminarians were interning in local parishes, Lou went to Germany to work as a *jugendarbeiter*, a youth worker. Even before we'd gone to Africa, I had begun to sense Lou's restlessness with his 25-year vocation as a parish pastor, his yearning for a different sort of purposeful adventure.

"I've been with this Chapel Hill congregation for eight years, and according to the terms of my call, I'm eligible for a three-month sabbatical. We could go to Africa for those three months."

"Where would we go? What would we do?"

Chicago is the headquarters of the Evangelical Lutheran Church in America, the five-million-member church in which Lou was an ordained pastor. I knew our national church had missionaries around the world and had even heard one of them speak a number of years ago, but I was completely ignorant about what modern missionaries did these days. Lou must have read my thoughts. He phoned the church headquarters the following morning, but neither of us expected a quick response. The wheels of ecclesiastical bureaucracy grind slowly. So we were caught off-guard when Harold, the Director for International Personnel, phoned us at home that evening. In a no-nonsense voice he barked, "There's a Lutheran seminary in Namibia that needs lecturers. All the classes are taught in English. Lou, you can teach pastoral counseling and Susan, they want you to teach English. They really want people for six months, but I

11

convinced them to take you. Be ready to go on February 5. We will mail you the tickets, and you can send us a check."

I didn't want to sound like a wimp—after all, this was the person who sent people to remote mission fields all over the world—but I still had pee-in-the-bushes worries. As delicately as I could, I asked about living conditions.

"Don't worry about that," he said. "The village where you'll be living has a nice big house for you, and we can probably find a car for you to use while you're there. Make sure your shots are up to date, and get yourself a three-month prescription for anti-malarial pills."

All the while, I had pretended I knew where Namibia was. The next day I found two guidebooks and a map in a local bookshop, and learned that Namibia was what my seventh-grade geography teacher had called South West Africa, a country twice the size of California with a population of only two million people. Its neighbors were Angola, Botswana, and South Africa. Unlike the tropical climate of West Africa, Namibia is arid, bordered by the Namib Desert in the west and the Kalahari in the east and south. When the country won its war for independence from South Africa in 1990, it had adopted English as its national language.

Our friends, Craig and Glenna, said they'd be happy to let Megan live with them for three months during the spring of her junior year in high school. Jason, who lived in an apartment across town, would take Fuzzy, our cat. We would not be paid, but Lou's church salary would continue. The university allowed me to take a three-month unpaid leave of absence.

The Lutheran Church's Division for Global Mission had had a longstanding relationship with Namibia. Rev. Dan Olson, DGM's Area Program Director for southern Africa, phoned us after Christmas to give us some background and tell us more about Paulinum Seminary, the place where we would be teaching. We were surprised to learn that 75 percent of Namibia's people were Lutheran, a result of the evangelization of the German and Finnish missionaries who went there in the nineteenth century. For many decades the leadership of Namibian Lutheran churches was firmly in the hands of their European mother churches. Over time, this leadership shifted to Namibian pastors, and the need arose for local training of these indigenous pastors. In 1963 Namibian Lutherans of various tribal backgrounds came together and formed this seminary for the training of their pastors.

By the 1980s the seminary had begun accepting women, a relatively rare phenomenon among African Christians. "The school has about 45 students, and they attend for four years," Dan said. "There are several Namibian lecturers and a German woman pastor."

It never occurred to me to worry that I'd never taught English to anyone. I had been an English major in college, and I still remembered how to diagram sentences. When Glenna, a high-school German teacher, gave me two of her ESL books, I figured I'd do just fine.

We bought our first laptop computer and a small printer for producing lectures and assignments. Dan had told us that Otjimbingwe, the village where we would be living, had electricity for only twelve hours a day, and we worried about power blips and about whether the country's 220-voltage would damage the laptop. Roger, our computer guru, assured us the laptop's built-in transformer could handle the conversion. Just to be safe, he created a transformer for us. "Once you get there, you will just connect your laptop to this box and then attach the box to a new car battery, and you'll be good to go." The contraption, a metal box with wires and plugs attached to it, looked like a bomb! I still wonder how we got it through customs.

When we arrived at Hosea Kutako Airport in Windhoek, Namibia, we calculated that we had been traveling for about twenty-seven hours, including a five-hour layover in Frankfurt and a shorter one in Johannesburg. Neither of us had slept on those flights. Now, it was mid-afternoon and we were eager to claim our luggage and get settled. Our mysterious metal box cleared customs with a nod and a grunt from the agent. As we walked into the tiny arrivals terminal, I was surprised by how clean everything looked. There were neat rows of orange plastic chairs for people awaiting travelers. Almost everyone was wearing Western-style clothes. This was nothing like the chaotic West African airports we'd known from our two previous visits to the continent. The smell was different, too. Or, rather, there was no smell. From what I remembered of the airports in West Africa, I'd expected dusty wood smoke with a touch of mildew, but the air was clear and dry. Through the doors to the parking lot, I saw a brilliant blue sky above the palm trees.

We had been told that the Namibian bishop would meet our flight, so we looked around for someone resembling a bishop. Taxi drivers kept approaching us, and we waved them away. "No thanks, we're being met." The bishop must have been delayed. Outside, a large bus was filling with passengers for City Centre. While we waited, I exchanged our currency into Namibian dollars. After half an hour, our only companions in the terminal were a few workers in blue jumpsuits, sweeping the floor.

"I'm going to look for a telephone and a phone book," said Lou. "Maybe I can find the number of the church office. You stay here with our luggage."

Twenty minutes later, he returned. "There was no answer when I phoned the church headquarters, but I found the listing for a Lutheran pastor in Windhoek and phoned him. He said we should take the bus into town, and he'd meet us at the City Centre bus stop and take us to the guesthouse."

We dragged our luggage outside and sat on the curb under a palm tree, sweltering in our winter clothes. We only had to wait half an hour for the bus to arrive, and soon we were on our way into the city, still wondering what had happened to the bishop.

The view from the window of the bus reminded me of our recent trip to New Mexico. The land looked parched and rocky. Waist-high grass and small thirsty thorn bushes lined the highway. In the distance were hazy granite mountains that looked as if they had been guarding this land forever. I remembered reading that although Windhoek was a mile high, it had actually been built in a basin surrounded by the Hochland Mountains. The German colonists had believed the mountains protected them from invasion. Occasionally, we passed what appeared to be a ranch or farmhouse, but I couldn't see any livestock. How different this was from West Africa. For one thing, the road was smooth and wide with very little traffic. For another, no one was hawking wares, either at the airport or along the road. Where were all the vendors? The word that came to mind was desolate, but perhaps that's because we'd been traveling for two days and hadn't been met at the airport. Our two previous trips to this continent had taught me not to become overwhelmed by first impressions. Or underwhelmed.

As we entered the outskirts of the city, the barren land gave way to tidy, adobe-style homes and little shopping centers. The sidewalks were wide and clean; palm trees and brilliant fuchsia bougainvilleas replaced the brush and acacia trees. Neat little signs along the road advertised lodges and hotels for the weary traveler. No longer weary, I pressed my nose against the window. Windhoek could have been any city in Western Europe, with its fashionable shops and well-dressed pedestrians. The driver eased the bus into a tiny parking area on what looked like Windhoek's main street. I glanced across the spacious boulevard at a modern, multi-storied building with a cheerful, sun-shaped sign, the Kalahari Sands Hotel. And here were the vendors. Not pushing and grabbing at us, but sitting quietly on the pavement with their beads, batiks, drums, and carvings neatly arrayed on cheerful red, yellow, and blue ground cloths.

Pastor Frederick was waiting for us when we stepped off the bus. A tall, stern-looking fellow in black clerical garb, he formally shook hands with each of us and shoved our luggage into his tiny car. Lou folded himself into the front seat and I climbed into the back seat. The pastor said the guesthouse was only five minutes away. As he drove, he explained that the guesthouse was actually part of the downtown Lutheran church headquarters that included administrative offices, an old stone church, and the bishop's residence. We drove through a gate in the ten-foot-high chain-link fence surrounding a cluster of old, Teutonic-looking buildings and houses. The place looked like an old German missionary compound which, I realized, it probably was. Pastor Frederick went inside a cement block building to find the matron.

He emerged accompanied by a tiny lady in a crisply starched, blue print housedress. "This is Sister Agnes," he said. "Unfortunately, she said she doesn't have a double room, but if you don't mind, she can put you into a single room. Her staff has gone home for the day, so we'll need to help her carry the bedding over there." He nodded toward a block of flats at the edge of the compound that resembled a motel. Lou and the pastor hauled an old iron bed to one of the flats, and I followed with sheets, pillow, and duvet. Sister Agnes stood watching us with her arms crossed. I had the feeling I should be apologizing for being a guest at her guesthouse. When we'd dumped our gear into the flat and thanked Pastor Frederick for his assistance, I asked Agnes if it would be possible for us to have supper in the dining room.

"You do not have a reservation for supper, but maybe I can find enough food for you," she said.

Despite the inauspicious beginning, we tried to remain hopeful and optimistic. The following morning, feeling refreshed and hungry, we made our way to the dining room in a building across a small courtyard from the church administrative offices. Two rows of rectangular tables covered in crisp white tablecloths were set end-to-end. On a heavy, dark wood sideboard were several boxes of cereal, large jugs of milk and juice, a loaf of bread, containers of margarine and marmalade, and a basket of hardboiled eggs. I was crumbling my Weetabix brick into a cereal bowl when a slender, gray-haired man in a deep purple clergy shirt approached our table. His skin was the color of Kraft caramels, and an ornate silver pectoral cross on a heavy silver chain glistened on his chest.

"I am Bishop Diergaardt," he said, a friendly smile crinkling his weathered cheeks.

He apologized profusely for neglecting to meet our flight. "I had written this in my date book, but I suddenly had to conduct a funeral and, uh, I forgot that I needed to go to the airport." Lou assured him that we had managed very well. He didn't mention Sister Agnes.

We spent a week in that Windhoek guesthouse, walking into town and enjoying this capital city that travel writers consider one of the continent's cleanest and prettiest. We peered at the latest fashions in the wide department store windows, found the banks, ATMs, and coffee shops. I stood in a queue at the main post office and stocked up on overseas airmail stamps. If it weren't for all the African faces and the street vendors selling carvings, drums, and batiks, it would have been easy to forget that this was Africa. A German fellow we'd met at the guesthouse explained that the South Africans, for all the misery they'd caused the Namibians with the imposition of apartheid, had at least left behind a decent infrastructure: roads, bridges, and a good water system. "You can drink water from the tap here, you know."

One morning, we joined several members of the bishop's staff for their mid-morning tea break in a garden area within the compound. A portly fellow with a wide smile and the same caramel-colored skin as the bishop joined the small group at our table. "You must be the Bauers," he said, extending his hand. "I'm Dirk Cloete. The seminary's governing board has just elected me to be principal of Paulinum Seminary for the next three years, and I wanted to be the first to officially welcome you to our faculty."

Dirk showed us the car that DGM had made available to us, a blue, eight-year-old Jetta, and suggested we might want to practice driving it before we left for Otjimbingwe. "I know it takes Americans a little while to get used to driving on the left side of the road."

That afternoon he gave us a tour of the city. In a suburb of Windhoek called Pionierspark, he said, "This is the site of the new seminary. As you can see, they've just broken ground, but we've been promised all the construction will be finished by 1997. When you get to Otjimbingwe, you'll see why it's so important for us to move into town." I wondered what he wasn't telling us.

I told Dirk that his English was excellent. "I studied in Pennsylvania, and received my Master of Divinity from Gettysburg Seminary," he said.

Lou practiced driving around town the following morning, once Windhoek's rush hour had subsided. While Lou drove, I paid attention to the traffic lights, which the locals called "robots." The tricky parts were learning how to shift gears with his left hand and making left-hand turns. More than once, after turning left, Lou would automatically drive into the right lane, and I'd yell, "Get left! Get left!"

We found a supermarket and stocked up on canned goods, cereal, and boxes of milk with a long shelf life. The store had its own bakery, and the favorite item seemed to be small crusty rolls called brochen. The meat department offered an ample array of fresh sausages of every kind. Most of the grocery items on the shelves seemed to be British. I decided not to buy any Marmite, but I did purchase a few jars of Crosse and Blackwell chutney and several packets of cookies. I'd have to remember to call them biscuits. On the next aisle I spied a pedestal fan. "Get it!" I said. Even though the climate wasn't humid, as it had been in West Africa, we'd lain awake on sweaty sheets the past few nights. February in Namibia was the middle of summer.

Our next stop was the U.S. Embassy where we needed to register as temporary guest workers. We drove to the residential Ausspannplatz neighborhood, just a few blocks from the center of the city. I remembered the grand embassy buildings I'd seen in Washington, D.C., with their marble block construction, tall wrought-iron fences, and immaculate landscaping. By contrast, my country's embassy in Windhoek was a smallish, nondescript structure. If we hadn't seen the American flag, we would have driven right past. No lawn or fence separated the building from the sidewalk. We stepped inside and a laconic Namibian guard at a table shuffled through my handbag before directing us to the consular affairs window. Behind the counter, a friendly, middle-aged Namibian woman in a smart navy blue suit and crisp white blouse made photocopies of our passports and wrote down our contact information. Our final morning errand was a visit to a petrol station where we purchased a car battery for our computer's transformer.

Our week as tourists was over, and it was time to do what we'd come here to do. We sat down in the church courtyard with Dirk and our Namibian map. We needed to know how to find the seminary where we'd be living for the next three months.

"It's about a three-hour drive from here," he said. "I would accompany you, but I need to remain in town for a few more days. You just take the B-1 out of Windhoek. It's a good, tarred road. After about two hours, when you get to Karibib, you'll see the sign for Otjimbingwe. It's next to the turn-off to the Navachab Gold Mine. Follow that gravel road for another hour. You can't miss it. Oh, and be careful when you drive through the rivers. Don't stop halfway through or you're likely to get stuck."

When Dirk had said, "gravel road," I'd expected something like my Chapel Hill driveway: a three-inch layer of grey, pea-sized pebbles. The only substance resembling gravel on that washboard road from Karibib were the boulders that threatened to puncture our tires. I was beginning to believe the entire country was nothing but rocks and mountains. Although Lou never exceeded thirty miles an hour, he struggled to keep the Jetta on a straight course. His knuckles were white on the steering wheel. Drops of sweat rolled down his cheek and disappeared into his beard. The smoothest part of the road was the middle, which was fine because there was no other traffic. There weren't even any houses or villages, just parched brown grass and stunted thorn bushes. Had we made a wrong turn somewhere? We saw a small dusty sign with a wavy blue line. We must be approaching the river. How deep would the water be? How much clearance did this little car have, laden as it was with all our luggage and supplies?

The river turned out to be a twelve-foot-wide strip of deep sand bisecting the road. Lou stopped, chewed his lower lip, backed up, and pushed the gearshift into second gear. "I've driven through sand like this before," he said. "Dirk was right. You can't stop in the middle."

The hot wind was blowing fine grains of sand through the open windows, and I wiped my face with a bandana. Sweat was dribbling down my neck, and the back of my dress was soaked. Even Lou, who always told me he liked hot weather, had big dark circles under his arms. What sort of impression would we make when we finally reached the seminary?

I kept looking for a village like the ones we had seen in West Africa: mud-brick huts with thatched roofs all crowded together. What we saw, instead, was a smattering of tiny tarpaper shacks with corrugated tin roofs. Beyond the shacks was a cream-colored brick church with an ornate white steeple that looked as if it had been transplanted from Bavaria. I recognized it from the picture in the guidebook as the 130-year-old Rhenish Mission Church. We turned right and followed a small sandy car track leading into Otjimbingwe. In the distance, beyond a tall barbed-wire fence, was an assortment of institutional-type buildings, all of them tan with rust-red roofs. This must be the seminary. Little barefooted children came running out of their homes to wave at us. Their mothers, in headscarves and simple, calf-length dresses, stopped hanging laundry on bushes and stared. The few men sitting outside their homes never looked up.

The gate into the campus was open, and when we drove through we saw three large houses ahead of us: solid, single-story, cement block structures with dark green tiled roofs and sturdy wood doors. Maybe one of them was ours? We saw no one walking around, so we stopped in front of the house that seemed the most lived-in: laundry on the clothesline, a flower garden in the front, and patches of tousled corn and healthy tomato plants in a side garden. We knocked on the front door. The gentleman who answered was tall and slender, very dark skinned, with a neat white beard. He smiled broadly, grasped our hands, and told us his name was Tomas Shivute.

"Welcome to Paulinum! You must be Lou and Susan. We are so very glad that you are here." He peered more closely at Lou and the two men laughed. They looked like negative and positive images of each other.

"I think I have just met my African double," said Lou.

Tomas produced a set of keys, and pointed to one of the large houses we had passed. "That one is yours for the next three months. Please feel at home. There isn't anyone else on campus now except my family and the treasurer, but the students and other faculty members will be arriving in a few days. My wife teaches primary school here in the village, so we live here year-round. What else can I do to help you feel at home?"

"Can we drink the tap water here?" I asked.

"Oh, yes. The water is safe to drink."

"And what about electricity?" asked Lou. "We were told there is only electricity for twelve hours a day."

Tomas smiled widely, "You are in luck! As of last month, Otjimbingwe now has electricity twenty-four hours a day."

As tired as we felt from the long, hot drive, we were eager to set up housekeeping in our new home. The house was more spacious than I had expected, and with its thick, white plaster walls and tall ceilings, it felt twenty degrees cooler than the outside temperature. There were plenty of kitchen cupboards and drawers. When I pulled out one of the drawers, an enormous cockroach scurried down the side of the cupboard and disappeared under the baseboard. I swallowed hard, determined not to be a wimp, and rooted around in our plastic shopping bags for the green and yellow can of Doom insecticide. I was pleased I'd remembered to bring plenty of plastic zip-lock bags for our dishes, cutlery, and food. There was no stove, only a two-burner hotplate, but since DGM had negotiated with the seminary for us to eat lunch and dinner in the seminary's dining hall, I wouldn't be doing very much cooking. The tiny, half-sized refrigerator would be adequate.

The living room was spacious, but sparsely furnished with two faded blue upholstered chairs and two long wooden tables. There was no carpet on the brown linoleum floor, and no pictures on the walls other than a Bless This House needlepoint sampler. The air felt thick, so I pushed aside the heavy curtains opened the windows. Lou was already assembling the pedestal fan. We carried one of the tables to the far end of the room, and set it down in front of a window that opened onto the screened porch. There was plenty of room for two chairs at that table, and we set up the computer, printer, car battery, and the transformer box. This would be our workstation.

The house had three bedrooms, and the queen-sized bed in the largest one was made up with crisply ironed sheets and a blue-flowered duvet. The two wardrobes would easily accommodate our clothes. I had to swallow hard when I saw the bathroom. Squares of gray, powdery grout revealed where tiles were missing from the walls and floor. The sink was cracked and chipped, and the bathtub was stained with streaks of greenish mineral deposits. Next to the sink, a tiny shower emitted a pitiful dribble when I turned on the faucet. That first evening we discovered there was no hot water, even though we'd seen a hot water tank outside the house. The next week, when we asked a colleague whether it worked, she told us no one's geyser (she pronounced it, "geezer") worked. We discovered that if we wanted a warm shower, my preference for hair washing, we would have to shower in the late afternoon, after the water in the outside pipes had absorbed the heat of the day.

While we waited for the students to arrive, we put together what we hoped were acceptable lesson plans. In the evenings, when the heat of the day abated, we strolled around the dusty grounds of the campus. We peered through the windows of the tiny administrative office and adjoining library. One evening, Tomas joined us.

"We only see two classrooms," Lou remarked.

"Yes, because of our space limitations, Paulinum only accepts new students every other year. The students who will arrive in a few days are

P-two's and P-four's, second- and fourth-year students. The seminary used to train deacons and elders, as well as students studying for the ordained ministry. We don't do that anymore, but somehow the 'P' designation remained for our pastoral students. Let's walk over to the volleyball court." As we approached a sandy field on the edge of the campus, Tomas continued, "We have classes from eight o'clock to one o'clock each day. The students remain in those two classrooms you saw and their lecturers come to them. We have a half-hour tea break in the middle of the morning, and dinner is served in the dining hall at one o'clock. I think you will be eating your meals in the dining hall, right?"

We nodded.

"Are there afternoon or evening classes?" asked Lou.

"No, it's too hot. Everyone rests in the afternoons." He laughed. "When I was in Finland—that's where I studied for my doctoral degree— I was surprised that we had afternoon classes and evening seminars there. Even though it wasn't hot, I had a difficult time staying awake." He explained the daily chapel service schedule. "We have morning devotions at seven-thirty on Monday, Tuesday, Thursday, and Friday. There is a vespers service on Wednesday evenings and a service of compline on Saturday evenings. Our Sunday morning services are at nine o'clock."

Our walking tour had brought us to the front of the chapel. Adjacent to this small, attractive, sand-colored church was a tall, white bell tower with an intricate depiction of Jesus and his disciples painted onto one side. Tomas reached in his pocket for a ring of keys and opened the front door. The pulpit, lectern, and communion rail were constructed of sturdy blond wood, polished to a lustrous glow. The whitewashed walls gleamed. A ruby-red carpet runner covered the wide center aisle. It was apparent that a lot of foreign donor money had been poured into this chapel. As if reading my thoughts, Tomas said, "Our German friends helped us build this chapel. It's quite nice, isn't it?"

On our way back to our houses, a tall, robust man wearing a bright yellow shirt and knife-creased brown trousers emerged from a door next to one of the classrooms. He and Tomas embraced one another in one of those triple, European hugs, and the man said, "Comrade!" Tomas introduced us to his good friend, Matheus Hashoongo. "Matheus is the treasurer of our seminary. He has been with us for five years, since the end of The Struggle."

Matheus shook hands with Lou and me, bowing slightly from the waist. "You are most welcome here," he said in a deep voice. "Please feel at home."

"My friend was a freedom fighter during Namibia's long war for independence," said Tomas. "He has many diplomas in accounting and business. We are fortunate he has joined us here."

During the next few days, our faculty colleagues began arriving. We met Rev. Eino Amaambo, an elderly gentleman who taught Greek and pastoral counseling courses. He told us his wife, Esther, was living in their home in the north, tending their crops and taking care of the relatives who lived on their homestead. Rev. Michael Shangala was the next to arrive, a slender young man who appeared to be in his early forties. His wife, Lucia, was a nurse in Windhoek and lived there with the couple's two children. Eino and Michael had both studied at a Lutheran seminary in Minneapolis.

Rev. Angela Veii, a friendly, energetic woman with short, blonde hair, was a German pastor in her forties who lived in the house next to ours. Angela said she had been teaching at Paulinum for three years. She was married to Gerson, a Namibian who had his own small construction company in Windhoek. We were learning that it wasn't uncommon for married couples to live apart. In this country where unemployment was 40 percent, a person couldn't leave her job just because her husband might have a good position somewhere else in the country. We were surprised that Dirk had not yet appeared on campus, and assumed his Windhoek meetings had delayed his departure.

Mail was only collected once a week, whenever someone took the big canvas mail pouch to the post office in Karibib. We discovered that phone service was basically nonexistent. Matheus said if we wanted to make a phone call, we could phone the operator in Karibib and give her the phone number of our party. She would seek an open line, and call us back. "Sometimes that can take three or four hours," he said. Since we didn't know anyone in Namibia and never expected to make any transatlantic phone calls, that didn't seem to be a problem for us.

The dining hall was not yet open for meals and we were growing tired of canned spaghetti and tins of tuna fish. Our supply of Nescafé instant coffee was almost gone, and the tiny shop in the village sold little more than fresh bread, jam, lots of tinned sardines (pilchards) and soda—what the Namibians call cool drinks. We decided to drive the washboard road back to Karibib for supplies and offered to collect the mail. Matheus gave us the key for the mail pouch.

After less than a week in Otjimbingwe, driving into Karibib felt like reentering civilization. We stopped at the Caltex petrol station and remembered to tip the service station attendant who filled the tank. Next door to the service station, we stocked up on groceries at the little supermarket. Lou found a small styrofoam ice chest on a dusty shelf at the back of the market, and we filled it with a bag of ice, Cadbury chocolate bars, and three packages of hard cheese. We were preparing ourselves for the long, hot drive back to the village when we discovered a little Bavarian-style coffee shop. The return trip could wait while we enjoyed fresh filter coffee in china cups and gooey cream-filled pastries. That's when we decided to make this teeth-rattling drive into Karibib part of our weekly routine.

The students had begun to arrive, and so had Dirk. We were eager to start teaching, and Lou asked Dirk about the class schedule when we met him on campus. "Oh, sorry. I meant to tell you. The lecturers will be meeting in the library tomorrow morning at nine o'clock. That's when we will decide who teaches which course, and we'll set up the class timetable."

Lou glanced at me and raised his eyebrows. The faculty didn't know which classes they would be teaching?

Chapter 3
Life in Otjimbingwe

*I*was drying our few dinner dishes when I looked out the kitchen window and saw an old, dusty white Toyota entering the sandy yard surrounding our house. The vehicle coughed to a stop and two white people, a man and a woman, climbed out. They must be Peter and Solveig, the other American couple who would be teaching at the seminary this semester. We had been expecting them. Peter was a wiry fellow with thick, white hair and bushy black eyebrows. Solveig's gray curls were damp with perspiration. Laugh lines crinkled her eyes. She wore a white and navy calico-print muumuu dress trimmed with black rickrack. I asked if they had eaten supper. Peter said they hadn't, so I made peanut butter and jelly sandwiches, opened a packet of cookies, and poured us all large glasses of guava juice. Solveig surprised us when she said that our sons had both been students at the University of North Carolina and had met each other. They told us about their few days in Windhoek, we told them about being forgotten at the airport, and we all laughed about the road from Karibib.

Although we had only been in Namibia for two weeks, I was surprised how pleasant it was to hear an American accent. Solveig said they had visited Namibia twice before, during The Struggle, and that they had many close Namibian friends. The seminary in Iowa where Peter was teaching had offered full scholarships to Namibian students for almost twenty years. We told them about the next day's faculty meeting and planned to meet them in the library at nine o'clock the following morning.

Angela was dusting chairs when we arrived at the library five minutes before the scheduled meeting. No one else was there. The library wasn't much larger than our living room back home. Blond wood shelves lined the walls, and eight scratched and dented tables and matching chairs filled the rest of the room. The faculty had appointed Angela librarian the previous year. We helped her open windows and push together two tables to form a large, square workspace in the middle of the room. The other

24

faculty members began arriving, and we all shook hands and engaged in small talk while we waited for the principal.

Dirk hurried through the door at nine-thirty. The ample waistband of his trousers had lost control of his shirttail, and loose papers threatened to tumble out of the oversized three-ring binder he'd tucked under his arm. He looked at his watch.

"Sorry, sorry! I was busy at home and forgot to check the time."

Dirk offered an opening prayer and extended a generous welcome to the four visiting Americans. He suggested that we should each introduce ourselves. As I glanced around the table, I was surprised to realize that we five expatriates outnumbered our four Namibian colleagues. It was ten-thirty when Dirk opened his binder and distributed a sheaf of papers to each of us: an agenda for today's meeting, the minutes of the previous faculty meeting, a list of courses that would be taught this semester, and a chart labeled "Timetable."

"We have completed items one and two on our agenda, the prayer and the welcome," he said. "Now we will read the minutes of the previous meeting from last October."

Michael Shangala, faculty secretary, read aloud from the five-page, single-spaced document. When he had finished, Dirk explained the procedure to us newcomers. First, we would examine the minutes, page by page, for corrections. After that, we would start at the beginning, discuss each item raised at the October meeting, and, finally, take up any new business. Across the table, I saw old Rev. Amaambo's eyelids fluttering. Every few minutes, the elderly dean of students would awaken with a little jolt. It was nearly noon before we were able to check off "Minutes" from our list of agenda items.

"Why don't we stop now for a little refreshment?" asked Dirk.

He nodded to Angela to accompany him and hurried out the door while the rest of us stood up and stretched. A hot little breeze ruffled the curtains. The Namibians began talking among themselves in Oshiwambo, and Peter and Solveig walked around to our side of the table.

"I wonder if they always do the minutes that way," whispered Solveig.

Peter's bushy eyebrows were knit together in a puzzled frown. "Lou, does it seem to you that these faculty members have yet to decide who will teach which course this semester?"

"That's what we've been told."

Peter shook his head and walked away.

Dirk returned carrying a large platter of brochen, the small, crusty rolls we'd seen in Windhoek, filled with sliced tomatoes, cheese, and salami. Christa, the seminary's secretary, followed him with two-liter bottles of Coke, Sprite, and Orange Crush. Angela carried a tray of drinking glasses covered with an embroidered dish towel.

After we had eaten, we took up the task of matching lecturers to courses. It took less time than I'd expected. Each faculty member had his or her specialty. Lou already knew he would be teaching pastoral counseling to the fourth-year students, and Peter's field was New Testament, so he would teach two sections of NT. Solveig and I decided to share English classes. I would have the more advanced students. Filling the class time slots, six forty-minute classes per day, proved to be more of a challenge. Most courses met three times a week, and there was gentle wrangling about who would have a teaching schedule free from Monday or Friday classes. Seniority seemed to prevail. In the middle of the negotiations, Dirk jumped up and ran to the window, slamming it shut. A small, dusty cyclone was spinning across the campus. No one except us Americans found this unusual.

At three o'clock, we trudged back home, thinking only of a cool drink and a nap.

"Are faculty meetings always that long?" I asked Angela as we stood in the cool shade of the tree between our houses.

She laughed. "I have yet to attend one that is shorter than four hours. You have just been introduced to African time."

I am embarrassed to think of my terrible teaching during those three months. The seminary had no grammar books, and the previous English teacher had left no lesson plans, so I patched together a series of grammar lessons from the ESL books Glenna had given me. I know now that the hours I spent drilling the students on verb tenses were not their happiest moments. Fortunately, my Namibian students were forgiving and gracious. Learning my students' names, though, was proving to be as big a challenge as teaching them English. I kept my seating chart on the lectern, and while they were conjugating verbs, I would scribble notes next to teach student's name: *chipped front tooth, widow's peak, glasses, long braids, mole on forehead, tribal scar on left cheek.* My crib sheet worked well until the women students decided to change their hairstyles.

The week after classes began two male students whose names I couldn't remember knocked on our front door. The handed me a piece of paper: *You are invited to come to the Dinning Hall at 19h00 on Thursday for the welcomming party.* I made a mental note to discuss spelling rules the following week.

I was also learning about the variety of tribal groups on campus. Most of our students and faculty colleagues were from one of the eight closely related Ovambo tribes. These were the dark-skinned ones whose families farmed the fertile land in the northern part of the country. Theirs was the predominant ethnic group in the country. They spoke Oshiwambo, a Bantu language. The few Herero students were also dark-skinned. Our German colleague, Angela, had told us that her husband, Gerson, was a Herero. The Nama students were lighter, yellowish-skinned, with almost oriental features. I learned that the Nama people were related to the Khoi or Khoisan ethnic group, the Bushmen of southern Africa. Their ancestors were a nomadic people, and their culture seemed to lack the cohesiveness of the Ovambo people, whose ancestors had tilled the land long enough to establish kingdoms and formal governance structures. The Nama's "click" language was similar to that of the Damaras, yet another distinct ethnic group.

Angela taught us that it wasn't disrespectful to call someone "coloured."

"It's what they call themselves," she said. "Our principal, Dirk, is coloured. Mixed race. His first language is Afrikaans."

"Isn't that the language spoken by the South Africans?" I asked.

"Yes, most South Africans speak Afrikaans, but South Africa has more than ten official languages. For a while, missionaries to Namibia were told not to learn Afrikaans because it was considered the language of the oppressors, but almost everyone here speaks better Afrikaans than English. It's what the children had to learn in school for the past thirty years or so."

I was having trouble keeping all these cultures and languages straight. I had thought I could at least learn to greet my students in their mother tongue, but could I learn all of these different greetings in just three months?

The welcoming party introduced us to what the Namibians call a *braai*, the Afrikaans word for barbecue or cookout. For most of the afternoon we had been smelling the delicious aroma of meat roasting outdoors, and by seven o'clock, our stomachs were rumbling. Four long tables covered with white tablecloths had been set up end-to-end in the center of the dining hall. Platters of roasted lamb, chicken, and plump, grilled sausages were flanked by big bowls of potato salad and shredded carrot and raisin salad. Towers of canned soft drinks balanced the display on either end of the buffet table. The students guided us to the long head table where all the faculty members and their wives were assembling. Between every two places was a program. It resembled the agenda for the faculty meeting. Prior to item number seven, "Eat Dinner," were listed four welcoming speeches, each interspersed with a selection by one of the seminary's many small choirs. The speech by the principal was the last one.

"We are very happy to welcome each and every student back to campus," Dirk said. "I would like to extend a special word of welcome to our guests from America." He nodded at Lou and me at one end of the table and Peter and Solveig at the other. "When I attended seminary in America, I was not made to feel welcome, and I want to make sure that doesn't happen to you."

I had been looking at Dirk, but when I heard those words, I looked down at my lap. From the corner of my eye, I could see that Lou was doing the same. I found it hard to believe that a visiting African student would have been snubbed at an American seminary. Was this a welcome, or was it something else? I didn't have time to think about this further because Rev. Amaambo was offering a table prayer. It was eight-thirty, and we were finally going to eat!

A few days later I was sitting in Angela's living room. She had closed the thick brocade curtains to block the heat of the summer sun. The heavy dark wood cabinets and upholstered brown chairs seemed like clunky intruders in this African village where, outside the seminary's perimeter fence, people lived in tarpaper shacks. Angela had told us that when she had married Gerson, she'd had her furniture shipped here from Germany. "It was actually cheaper than buying new furniture here."

I had come to her house this afternoon to learn how to catalogue books for the seminary's library. Most of those books were secondhand acquisitions from the libraries of retired American pastors. The seminary library maintained a complicated record-keeping system. Information about each book, including the name of the donor, was recorded in three separate logbooks. By hand. Once Angela assigned the Dewy Decimal numbers to the books, the subject, author, and title cards had to be typed for the card catalog. Solveig had agreed to help with the typing, and I had told Angela I would help her with the logbooks. I kept thinking how simple it would be to computerize this task. Angela must have read my thoughts.

"Once Paulinum relocates to Windhoek in a couple of years, all of this data will be entered into the seminary's computer. Perhaps we'll also be able to find a missionary who is a retired librarian to help us." We worked together in silence for another thirty minutes.

"Do you know about the Basters?" Angela asked.

Had I heard her correctly? What bastards?

"I know it sounds like a naughty word, but the Basters are very proud of their heritage. They are descendants of the Dutch colonizers of South Africa and indigenous Nama women. When the White, apartheid government of South Africa separated the people of Namibia into eleven categories according to race and tribe, the Basters enjoyed the same status as other coloureds. They were one category removed from the whites."

There was a lot more to learn about this country than I had realized, but I was discovering that my students were eager teachers. One day Namusha knocked on the door of our house. Namusha was, by far, the poorest student on campus, his poverty both economic and academic. He was slight of build, with a generous grin that crinkled his eyes and puffed up his cheeks like a child caught with forbidden sweets. I was surprised when he told me he was thirty-one. He looked a dozen years younger.

"Meme Susan, it is a good thing for you to learn the greetings in our language. I have come to teach you."

Most of our students had begun calling me *Meme* (MEH-may), an Oshiwambo word that means "Mommy." Their word for father is *Tate* (TAH-tay), but they preferred to call Lou *Tatekulu*, which means wise old grandfather or elder. It must have been his white beard.

I had noticed that our Ovambo students exchanged a sort of ritualized greeting with one another whenever they met. This greeting accompanied the obligatory handshake, the omission of which, I had quickly learned, was an insult. Namusha sat down next to me on the sofa, helped me pronounce the words, and gave me the literal English translation.

"*Wala la-po?*" (Did you sleep well?)

"*Eh.*" (Yes.)

"*Nawa?*" (Very well?)

"*Eh.*" (Yes.)

He said that each person must also return this greeting to the other person.

I reached for my yellow legal pad and asked him to write down the words. He did, explaining that this was the morning greeting. There were two more I needed to learn: one for midday and a third for evening. He wrote those down, too. I taped the language lesson to the door of our refrigerator, and practiced these vowel-heavy greetings several times daily. After a couple of weeks, they felt comfortable in my mouth, and my Oshiwambo-speaking students grinned when I greeted them in their mother tongue. Feeling pleased with myself, I sought out students who spoke Afrikaans, Damara-Nama, and Otjiherero. My Damara-Nama-speaking students laughed good-naturedly when I tried to distinguish among the seven different click sounds of their language.

Life in Otjimbingwe slipped into a comfortable routine of chapel services, classes, mealtimes and household chores. Despite the gravel road to Karibib that was always eager to offer us a punctured tire—we'd had two already—we looked forward to our weekly shopping and post office trips, especially the stop for filter coffee and pastries at the little coffee shop. Peter and Solveig joined Lou and me for meals in the dining hall. We were the only lecturers who ate with the students. The students' tables rimmed the perimeter of the room, and our small table for four was set up in the middle of the hall. It was the Namibian custom to serve the bigger meal in the middle of the day. The meat was usually chicken, goat, or beef. When I thought about the grazing land we'd passed on our drive from Windhoek to Otjimbingwe, more thorn bushes than grass, I was surprised those poor creatures had any edible meat on their lanky frames. I always enjoyed Friday lunch: fried fish, spaghetti with tomato sauce, and potato salad, but my favorite meal was Sunday lunch: baked chicken legs, rice with gravy, stewed pumpkin, and cold, slivered beets. It was the only meal where dessert was served: a parfait of vanilla pudding, fruit cocktail, and Jell-O. Peter called it TND: Traditional Namibian Dessert.

When the matron rang the bell for supper at six o'clock, the dining hall had been soaking up the Namibian sun all day and it felt as if we were entering a sauna. Those suppers were either bowls of hot soup with slices of bread (no butter or jam) or steaming bowls of oatmeal or maize meal porridge. After the first week, Solveig and I started bringing cotton bandanas with us to supper, and after each bite, we'd have to put down our spoons and wipe our sweaty faces.

Doing laundry posed other challenges. I had observed the women in the faculty houses washing their clothes outside in galvanized tubs, but somehow I couldn't see myself washing clothes in the yard, so I used the bathtub in our house. Lou helped with wringing out bath towels and queen-sized sheets. The clothes baked quickly on the line, and even the thickest towels dried in an hour. I had failed to notice that those Namibian women always hung their clothes inside out. By the end of those three months, Lou's two pairs of dark khaki jeans had been bleached white by the sun.

One morning I hoisted my tote bag onto my shoulder, grabbed my wide-brimmed white hat from the kitchen counter, and stepped outside, ready for my nine-thirty English class. The morning's laundry was drying on the clothesline, and I thought I saw something moving behind the bath towels. A large black pig, no doubt a refugee from the village, was rooting in the ground. I wondered what he thought he'd find in that hard-packed sand. Suddenly I heard a shout. Gentle Tomas, who never shouted and never ran, unless he was playing volleyball with the students, was charging after the pig, a thick branch in his hand. He chased the porker out of our yard and through the seminary gate. He returned, breathless and the closest to angry that I'd ever seen him. "That pig was eating our maize! I've told the workers they must keep that gate closed. I'm sorry, Susan, if I startled you."

March 21 was a national holiday, Namibia's fifth Independence Day. Many of the students and about half of the faculty had hitched rides into Windhoek to see the parades and join the crowds at the huge soccer stadium on the edge of town. We felt fortunate to be in Namibia for this festive day and were tempted to accept Peter and Solveig's invitation to join them in Windhoek, but the prospect of that long, hot journey lacked the appeal of a leisurely day spent writing overdue letters to our family and reading. After lunch, Lou said that he was going to drive up to the little shop in the village to buy some Cokes. When he returned, his face was grim.

"I was coming out of the shop, and just getting into the car when two guys approached me. I could tell they'd been drinking, and they were shouting at me and waving their fists."

"What were they saying?"

"I couldn't tell. They were speaking Afrikaans. When I got into our car, they got into the one next to me and tried to block my way out of the parking area. The driver rammed the front of our car. I sped up, but they didn't follow me. I don't think the car is damaged, other than the bumper."

"Did you do or say anything in the shop that might have insulted them?"

"Of course not! I didn't even see them in the shop. They were just hanging around outside."

"Perhaps they weren't happy to see a white guy on Independence Day.

A case of being in the wrong place at the wrong time."

We went outside and examined the bashed-in bumper. We could probably get it repaired when we got back to Windhoek.

"Do you think we should tell Dirk?" I asked.

"I'd really rather not. Let's just drop it, okay?"

A week later, Lou happened to mention the incident to kindly Rev. Amaambo, the lecturer with whom he taught pastoral counseling. The next day Dirk knocked on our door. This was the first time he had come to our house.

"Why didn't you tell me about what happened on Independence Day?" He was scowling, and I immediately felt guilty, as if the bumper bashing had been our fault.

"Dirk, I really didn't want to make an issue of this," said Lou.

"You should have told me. This sort of behavior against a foreign visitor is inexcusable. Do you think you could identify the men who did this?"

"Perhaps. I don't know. Can't we just forget about it?"

"No, I'm going to raise it with the village magistrate."

Village life was feeling less idyllic. The next morning Dirk called Lou into his office and introduced him to the magistrate, a tall fellow in a tan suit. Two dark-skinned black youths were standing next to him.

"Are these the young men who damaged your car?" the magistrate asked Lou.

Lou said that they were.

"Someone saw what happened outside the shop that day, and it didn't take much investigation to find out who they were. They will pay you for the repairs."

Lou told me that he had started to protest, but a frown from Dirk kept him from saying anything. That evening we told Angela what had happened.

"That was an unfortunate racial incident," she said. "And I'm not talking about the car business. Look, I probably shouldn't say this, but you have to be careful around Dirk. He isn't as open-minded about racial equality as he would have you think."

I remembered Dirk's comment at the welcoming dinner. "Is it because of those long years of South African rule?"

"Yes, that's certainly part of it. Namibia's various ethnic groups were living together, more or less peacefully, before the South Africans took over, but what we're seeing here now is something new since

Independence. You see, now we have a SWAPO government. I think you remember that SWAPO was the name of the group of freedom fighters who fought for Namibia's liberation?"

I nodded.

"Their leader was Sam Nujoma, who is now the country's president. He's an Ovambo, and so are most of his ministers and cabinet appointees. The Ovambos are the predominant tribal group in the country. The people who used to be considered privileged, the whites and the coloureds, have very few seats in government. I suppose they feel dispossessed. On the other hand, there is still economic apartheid in this country."

"What do you mean?"

"Most of the businesses and the larger, productive farms are firmly in the hands of the whites."

I understood why those youths might have been angry to see a white man in their village, but I was still surprised by what Angela had said about Dirk. "Have you seen this racism on the seminary campus?"

"Oh, I could tell you stories." She paused. "Perhaps another day. There are a lot of cultural differences here. I think everyone is still learning how to live together again after those apartheid years. It isn't easy."

Another disappointing aspect of campus life turned out to be our daily chapel services. In the months before we'd come to Namibia, Lou and I had enjoyed listening to CDs of lively African choirs accompanied by strong, rhythmic drumming. I suppose I had been expecting our worship experiences to be as dynamic as those of the black gospel churches I'd visited in the States. We were startled to discover the seminary community using the "green book," the Lutheran Book of Worship that Lutheran congregations used in the United States. Not only did they use the same liturgies, they also sang the same hymns. When I asked our faculty colleague, Michael Shangala, about that, he simply shrugged and said that the LBW was the best English-language liturgy available.

"What do Namibian Lutherans use in their own churches? Those services aren't in English, are they?"

"No, I think there is only one other English-language Lutheran worship service in Namibia. It's the Sunday service at Inner City Congregation in Windhoek. I think you saw that church when you stayed in the guesthouse there. Our churches in the north have their own liturgies. Many of our hymns are ones we learned from the Finnish missionaries. The Southern Church's congregations have adapted their liturgies from what they learned from the German missionaries to those regions."

Michael's short explanation reminded me of what I had naively forgotten. Even though we had been invited to this campus and this country to teach, Lou and I were missionaries, albeit temporary ones. We were updated, American versions of a 150-year legacy of those German and Finnish missionaries to Namibia. I wonder why that thought made me feel so uncomfortable. Was it because I didn't want to be associated with those earlier evangelists whose Gospel message had arrived on the continent encased in cultural baggage? My students had already told me, "When the missionaries arrived they told us we had to stop wearing animal skins and the ladies couldn't be bare-breasted anymore. They said we couldn't use drums in our worship services and that we could only have one wife."

I'd felt proud, and perhaps a little smug, that *Americans* hadn't colonized or evangelized the country. Coming later, we could relate to our Namibian colleagues in modern ways. After all, we were teachers, not really missionaries. Weren't we?

Lou and I had brought with us a cassette tape and a printed copy of a contemporary Lutheran vespers liturgy, Marty Haugen's *Holden Evening Prayer*. We had thought it might be fun to introduce this to the seminary community. Now, we weren't so sure. Would this be yet another imperialistic intrusion received by Namibian colleagues who were too polite to refuse?

"Let's try," said Lou. "We'll ask the faculty."

"I've got a better idea. Why don't we invite them all to our house in the evening for refreshments so we can play the tape for them?"

We had arranged extra chairs in a circle in the middle of the living room and offered our guests mango juice and an assortment of cookies. Lou spoke a few words of introduction.

"We would like to give you the opportunity to listen to a new version of the vespers liturgy. Essentially, it is the same as the one in the green book that you are using for the Wednesday evening services in the chapel, but the words and the music are a little more up to date. It's a liturgy I have used in my own congregation in North Carolina. We'd like to know what you think."

He switched on the tape player and we held our breath as our colleagues listened intently to the music. Would their conservative upbringing find this offensive? As the voices and guitar segued into the final litany, Rev. Amaambo was smiling. Tomas Shivtue had closed his eyes and was gently nodding in time to the music. Dirk Cloete was tapping his foot. Lou turned off the tape player and looked expectantly at the principal.

"Wonderful!" said Dirk. "You must teach this to the students. Let's do it next week!"

"Well," said Lou, "it might take a little longer than one week. We will need to get more copies of the liturgy. Perhaps fifty. I think I saw a place in Windhoek that could photocopy these for us."

"We could invite the students here to our house, in small groups, to listen and practice singing along with the cassette," I added, mentally calculating how many bottles of juice and packages of cookies we'd need to buy.

Three weeks later, rehearsed and eager, everyone gathered together on Wednesday evening for vespers. I held my breath. We'd be singing this service *a capella*, as we did all services in the chapel. Would the students remember what they'd been taught? I have a powerful voice, a voice that used to embarrass my children when they sat in the pew next to me, and I felt myself vocally pulling the community through the rough patches like a woman hauling water jugs from the well. What I hadn't expected was the harmony. I'd become accustomed to the students' spontaneous four-part harmonization of those old workhorse hymns in the green book, but here they were, harmonizing music they scarcely knew.

Everyone agreed the new vespers service was a success. I wondered if the seminary community would ever use it again. Since we would be returning home in a few weeks, I'd never know. Maybe it was enough for them to have learned that it was possible to try new ways of worship. Did that make me a missionary?

Once the students realized we would soon be leaving, their visits to our home increased. One afternoon, when it was too hot to sleep, too hot to correct assignments, too hot to do anything but sit in the shade of a tree and sip lemonade, Namusha stopped by. I poured him some lemonade and asked him about life in his village

"Oh, Meme," he said. "It is very difficult. We are ten, my sisters and brothers and I, and my mother is a widow. The money, it is not so much. Last year—my first year here—I used to get potato bags from the kitchen, iron them, and use them for paper for my assignments." He raised his leg to show me his sandal. "I make these shoes from old car tires," he said. "Sometimes I sell them."

I asked him to wait in the yard. Inside, I gathered up all our extra paper, notebooks and pens and brought them outside to him. From the grin on his face, I had the feeling Namusha hadn't received very many gifts in his life.

A few days later Menthos came to visit. This tall, handsome fellow was also a second-year student who occasionally played the piano for our chapel services. He wanted to know if we could give him money to buy a new trumpet so he could play in his church's brass band. Sorry, Menthos.

One evening Annelie came to see Lou. She was a stout, matronly fourth-year student. I had noticed that the younger students respected her as they would an elder. My husband told me that this would be a counseling session and asked if I'd mind waiting in our bedroom. Three hours later, Lou opened the door.

"What a sad situation." I pushed the notebooks and grammar papers aside, and he sat down on the bed next to me. "When she was a child, Annelie lived with an uncle who sexually abused her. She had never told anyone until this evening. I asked her if there were an older pastor with whom she'd feel comfortable discussing this, or maybe one of the women deacons in the church. She really needs more counseling than I can give her in the next two weeks."

I was to celebrate my forty-eighth birthday the week before our departure. Lou must have mentioned this to one of his classes because when Angela heard about it she alerted me to a seminary tradition. "The students gather outside your bedroom window before dawn to awaken you with songs. When they finish singing, you are expected to invite them inside for coffee and tea."

The night before my birthday, I made sure I had plenty of instant coffee, teabags, and cookies on hand. Once again, Angela lent me dishes. The village roosters usually awakened me with their morning chorus an hour before dawn. As I lay in bed, I heard soft giggles and, "Shhh, shhh!" outside the bedroom window. The serenade of hymns lasted twenty minutes. I grabbed my bathrobe, and when I welcomed all forty-four of them into our house, they burst into a rousing chorus of "Happy Birthday to You!"

"It's how we honor our parents," Annelie said. I thought I saw tears glistening in her eyes.

Chapter 4
Doubt and Desire

*O*ur last night in Otjimbingwe, Lou and I lay in bed unable to sleep, recalling our experiences of the past three months. We could smile, now, at the memories of our sweaty suppers in the dining hall. And the day the campus had run out of water. We all waited two days for the flat bed truck with its big rubber bladder filled with water and gathered round with our pots and pans and buckets. We wouldn't miss the scary kitchen cockroaches. (Lou chopped in half a particularly huge, horrid specimen one night before we went to bed, and the next morning the two halves were still writhing, as if trying to rejoin themselves.) We laughed at the Good Friday service in the village church: the woman pastor had announced it was a day of silence, but she could scarcely be heard above the bawling of the thirty infants who were being baptized that morning. It was difficult to imagine that in less than a week we would be back in our Chapel Hill home, shouldering the demands of our Chapel Hill jobs. We listened to the chirping crickets, shivered, and snuggled together under the duvet. It was April, and the cool breeze through the windows reminded us that winter was coming to Namibia.

The rising moon brightened the bedroom, and we talked on. Did we think we had contributed something useful to this seminary during the three months? Yes. Could we handle the difficulties and the distance from our children and our home country? Probably. Was it fun? Absolutely. We felt such a strong tug to cast our lot with the people of Africa, but was this the sort of thing reasonable, middle-aged people did?

"Listen," said Lou, "why don't we have a short talk with Dirk tomorrow morning before we leave? In a couple of years Megan will be in college and this seminary will have relocated to Windhoek. Doesn't it make sense to ask if they'd like us to come back? If Dirk says yes, we can talk with the folks in Chicago and see if a longer term appointment would be possible—paid positions, of course."

Lou's suggestions made sense. We wouldn't be making any sort of commitment, but I liked the idea of propping open the door. The next morning, while Lou finished loading our suitcases into the car, I made a final check to be sure we hadn't left anything behind. In the corner of the living room I had assembled the items we'd be leaving for certain faculty friends: bath towels, small kitchen items, and the pedestal fan we wanted to give to Matheus, the treasurer.

"Wonderful!" Dirk said when we asked if the seminary would like us to come back. "Lou, Rev. Amaambo will be retiring soon and you could take the pastoral counseling course. And, Susan, Paulinum really needs a native-speaking English teacher. I will send a letter to DGM right away and tell them we want you to come back."

We thanked Dirk and told him we would look forward to seeing him in Windhoek in two days for the meeting of the Relocation Committee, our last official duty before we left the country. As we were walking out the door, Dirk said, "Oh! I almost forgot. You wouldn't mind leaving me that pedestal fan of yours, would you?"

Lou and I quickly looked at each other. "Sure, Dirk," said Lou. "We'll leave it for you in the house." We returned to our house only long enough to remove from the fan the note with Matheus' name on it.

Sister Agnes welcomed us back to the Windhoek guesthouse as if we were dear friends. Had we passed some sort of test? She escorted us to a roomy flat with a kitchenette where we would stay for our final few days in Namibia. Now that we were thinking about returning, we had a particular interest in the meeting of the committee to plan the relocation of the seminary from Otjimbingwe to Windhoek.

We joined our faculty colleagues who gathered the next morning in the large conference room of the Southern Church's headquarters, just around the corner from our guest flat. We found two seats next to each other at the conference table. Dirk formally introduced us, along with Peter and Solveig, to the bishops and general secretaries of the two Namibian Lutheran Churches, and to Jurgen Borchard, the young man from Germany who had been appointed the head of the Relocation Task Force. I noticed a gentleman at the far end of the table to whom we had not been introduced. He was coloured, like Dirk. His hair looked as if it had been stretched tight and glued to his scalp. He smoothed his already tidy mustache with his index finger and scowled at the stack of papers on the table in front of him. The group spent two hours talking about such things as what pieces of furniture and equipment to transport to the new facilities and whether the maintenance and kitchen staff would also make the move or remain in Otjimbingwe. Mr. Borchard suggested there might be major construction delays because the electricians and plumbers seemed unable to meet the contractor's timetable. The man at the end of the table exploded.

"Delays are unacceptable! We need to get the seminary into the city as soon as possible. As an academic institution, Paulinum just isn't taken seriously as long as it remains in the middle of the desert. It's like a remote mission outpost that everyone has forgotten about."

Rev. Amaambo agreed. "You don't understand," he said, glaring at the church officials. "It's like being in a prison out there."

During tea break, we introduced ourselves to the mustached man we hadn't yet met. I was surprised to see that he was such a short fellow.

"My name is Dr. Johan van Wyk," he said, lighting a cigarette. "I used to be on the Paulinum faculty, back in the days of The Struggle." He took several deep drags on his cigarette, like a parched traveler gulping water. "The seminary has the potential to become one of the best in Africa, and I intend to see that it does." Dr. van Wyk said he was presently the principal of a Lutheran high school.

The following morning Angela and Gerson drove us to the airport. I told Angela that I had been impressed with Dr. van Wyk and wondered if he might be reappointed to the seminary faculty. I was surprised by her silence. When she finally spoke, she said that such an appointment may not be a good idea, but when I pressed her, she refused to elaborate. I wondered what there was about Dr. van Wyk that she wasn't telling us.

Back in Chapel Hill, our job and family responsibilities swallowed us whole. In addition, we were worried about Esther, my mother-in-law, whose health was failing. Lou and I had hoped to have time to more fully examine our Namibian experience with each other, but something else always seemed to need our attention. As the months passed we started questioning our earlier desire and our motivation. Did we really want to work in Africa, or were we simply in love with the image of doing so? Was this a religious commitment—a call—that we were trying to discern, or was it the yearning of two aging baby boomers to be what their generation had always prized: relevant? I've never been one of those Christians who claims that God talks to her. Although I'd never heard any thunderous commands or even gentle whispers, I couldn't dismiss the thought that, somehow, Lou and I were being invited to pack our bags for a lengthy spiritual journey. When Lou's parishioners had asked him why he was going to Africa, he told them, "It seemed to me that God was saying, 'Come to Africa. I have something to show you.'" That felt right, but now I was asking God, "Okay, but do you *really* want us to move there?" As usual, God was silent.

And then, there was the "missionary" label. Despite our mostly positive experience in Otjimbingwe, I couldn't help thinking of those dreadful stereotypes of pious, homely folks living in crude grass shacks trying to teach Bible stories to nearly naked heathens. And, of course, there's the unfortunate cartoon in everyone's head of the cannibals with bones in their noses dancing around the poor missionary stewing in the cooking pot. It seemed as if modern missionaries, at least in the Lutheran Church, didn't proselytize. They worked alongside indigenous people as teachers, administrators, nurses, and doctors.

When Megan began her senior year of high school, we made our decision. We contacted the Division for Global Mission and told them we were ready to return to Africa, to be employed as contract missionaries. Perhaps we felt freed, too, by the passing away of my dear mother-in-law. Esther had always worried so much when we had taken those three previous trips to the continent, fearing we would never return. We had never told her about our quest to discern new vocations overseas, and I doubt we could have undertaken such a venture had she still been with us.

Despite his promise to contact DGM, Dirk hadn't done so, and we found ourselves in the awkward position of having to write to him. Without a specific request from the Lutheran Church in Namibia, DGM would not send us back there. When DGM finally received Dirk's letter, they had to approve funding for our positions. That took another six months. Eventually, we were approved for faculty lecturer positions in Namibia. We signed contracts for two years, with the option to renew them.

"Oh, you're so brave!" people told me. Was it because they thought we would be living in a dangerous place with wild animals and unpredictable natives? Maybe, behind our backs, they shook their heads and thought, "What a foolish thing to do at this stage in their lives."

Steve, one of Lou's friends from divinity school days, said, "You know, Lou, you have really done a daring thing to take yourself out of your professional career track. You'll never get back in." Even clergy have career tracks. I suppose Steve's admonition meant that Lou would never be called to a larger, more prestigious congregation, but I doubted that would bother him.

And yet, Steve's comment gave me one of those stomach-lurching, what-have-I-done feelings. Ten years earlier I had finally found a career that satisfied my need for vocational meaning. I felt that my work at the medical school made a difference in the lives of desperately ill patients, and leaving this position would not be easy. Could I reenter the field after a hiatus of two, or more, years? Would I want to?

Frederick Buechner locates vocation as "the place where your deep gladness meets the world's deep need." Our deep gladness had met the raggedy children playing with toys fashioned from empty Coke cans. It had met the serious young women, infants swaddled on their backs, selling their tomatoes, peppers, and onions by the side of the road. My deep gladness had also met those Namibian students in the predawn darkness of my forty-eighth birthday when they gathered outside my bedroom window to serenade their English teacher.

It isn't easy to explain a "call" to nonbelievers. My heart was pounding when I picked up the telephone to tell my elderly parents that we would be moving to Namibia for at least two years. Our family had emigrated from war-ravaged England when I was a small child, and my parents were grateful for the jobs that fed and sheltered their young family. Mom and Dad understood sacrificing and striving for financial security, a goal they had achieved. What they had trouble understanding was the concept of a religious vocation. When I was a child, they would drop me off at Sunday school and pick me up when the hour was over. When I could drive, I took myself to church and to youth group activities. They seemed to like Lou well enough, but I know they were embarrassed to tell their friends that their eldest daughter had married a minister.

Consequently, I was uncomfortable using religious language around my parents. And yet, this was the only way I knew to explain the reasons for our decision. I told them that, in the Bible, the prophet Micah offers a simple requirement for a life lived faithfully: "...and what does the Lord require of you but to do justice, and to love kindness, and to walk humbly with your God." I mentioned, as well, the concluding words of Jesus in his parable of the sheep and the goats: "Inasmuch as you did it to one of the least of these my brethren, you did it to me." I told Mom and Dad that we had met so many African people struggling to survive and thrive with so little. Where was the justice in this? "Lou and I couldn't rest easily with those images, knowing the relative ease of our own lives. We won't be doing actual relief work, but we are hoping that, in some way, our teaching will help. Do you understand?" They said very little. I suppose they knew something like this was coming, given those previous three trips, but I could tell they still thought our decision was frivolous, and I know they genuinely feared for our safety.

With our sights set toward Africa, our own lingering fears and doubts began to fade. The preparations seemed endless: visas and vaccinations and many months of waiting for Namibia's Ministry of Home Affairs to approve our work visas. In the midst of our packing and leave-takings, I began combing the bookstores for useful books about teaching English as a Second Language, and Lou selected several large boxes of books from his professional library at the church. The others would be placed in storage. We hired the services of Missionary Expediters, a company specializing in shipping missionaries' belongings overseas. We filled twelve cartons with our books, medicines and toiletries, sheets and towels, family photographs, extra clothes, zip-lock plastic bags of all sizes, and lots of packets of Lipton's Chicken Noodle Soup, my favorite comfort food. Missionary Expediters assured us our belongings would arrive in Namibia, by airfreight, the week after we did.

Time collapsed. Our realtor told us she'd found a buyer for our house. We sold our cars and attended various farewell parties. On our last Sunday in Chapel Hill, Dan Olson flew in from Chicago. During the morning worship service at our church, he officially commissioned us to be missionaries on behalf of the church-at-large. Unlike my husband, who had been through services of installation whenever he was called to a new parish, this was a new, solemn moment for me. It almost felt like a wedding ceremony. The Chapel Hill News sent its religion editor to our home to do a feature story about us. The big color photo that appeared above the fold showed us stuffing clothes into storage boxes. The family-owned moving company we'd engaged also operated a storage facility where our furniture, winter clothes, toaster, bathroom scale, and washing machine would reside in climate-controlled comfort for two hundred dollars a month. I wondered what sort of a person I would have become when we unpacked all our stuff at the conclusion of our adventure.

In July, prior to our departure, we were required to attend a month-long orientation for new missionaries in Chicago. With all our preparations completed, we decided that we would simply leave for Africa directly from Chicago. The training took place on a college campus where we spent four weeks attending workshops and lectures and getting to know about fifty fellow missionaries, both Lutheran and Presbyterian. We received briefings about what to do if we became ill, how to correspond with the American congregations that supported us, and how to adapt to being strangers in a strange land. Our instructors filled our heads with advice and admonitions. We learned politically correct language: never use the words *hut*, *native*, or *tribe*—these words are disrespectful. Our most valuable advice came from an elderly Jesuit missionary, Tony Gittens.

"You're going to have to learn to manage the transitions," he said. "We Americans don't like transitions. We like to manage them and get over them. Your journey starts now. In your home country. You will feel like Alice in Wonderland. Your perceptions of what is real will be shattered. Many things will be taken away from you: privacy, personal space, hygiene, being understood. You must remember that you will be in permanent transition, and you're going to try to control that again and again. The question to which you must find the answer is this: how do I live this way when my culture and friends are all about permanency?"

I scribbled page after page of Father Gittens' words into my little notebook. I felt as if I were taking an advanced graduate course and I guess, in a way, I was. The test of how well I learned this stuff would be real life, lived in a country thousands of miles from home. I had been feeling a little smug those first few days telling our new missionary friends that we'd already spent three months in Namibia. Now I felt as if I knew nothing.

Gittens told us that we would find ourselves wondering and worrying about whether we would be considered irrelevant by our indigenous colleagues. "Missionaries who create their own agendas can busy themselves every day, but still be irrelevant," he said. He reminded us that life in our new countries was going on long before our arrival, and that it would continue long after we departed. "Remember that you are encountering people with their own history and context. And you are arriving with yours. Don't forget to fill yourselves in for the local people. They need to learn you as much as you need to learn them."

I had studied such concepts as socialization and acculturation thirty years earlier as a college student. Now the lessons were real. Father Gittens was intent upon stripping away our illusions and romanticizations, but he also assured us that, in time, we'd know when were "on the agenda."

One weekend my parents drove in from Cleveland to see us one last time before we left the country. They seemed to be easier with our decision, and we shared some wonderful dinners at their hotel restaurant, laughing at Dad's stories about their own travels abroad. The next weekend, my sister, Candace, flew in from Denver. These family farewells plus all our training sessions reminded me that this really was a

Big Deal.

I felt a mixture of excitement, trepidation and numbing fatigue when we finally stepped off the plane at Hosea Kutako Airport on that chilly winter evening in July 1997. We'd been traveling for twenty-one hours. No one could accuse the Namibian immigration clerks of inattention to detail. After thirty-five minutes, we reached the front of the queue, only to have the immigration officer tell us that since we had work visas we would have to meet privately with her in her office after she had finished processing the other passengers. We stepped aside and peered through the large plate glass window at the side of the terminal where crowds of people were waiting to greet the passengers. I remembered our last arrival at this airport when the Bishop had failed to appear, and I hoped to see at least one familiar face. There, waving to us behind the window, was our friend Angela—and her husband Gerson. I also recognized our faculty colleagues Tomas, Michael, and Rev. Amaambo, along with the seminary treasurer, Matheus, and many students we recognized from two years ago. We had not been forgotten!

When we were finally able to greet our friends, I counted twenty-eight people from Paulinum. Handshakes and African double-hugs for everyone. Just outside the terminal, the students told us that they wanted to sing two hymns for us, and they offered a prayer, thanking God for bringing us all together again. We paused for a moment to inhale the dusty familiar scent of Africa while the students argued with each other to determine who would carry our four heavy suitcases to the waiting vehicles. I shivered in the chilly night air and was glad I'd tucked a sweater into my carry-on bag. The students were all wearing heavy winter coats.

"Why don't you and Lou ride with Gerson and me?" suggested Angela. "We can use the time to catch up on things." The rest of the faculty members and students climbed into three cars and the seminary's shiny new combi, the Namibian name for a mini-bus.

"I didn't see Dirk," said Lou.

"He's at home, recovering from appendicitis," said Angela. "Uh, perhaps I shouldn't say this, but you'll probably find out anyway. Dirk had told the students they weren't permitted to come to the airport this evening."

"Really?" I asked. "Did he say why?"

"No, but that's just the way he is sometimes. You remember."

I wasn't sure I did. Other than that bit of unpleasantness about the bashed-in car bumper in Otjimbingwe, Dirk had always seemed friendly toward us.

"They came anyway, didn't they?"

"Of course! The ones who were your students two years ago were excited that you would be returning. They've been telling the newer students all about you."

Gerson turned onto the highway leading to town and Angela chattered on, bringing us up to date on the lives of our faculty colleagues. I was sorry to hear that she was no longer on the seminary faculty. She'd been appointed to a multi-church task force created to bring about a merger of the three Lutheran church bodies in Namibia. She told us that Johan van Wyk, the intense little man with the mustache and cigarette we'd met at the Relocation Committee meeting, was now a faculty member.

"That's a good thing, isn't it?"

"No, Susan, it is actually a terrible thing."

"He seemed like a thoughtful, educated person. Why wouldn't he be a good addition to the faculty?"

"It's rather a long story. I suppose I can give you the short version. You probably don't know this, but van Wyk used to be the bishop of the Lutheran Church in the South. During The Struggle—I think it was in the mid-eighties—he turned his back on indigenous Namibians. He went to work for the South African government department that was administering Namibia. He treated the black Namibians very badly. He even denied the new, black bishop a visa to travel to America. The Church excommunicated him, but later, when Namibia became independent, the Church welcomed him back, in a gesture of reconciliation. It's really too bad that they did, because he has been nothing but trouble ever since."

"I thought he was a high school principal. That's what he told us when we met him two years ago."

"Yes, he was, but the Church audited the school's books and found financial irregularities. There were rumors that he had misappropriated funds, but he resigned and the Church decided not to pursue the matter. The Church Board tried to assign him to be a pastor of a congregation, but none of the congregations would take him. When the seminary relocated, the Church Board decided to appoint him to the faculty. Bishop Diergaardt has told me the Church Board thought van Wyk would be better off in a situation where others could keep an eye on his behavior.

There are some other things I will tell you later."

We were entering Windhoek. Gerson turned onto Robert Mugabe Avenue, and I peered through the window to see if the place still looked the same as I had been remembering it. I couldn't see much because night had enshrouded the city in darkness and the streetlights were few. There weren't many cars on the road, and I recalled that this is a town that falls asleep after dusk. We were only about a mile from the new seminary, and I was eager to see what had become of the construction site Dirk had shown us in 1995.

The twenty-acre campus was located in Pionierspark, an upscale suburb of Windhoek. A strong chain-link fence topped with coils of razor wire encircled the entire perimeter of the complex. Our four-vehicle convoy stopped outside the fence, and a worker emerged from a small guardhouse on the left and unlocked the gate. Lampposts positioned throughout the campus shone enough light to reveal a collection of tan-colored brick buildings, all with red tiled roofs. Angela identified the buildings for us.

"These three buildings just to our right are the student dormitories, and the big building beyond them, just past this volleyball court, is the dining hall and recreation room. Over there," she gestured to her left, "are the classrooms, library, and offices."

Gerson continued driving straight, past a large chapel in the center of the campus. In front of the chapel was a huge open space, an amphitheatre, with a stage at one side and tiered rows of cement seats at the other. The road forked, and Angela continued. "The houses in front of us and up the hill to the left are all faculty houses. There were supposed to be seven, but at the last minute, the builder decided he could fit one more in."

Lou and I had been told we'd be living in an apartment, not a faculty house, and I was beginning to wonder where it was. Gerson turned right and I saw a two-story brick building with four little patios behind each of the ground-floor units and four small balconies extending from the units above. Behind the building was a large parking lot, with a long clothesline at one end. A carport with a corrugated tin roof was at the other side of the lot, opposite the apartment building. I counted spaces for ten vehicles. "This is the block that was built for guest lecturers and married students." We were home.

The students had already climbed out of the combi and had begun to haul our suitcases up the outside staircase. "Your flat is on the second floor," one of them said. "Meme, you and Tatekulu will be the first people to live in this flat." We followed a tall, slender young man who had told us his name was Jonah. He set the suitcase down in front of the flat at the far end of the building. In front of the door was a sturdy metal gate.

Angela reached into her handbag, extracted a set of house keys, and unlocked the security gate and the door. "Gerson and I came here earlier today and left you a few groceries." She gestured to a narrow galley kitchen to our right. "I know you're tired, so we'll go now and let you rest."

It didn't take long to explore our new home. Straight ahead was a small sitting room sparsely furnished with a dark blue, upholstered sofa and matching chair and a blond wood coffee table, both brand new, with simple, modern lines. I opened the door onto the balcony and saw that we had a panoramic view of the entire campus. There was no dining area, but built into one end of the sitting room was a long counter. Above that counter, a small window with a sliding door opened into the kitchen. For seating, tucked under the counter, were two old wooden chairs, like the ones I remembered from the Otjimbingwe library and dining hall. There were two bedrooms, a queen-sized bed in the larger room and two twin beds in the other. At first I was surprised to find no chests of drawers or dressers, but then I discovered that both bedrooms had large, built-in cupboards with lots of shelves for storage. The empty plaster walls and bare linoleum floors reminded me of a college dormitory on moving-in day. The flat exuded a sweetish, musty odor, not exactly unpleasant but not the fresh-paint smell I would have expected in a brand-new apartment. Perhaps it was the combination of plaster and linoleum. All the windows were dressed with crisp, gaily patterned African print draperies and sheers. As tired as I was, I had already begun planning how much better the place would look with rugs, plants, pictures, and a bit more furniture.

I always have trouble falling asleep the night after a transatlantic flight. I kept remembering fragments of what we had been taught in Chicago, just a few days earlier, and I recalled Angela's strange story about Dr. van Wyk and Dirk's admonition to the students not to meet us at the airport. I thought about Jason and Megan, about my parents, and about the North Carolina town we had called home for eleven years, now six thousand miles away.

Once Lou and I had decided we would move to Africa, I liked to tell people we were pulling up our roots. It sounded dramatic, but it wasn't really accurate. The weeks and months ahead would show me that our roots had never left their American soil. What we had done was to take a cutting of ourselves—a slender stem with a few leaves—with the hope that it would thrive for a while in the earth of Africa. Transplants are fragile. I had forgotten that propagation-by-cuttings often means that the original leaves attached to that thin stem will die before new ones start to grow. It might have been helpful if I had remembered that during those early months.

Chapter 5
Strike!

*I*t was still dark at six o'clock the next morning. When my feet touched the floor, I groped for the socks I'd tossed in a corner the night before. No one had told us Namibia was so cold in the middle of the winter. I leaned across the bed and shook Lou awake. "We need to get dressed so we can go to the chapel service at seven-thirty." He groaned and grumbled and pulled the duvet up to his beard. "No, really," I insisted. "We ought to make a good impression on our first day here."

On my way into the kitchen I stopped in the hallway to switch on the portable oil-filled space heater that looked like an old-fashioned radiator on wheels. I found an old saucepan in one of the kitchen cupboards. While I waited for the water to boil for coffee, I made a mental note to buy an electric kettle when we went to town. Then I heard a shout from the bathroom.

"There's no shower!"

"Yes there is—just sit in the tub and use that spray attachment on the faucet."

More grumbling.

We were already walking to the chapel in the center of the campus when the urgent clanging from the bell tower startled the birds in the acacia trees. I wondered how the residents of this upscale neighborhood felt about the daily reveille from their new neighbor. Lou was still muttering about his sit-down shower.

At the conclusion of the service, Rev. Amaambo, who was also the dean of students, stood up and introduced us to the students and faculty. Everyone applauded. While the students hurried off to eat breakfast or get ready for their classes, Lou and I lingered with several of the lecturers outside the chapel. I noticed that neither Dirk nor Dr. van Wyk was among them. Michael Shangala, whom we knew from Otjimbingwe, introduced us to the other missionaries. Marjorie, who lived in the flat next to ours, was a retired librarian. Her wrinkled cotton blouse and flyaway grey hair announced that she had more important things to worry about than her appearance. She offered a no-nonsense handshake and told us she had recently worked as a seminary librarian in Indonesia, and that she'd be here in Windhoek for two years. "You're welcome to use my car for shopping until you get yours," she said.

The Lessings—Hanns and Ute—were both pastors from Germany. Hanns was a slightly built fellow with streaks of stubble on his chin that looked like a hastily plowed field of maize. His wife, a hefty woman in tight Levis, was trying to juggle a sheaf of papers under one arm while resisting the insistent tugs of a three-year-old daughter. They told us they had moved into "our" house in Otjimbingwe two months after we had left, and had been teaching at the seminary ever since. I heard Lou asking Hanns if he knew the location of a plumbing supply store when Michael motioned that he wanted to have a word with me.

"Susan, I have been teaching the two English classes this year, but now that you're here I want you to take these classes. I already have more than I can handle with the other courses I'm teaching this semester, so I'll tell the students that you will begin teaching them on Monday."

"Uh, yeah. Sure."

Dan, our area program director in Chicago, had told me that since the semester was half over, I wouldn't start teaching until the start of the new school year, in about five months. He'd said I could use those early months to plan my curriculum and assist the seminary in other ways. Monday was only five days away, and all my ESL books were in our shipment of boxes that had not yet arrived. I'd have to make it up as I went along.

Each day there was a mid-morning tea break. The students gathered in the dining hall for tea and bread with jam, and the faculty met in the staff room. We expected to meet the principal there, but when Dirk failed to appear, Lou suggested we pay a call upon him at his home. Perhaps his recovery from appendicitis was keeping him housebound. We couldn't forget what Angela had told us about Dirk's refusal to allow the students to meet us at the airport. And the students' blatant disregard of his injunction. We wondered if we would receive a chilly welcome.

To our surprise, Dirk couldn't have been friendlier. He apologized for not having come to see us as soon as we arrived and told us the seminary staff had been looking forward to our joining the faculty. He paused, and the smile left his face.

"To tell you the truth, there doesn't seem to be a good spirit on this campus these days. The students are always complaining, and we seem to have more problems than we did in Otjmbingwe. I will be glad when my term as principal is over in January."

I wondered what the students had been complaining about. Lou and I had already noticed that half of them failed to attend the daily chapel services which were supposed to be mandatory. Perhaps we would hear more in a few days at the first faculty meeting.

Meanwhile, we felt like newlyweds trying to create a home in their first apartment. By the end of the week Lou had installed a real shower and even a shower curtain rail using a drill he had borrowed from Hanns. Game, a discount store that we dubbed the Wal-Mart of Windhoek, supplied us with another space heater, a coffee maker, dishes, and rugs. We made contact with an American couple at the University of Namibia who were preparing to leave the country. From them we purchased a bamboo, glass-topped coffee table and two matching end tables, pots and pans, a TV set, and an old VW Jetta, not unlike the one we had driven two years ago in Otjimbingwe. Our Division for Global Mission had given us permission to buy this car, for which they'd reimburse us, until the new car they had ordered for us became available.

I wasn't sure that we really needed a TV set, but the price was right and Lou's brother had told us he'd be sending us videos of our favorite TV programs. In Namibia, if you don't subscribe to cable TV, there is one channel available, NBC (Namibia Broadcasting Company), and its offerings were sparse. However, twice a day there was a half-hour broadcast of CNN International. We discovered that we would need to buy something called a universal VCR in order to watch American videos. After a frustrating Saturday afternoon trying to hook it up, we were getting ready to throw the thing off the balcony.

"Wait," I said to Lou. "Don't people always say that you should ask a teenager to do this sort of thing?"

"You're right. Let's ask Elvin." Elvin was the sixteen-year-old son of one of our married students. Within half an hour Elvin and his friend had everything hooked up, and soon we were all watching the Saturday afternoon soccer match.

Our second bedroom became our office. We hauled away the two twin beds and outfitted that tiny room with two desks, a computer on each, and a bookcase. In the corner, between our desks, we placed a small photocopier that we had purchased from an office supply shop. The seminary still had no English grammar books, so I typed and photocopied all my lessons, worksheets, and homework papers. There was hardly room to move. If Lou and I were both working in our office together, we had to learn not to back up our desk chairs simultaneously to avoid crashing into each other. This was intimacy taken to a whole new level.

Meanwhile, we awaited the arrival of our shipment of twelve cartons of personal possessions from the USA. It felt like Christmas the day they were delivered. There was just one problem. There were only eleven cartons. We initiated tracking procedures with the shipping companies on both sides of the Atlantic, but to no avail. We learned that the errant box had arrived in Johannesburg, but from there the trail grew cold, and we had to resign ourselves to the loss of our good camera, many audiocassette tapes and, worst of all, my husband's favorite pillow.

Lou and I continued to wonder and worry about Dr. van Wyk. We were having trouble reconciling what Angela had told us with our impressions of the dapper little gentleman who was obviously well educated and concerned about the academics of the institution. It didn't take long for us to see other aspects of his personality. Within our first week on campus, we attended not one, but two, five-hour faculty meetings. The first was the regular monthly meeting; the second, a specially called meeting to deal with a student disciplinary problem. There were rumors that Daphne and Menthos, both fourth-year students, had been sleeping together. If that were the case, the seminary's code of conduct required their suspension.

The bishop had told us American and German expatriate members of the faculty that we should consider ourselves full-fledged faculty members. He said he expected us to fully participate in the deliberations of the Lecturers' Council. Nonetheless, neither Lou nor I felt comfortable offering any opinion on as delicate a matter as this. Each student was asked to appear individually before the Council and face interrogation. When the faculty reconvened to determine a course of action, it soon became clear that there was a strong division of opinion within the faculty between those who thought the students should be disciplined and those who were uncertain about their culpability. Dirk and Dr. van Wyk argued strongly for discipline. When our German colleague, Ute, suggested leniency, Dirk immediately barked, "That is not the African way!" He continued, saying that non-Africans could not possibly know or appreciate the way such matters must be approached.

The Ovambo faculty members, Michael, Tomas, and Rev. Amaambo, all stared intently at the papers on the table in front of them, obviously embarrassed by their colleagues from the Southern church. I glanced at

Hanns and Ute and saw angry frowns. For the longest time no one said a word. Finally, the discussion resumed and Tomas, in his gentle way, managed to achieve a consensus: there was simply insufficient evidence to suspend these two students. They would each be issued letters of warning, with copies placed in their student files. The Council also determined that Ute should speak with Daphne and Lou with Menthos, to counsel them about their behavior as future pastors of the Church.

In Otjimbingwe, we had come to appreciate the students' impromptu, a capella harmonization at our daily chapel services. They even managed to season dreary, nineteenth-century European hymns with an African flavor. The old spinet piano, rarely used in Otjimbingwe, had been relocated to this Windhoek campus and seemed to have suffered from the journey. Did anyone besides me hear how badly out of tune it was when Dr. van Wyk sat down to play at each service? Sadly, the vigor with which this little man attacked the keyboard only added to the auditory insult. I winced at each wrong note, and the students—those few who sang at all—sang listlessly. What had quenched the enthusiasm and energy we'd experienced only two years earlier?

Troubled and puzzled, I turned my attention to lesson plans with the goal of staying one week ahead of my students. I told the students they were always welcome to visit us at our flat. One of the first students to respond to my invitation was Namusha. He was a senior now, and he told us his sister was helping him with his expenses. No more ironing potato sacks for paper. He still enjoyed instructing his American teachers, and gave me a new lesson, probably the best lesson I ever received. He told me a story about a woman who attended a wedding. She arrived at the celebration with her baby bound tightly to her back in a swatch of brightly colored cloth. During the festivities, she discreetly stepped behind a bush to relieve herself. When she returned and resumed her vigorous dancing, she was unaware of the crowd that had gathered around her, laughing and pointing. She did not know that she had inadvertently tucked the hem of her dress into the cloth that bound the child to her back, exposing her backside to the crowd each time she bent over. "The moral of the story," Namusha said, "is always be aware of what other people are saying about you because you might learn something valuable."

Pico Iyer, in *The Global Soul*, observed that when you travel to another country you step on the plane as one person and step off as another. Most people, upon reaching their middle years, have acquired a good measure of competence and self-confidence. Self-identity is well defined; you feel comfortable in your own skin. A decision to live and work in another country, especially a developing country, feels like a fast trip back to adolescence. Cultural norms must be relearned, sometimes in embarrassing ways. Our month-long orientation in Chicago had filled our heads with advice and admonitions. I reminded myself never to use the words *hut, native* or *tribe*—these words are disrespectful—so I was surprised when I heard the students themselves using the word *tribe* to describe their different cultures. One day, in English class, I bluntly asked my students, "Do you feel insulted if someone refers to your cultural group as a tribe?" They looked at me as if I might have recently dropped in from another planet. "How else should we refer to ourselves?"

Paulinum trained young men and women from the Northern Church and the Southern Church. The differences between the two churches reflected both diverse tribal populations and also differences in missionary heritage. The larger Northern Church was still partially supported by the Lutheran Church in Finland. Its members were predominantly the Ovambo people, Namibia's largest tribal group. The Southern Church received support from Lutheran and Reformed churches in Germany. The members of this Church were a mixed lot: Damara, Nama, Hereros, Basters, and other people who called themselves coloured. The seminary's Governing Board sought a balance of faculty members from both churches, in addition to a few foreign co-workers such as the Germans and us. The two top leadership positions, the principal and dean of students, were three-year term positions chosen from members of the faculty by the Governing Board, and every three years the people in these two positions alternated between faculty members from the Northern and Southern Churches. In January, the Governing Board would convene to select a new principal from the Northern Church and a new dean of students from the Southern one. Dirk would no longer be the principal, and Rev. Amaambo would be replaced as the dean of students. We would soon discover how significant this information was to become for our lives.

One Wednesday evening, a month after we arrived, we met our next-door neighbor, Marjorie, as we were walking to the chapel for the evening vespers service. She was carrying a large blue banner appliquéd with the word, "Peace," in big silver letters.

"It's a gift from my congregation back in Florida. I'm going to present it to the seminary at the conclusion of this evening's service."

As we entered the chapel, I heard the students singing a lively African hymn, accompanied by the piano. Dr. van Wyk? No, it was Menthos—the student who had recently been grilled before the lecturers' council. The same one who had written to me in 1995, asking for money to buy a new trumpet. I looked around and saw a larger than usual crowd and two strangers, fair-haired men in short-sleeved sports shirts and neatly pressed trousers, tapping their feet in time to the music. Dr. van Wyk strode up the center aisle and slammed his stack of music books down on the top of the piano. With a backward swipe of his hand, like someone batting away a pesky fly, he told Menthos to get up. The students ceased their singing, and the two strangers studied the hymnals on their laps.

At the conclusion of the service, during the time reserved for announcements, Marjorie presented her banner to the seminary community, and Ute introduced the visitors, two pastors from Germany. When Dirk asked if there were any more announcements, Dr. van Wyk emerged from behind the piano. His face was twisted in an angry scowl.

"I will not—will *not*—have this piano played by goats!" He glared at Menthos, who held his gaze. Up and down the rows of chairs, shoulders stiffened. Van Wyk scooped up his music books and marched down the aisle and out of the chapel. Everyone else filed out in silence, and no one gathered outside, as they always did, for the usual conversation, jokes, and fellowship.

The following afternoon Hanns came to our flat to help us set up our Internet connection. When he crawled out from under the desk, where he'd been attaching the modem, I asked him if he'd like a glass of juice.

"Yes, thanks. I'd actually been hoping to have a chance to talk with you both, somewhere other than in the staff room." He sat on the edge of the sofa, thrust his hand between his knees, and leaned forward.

"You need to know that there's serious trouble brewing on the campus. Some of the students have told me that they have drawn up a list of grievances against the principal and his uncle."

"Who is Dirk's uncle?" asked Lou.

"Dr. van Wyk. Didn't you know that?"

We shook our heads, and Hanns continued.

"Yes. Well, it seems the students are demanding their removal from the faculty. They're saying that if the Governing Board doesn't meet their demands, they will go on strike."

"Have you seen their list of grievances?" I asked.

"Not yet, but one of the students said he'd give me a copy. This doesn't look good. It's what happened about twenty years ago when van

55

Wyk was principal of Paulinum. The students rebelled against him and went on strike. The bishops and the Governing Board shut the seminary down, and everyone was sent home."

By the end of the week, the students had another item to add to their list of grievances. In a homiletics class, Menthos had failed to preach a sermon for the requisite number of minutes and had exchanged angry words with his lecturer, Dirk. The faculty convened for yet another meeting.

"This is gross insubordination!" sputtered Dirk.

"This student persists in demonstrating disruptive behavior on this campus," added Dr. van Wyk. "He argues constantly in the classroom. He abuses the piano in the chapel. We know he is taking sexual liberties with at least one of our female students, even if we can't prove it. And…he refused to greet my wife." Mrs. van Wyk was the matron. She was responsible for the kitchen, dining hall, and dormitories, and she supervised the seminary's cooks and cleaning staff. We had been in Namibia long enough to recognize that a refusal to greet someone was a grave insult.

Hour after hour the faculty deliberated, along the same lines as in the previous meeting. Dirk and van Wyk were insistent that Menthos be expelled. The Northern Church faculty—Michael, Tomas, and Rev. Amaambo—found that punishment excessive. So did the Germans and the Americans. At one point, Lou ventured a suggestion.

"Couldn't we just vote?"

"That isn't the African way," snarled Dr. van Wyk. "We decide matters by consensus."

There it was again: *The African Way.* Did these two colleagues from the Southern Church resent our being here? It had become clear that consensus, to Dirk and van Wyk, meant hammering their colleagues into compliance. In a soft voice, Tomas ventured that one of the hallmarks of a Christian community was grace.

"Bah!" said Dr. van Wyk. "That would be nothing but cheap grace. The gospel without the law. This seminary has a code of conduct, and this student has clearly violated it. He must be removed."

Finally, Hanns offered a compromise: suspend Menthos for the remaining two months of the academic year, but allow him to sit for his final exams. Dirk and van Wyk reluctantly agreed, and the meeting concluded at nine o'clock. As soon as we had returned to our flat and collapsed in the living room chairs, we heard a knock on the door. It was

Menthos. He pleaded with Lou to tell him the outcome of the faculty meeting, but Lou could only say that the principal and dean of students would tell him tomorrow morning. Twenty minutes later, Hanns came to the flat. Hanns seemed to have an inside track to information, probably his friend, Bishop Diergaardt. Hanns told us that both Dirk and van Wyk were being considered for congregational positions outside the seminary. If the Southern Church could find faculty replacements for them, they might be gone when the new academic year began in January.

The following afternoon, after classes had ended for the day, we sat on our balcony watching students gathering in little clusters around the campus. We heard them shouting and watched them waving their arms in anger. The phone rang. It was the seminary's secretary telling us that Bishop Diergaardt was in the staff room, and all the faculty members were to come immediately for an emergency faculty meeting. When we had all convened around the conference table, the bishop implored the faculty to grant Menthos leniency, but Dirk and van Wyk refused to budge. Menthos would remain on suspension. Bishop Diergaardt, looking sad and defeated, said he would abide by the faculty's decision.

That evening Lou and I went out to dinner with Ray and Lois, two career missionaries who had been teaching at a private Lutheran high school in the North for the past three years. The couple had worked as missionaries in several other African countries for thirty-five years and would be retiring at the end of this year. We met at our favorite Windhoek restaurant, Gathemanns, well known for its fine German cuisine and generous portions. The waiter seated us on the balcony overlooking Independence Avenue. At seven o'clock there was almost no traffic on the boulevard. Tiny lights twinkled on the trees in the park across the street. Lou and I ordered kingklip, a sweet, succulent white fish from the cold waters of the southern Atlantic.

Ray and Lois described the boarding school where they were teaching. How welcoming those Midwest American accents sounded. Although our campus was only a few kilometers away, I felt as if I had re-entered a world of normalcy and civility. I sipped a chilled Appletiser and fingered the crisp white tablecloth while Lou told our friends what had been happening on campus.

"It hasn't been an easy assignment for us either," said Ray. "Oh, nothing like a student strike. It's just that, of all the places we've worked in Africa, we have felt the least welcome in Namibia."

"Do you think it's because of the history of apartheid?" I asked.

"Perhaps. I'm not sure."

"I just remembered something else," said Lou. "Susan, do you remember what Tom said to us?"

I nodded. Tom was a high school principal in Oregon and a former missionary to Namibia. Before we left North Carolina, we had phoned him to ask about his experiences in Namibia. He had been surprisingly reticent.

"Tom cautioned us not to get involved in local disputes. 'Just go and do your job,' he said."

"What I'm having troubled with," I said between bites of broiled fish, "is how you can be a missionary and remain disengaged from the community you have come to serve. That's not what we were taught during our orientation."

"Let me give you some advice," said Lois. "And you probably weren't taught this, either. I know we missionaries are supposed to live at the level of the local people, but let's face it. We cannot be them. We are still Americans, and when we come to Africa to live and work, we straddle two cultures. That's not easy! Every six weeks or so, leave the campus and go away for a weekend. Go to a guest lodge, or the game park, or to the ocean. Don't be afraid to be tourists for a while. You'll find that you'll be much more effective missionaries."

We parted, agreeing to visit them in the North for Thanksgiving. The next morning, Wednesday, when the students failed to appear for classes, Dirk called an emergency meeting of the Lecturers' Council. He told us he had received a petition signed by thirty-eight of the forty-four students enrolled in the seminary. He did not make the petition available to the rest of us, but said that students would continue to boycott classes until the Paulinum Governing Board met with them. They demanded a Friday meeting. This seemed highly unlikely. Half the members of the Governing Board lived in the far North, at least an eight-hour drive from Windhoek. Dirk said he would bring the student's request before Bishop Diergaardt and would tell the students that their lecturers would all be in their classrooms the next morning, prepared to teach.

That evening, we walked across campus to the chapel, wondering if any students would appear for the regular Wednesday night vespers service. Not only did they appear, they were the most spirited we had seen them since we'd arrived, laughing and joking with each other on their way into the chapel. The service sizzled with their energy, but when I looked around, I noticed that Lou and I were the only faculty members present. At the end of the service, as we were leaving, Tomas Shivute hurried up the steps of the chapel.

"Please come to the staff room. The two bishops are there and wish to meet with the faculty."

Our colleagues were all seated around the table, and at the head of the table was a man I immediately recognized from his photos, Rev. Dumeni, Bishop of the Northern Church and chairman of the seminary's Governing Board. This was a man who had dared to stand up to the South Africans during the apartheid years and had achieved international recognition. During the War for Independence, his daughter had been killed by a bomb blast that demolished a bank. I had the odd sensation that I should curtsey. He wore a rich purple African-style shirt trimmed with gold embroidery. An ornate gold pectoral cross gleamed on his chest. Chalk-white hair crowned a dark black face, its brow deeply furrowed. Dirk introduced us.

"Ah, the lecturers from America. Yes, I have heard about you." He paused and looked at the lecturers seated around the conference table. "What I don't understand is this. Two weeks ago, you had a meeting about this student, and it was agreed that Reverend Bauer," he nodded at Lou, "would counsel this student. Now you are telling me he has been suspended. What has happened since then?"

An uncomfortable silence.

"Come now, speak up! I want you to tell me honestly what happened."

Those of us who had disagreed with the decision to suspend Menthos knew there would be hell to pay if were to break rank and even hint that we had been bullied into approving the suspension by our Southern Church colleagues, Dirk and van Wyk. Finally, Dirk explained what had happened, pleading that the faculty had had no choice. At the end of three hours' deliberation, the faculty and the bishops decided that Menthos's suspension would be reduced to three weeks, the Governing Board would meet with the students the next month, and the students would return to their classes. At eleven o'clock, Hanns rang the chapel bell, to summon the students.

Bishop Dumeni, in his sternest voice, addressed the student body, informing them of the decision that had been reached and ordering them back to classes. I had expected the students' assent, but one after another stood up to object. They began shouting, saying that they had asked the Governing Board to meet with *them*, not with the lecturers. Bishop Dumeni gripped both sides of the lectern. He was not someone accustomed to being crossed. In measured tones he replied that he and Bishop Diergaardt were not the entire Governing Board, that it would take the other members time to adjust their schedules and arrange transportation to Windhoek. When the meeting ended after midnight, it was unclear whether the students would comply with the decision.

The students failed to appear for any classes Thursday or Friday. Once again, the faculty came together in the staff room. Dirk showed us a new petition from the students. They were demanding the immediate suspension of the principal for three weeks, and if that did not happen the students said they would "employ forces from outside to strengthen our goal." We all agreed there was nothing more we, as the faculty, could do.

"My fear," said Dirk, tears in his eyes, "is that they will take this to the media. Then what will become of this seminary?"

Of course, what he was really saying was "What will become of me?" On Friday afternoon, we watched from our balcony as students piled into the back of Karsten's shiny red pick-up truck. Karsten was a second-year student. Bishop Diergaardt was his father. We knew they were driving into town to deliver their petition to the bishop, and we hoped they weren't also planning to stop at the office of the Namibia Broadcasting Company. We were eating supper when Dirk phoned.

"The students have met with the bishop. He told them that if they do not return to classes on Monday, the Governing Board would be forced to close down the seminary. There would be no final exams given, and the fourth-year students would not graduate. We will see what happens."

Chapter 6
New Friends, New Places

*B*y the end of every week, soft sand had powdered our floors, tables, and windowsills, so Lou and I developed a Saturday morning routine. We removed all the rugs in the flat and shook them outside. I hung the larger ones over the railing on our balcony and beat them with a broom, hoping no one was standing on the patio of the flat below. We would sweep and wash the linoleum floors and dust all the furniture. On Saturday afternoons, I would finish creating my lesson plans for the coming week, and photocopy handouts for all the students. We had begun buying copier paper by the case. I looked forward to these mornings of good, physical labor and the afternoons of designing my own English curriculum. But this Saturday, Lou and I could do little more than drink pots of coffee and rehash the events of the week. What would we do if the seminary closed for the rest of the year? It was mid-September and the next academic year wouldn't start until the end of January. Would DGM bring us home? Send us on another assignment? Tell us to sit tight and wait? Maybe they would send us to the North to replace Ray and Lois when they retired and left Oshigambo High School. Normally, I would be working on my lesson plans, but because of the strike, I was two weeks ahead. Should I prepare lessons for future classes that might not even happen?

Hanns stopped by in the afternoon to bring us copies of the students' petition. They accused Dirk of treating them disrespectfully and said he behaved like a dictator toward the foreign lecturers at faculty meetings. Their complaints against van Wyk were even more pointed. They quoted what they claimed they had heard him say: the bishop was sexually promiscuous; the bishop's wife was a gossip; the Ovambo students were baboons; the secretary was a stupid donkey; Matheus, the seminary's treasurer, didn't know anything; and our colleague, Rev. Amaambo, was "just a breath and not human." The students' petition concluded with a statement to the Governing Board that they feared reprisals by the principal and Dr. van Wyk who, they thought, might unfairly mark their final papers and examinations.

By evening, we were still sitting in our dusty living room when Lou finally gave voice to the question that had been hanging between us all day: had we made the biggest mistake of our lives? We examined all that we had relinquished: our jobs, our home, intimate contact with our children and our friends. Lou reminded me of something we had learned during our orientation in Chicago. Missionaries tend to go through a predictable pattern when they arrive in a foreign country. The energy and euphoria of the first few months usually plummet to feelings of disillusion and disappointment. Eventually, for most missionaries, there is a leveling of emotions and the missionary can get on with the work at hand. Unfortunately, the campus chaos had coincided with our downward trajectory.

"So what are we supposed to do?" I asked my husband. I had to blink quickly to keep the tears away.

"First, we send an e-mail to Benyam and tell him what's going on here." Benyam was our new area program director in Chicago. Our boss. We would be seeing him in two weeks when all the Lutheran missionaries gathered for a retreat at the coast. "We need to remember that these campus problems were here before we arrived. There is a lot of deep-seated tribalism and racism underneath them, and there isn't anything you or I can do about that. As I see it, our primary responsibility is to the students, so we devote our attention to them. Give them good teaching, maybe set up small groups of students to come to our flat on a regular basis. Other than Tomas Shivute and Rev. Amaambo, it doesn't look as if the faculty spends much time getting to know these students. They don't even have faculty advisors."

"Yes, that makes sense. And let's remember what Ray and Lois said to us about making sure we get away from here from time to time. Become tourists for a weekend."

We continued to hear complaints against van Wyk. The seminary's accreditation board in South Africa required all theology students throughout southern Africa to write Common Assignments, lengthy term papers that would be read and marked first by their seminary lecturer, and later by an external examiner in South Africa. Instead of receiving these assignments in class, van Wyk told his students they must deliver them to his house on campus. The students told us that when they brought him their papers, they were individually interrogated about the complaints they had lodged against him in their petition. If van Wyk wasn't satisfied with a student's answer, he refused to accept that student's paper, in effect dooming that student to fail the course.

The eight members of the Paulinum Governing Board (PGB), including Bishops Dumeni and Diergaardt, came to the campus. The board members sequestered themselves in the staff room and began their meeting at 9:00 a.m. They met all day, breaking only for a short lunch in the dining hall. After supper, the bishops called the lecturers together, without Dirk Cloete and Johan van Wyk, and asked for honest opinions. We all examined the grain of wood on the conference table for several uncomfortable minutes, but it was impossible to ignore the heat of Bishop Dumeni's eyes. Feeling nervous but relieved to have the opportunity to speak openly, we four foreign lecturers told about our experiences and perceptions. The two older African lecturers, Rev. Amaambo and Dr. Shivute, were silent. Michael, the youngest African lecturer, emboldened by the directness of the foreigners, said how hard it was for the community to function in the climate of suspicion and distrust that seemed to be stirred up by those two.

It was close to midnight when the bishops sent for Cloete and van Wyk, and a resolution was finally brokered. The bishops required public apologies from both lecturers and also from the student body. They said that if the students did not cease their sporadic boycotts of classes, they would close the seminary for twelve months. Hanns rang the chapel bell, and we all waited for the students to show up. We doubted any of them had been sleeping. When everyone had assembled in the chapel, Bishop Dumeni told the students what was required. Dirk walked to the front of the chapel and said he was sorry for his "mistakes." Van Wyk said his door was open and he would accept the students' papers. We all looked around at each other. This was no apology. But the bishops seemed satisfied. Finally, the president of the student body said the students were sorry for their behavior. As I read their faces, I knew they were not, but the threat of the seniors not graduating was a sufficient reason for them to acquiesce, as the bishops had known.

After a few weeks, the students regained their good spirits, and everyone seemed relieved that life would return to normal. I tried to keep in mind Lou's suggestion about focusing on the students. I was talking with Anthony, a second-year student, after English class one day and mentioned that I had been hungry for pancakes and thought I'd try to make some for supper that night.

"Oh, I love pancakes! Can I come to your flat for supper?"

I laughed and told him he was welcome to join us, but I didn't have a pancake recipe and would be making them from memory.

"That's okay. I even like the flops."

When CNN broadcast the funerals of Princess Diana and Mother Theresa on consecutive weekends, we discussed them in class and I assigned an essay comparing the two public figures. Lou, who was teaching pastoral counseling, used the events as an opportunity to discuss funerals and ministry to the bereaved.

I was returning to our flat about five o'clock one Friday afternoon, wondering if I had enough ingredients on hand to put together a salad for our supper. Half the student body had already left campus for a three-day holiday weekend, grateful to trade the classrooms for a few days in their villages. Those who remained on campus either lived too far away for the journey or lacked the bus fare that would allow them to see their parents and siblings. The heat of the day was slowly releasing its grip, and the long purple shadows of the volleyball players looked like vigorous, sleek-limbed apparitions on the court in front of the dining hall. Nokokure was sitting outside the ground floor flat she shared with her husband, Japhet. As our eyes met, she waved me over.

She wore a lime green, two-piece maternity dress, a style popular in the 1950s in the States. Her baby was due in three months, sufficient time for her to complete her final year at the seminary. As I walked through the tall, brown grass, I remembered that this would be the couple's second child. Gerald, their first baby, had been conceived when Noko and Japhet were second-year, unmarried students. The seminary's strict code of conduct had suspended both of them for two years. They had returned to their studies the previous year, and following their graduation and six months as vicars, both would be ordained as pastors in the Southern Church. Gerald would remain where he was now—in the village with Noko's mother—until his parents received their parish assignments from their bishop. These were two of Paulinum's brightest students, and I hoped they would be placed in good parishes where their skills and abilities would be recognized as strong assets.

Noko greeted me and nodded to the empty wooden chair next to her. I sat down and watched her fingers flying over the tiny yellow garment she was crocheting. On the dusty cement slab next to her chair were a pair of matching booties and a cap. Over a hundred years ago, wives of German colonists and missionaries had taught Namibian women how to crochet. Whenever I visited a Namibian home, I was startled to see evidence of this legacy. Crocheted doilies covered every table; antimacassars adorned the back of every chair and sofa; each roll of toilet paper and every box of tissues wore its own lacy jacket.

"I've always wanted to learn how to crochet," I told Noko. "My mother-in-law used to crochet brightly colored afghans, and I have always been sorry I never took the time to ask her to teach me. When she passed away, I kept her little packet of crochet hooks. I even bought myself a book of instructions, but I haven't been very successful in figuring them out."

"Would you like me to teach you?"

"Noko, that would be wonderful. In fact, I have those crochet hooks upstairs."

"If you will bring them to my flat tomorrow morning, I will give you a lesson."

Nokokure was a strict teacher.

"No, no—the yarn is too tight (or too loose). Take it out and do it again." Within a few weeks, I was producing granny squares that eventually became an afghan for my daughter, Megan. In exchange for my lessons, I spent a Saturday afternoon teaching Noko and her friend, Daphne, how to make apple pies. I couldn't find Crisco in any of the Windhoek grocery stores, so we used lard for the crust. I suggested that we make three pies: one that they could share between themselves, and two for the English-class students. We gave thin slices to the students on Monday morning, and they unanimously agreed that apple pie was their new favorite dessert. They said they hoped I would cook more American food for them.

One Sunday evening we were invited to dinner at the home of Matheus, the seminary treasurer, to celebrate the confirmation of Matheus's sister-in-law. As is the custom in Ovambo homes, everyone left their shoes by the front door. The menu was fried chicken, soft drinks, and cake, but before we ate, Matheus's wife, Ndeshi, passed around a dishpan full of soapy water and a towel so we could all wash our hands. Ndeshi did not speak at all during the meal, except when addressed briefly, in Oshiwambo, by Rev. Amaambo. The guest of honor remained out of sight behind the closed door of the kitchen where she ate with the children. The evening taught us that in the Ovambo culture everyone has his or her place.

A few weeks later I invited our friends, Angela and Gerson, to come for dinner. I enjoyed shopping for this first dinner party in our new home and decided to prepare my favorite Indian chicken curry recipe, accompanied by rice, marinated vegetables, and a fruit tart for dessert. Since our flat was so tiny and we had no dining room table, it was a buffet supper. We enjoyed listening to Angela's description of her new job with the Namibian office of Lutheran World Federation. Gerson talked about his work as a plumber and building contractor, skills he had learned while he was in Germany. He had been one of many Namibians who had gone into exile during the country's long struggle for independence. Today, he said, their home was a refuge for the children and grandchildren of Gerson's first marriage. I knew they worked hard to accommodate their two vastly different cultures, German and Namibian Herero.

We had finished dinner and were sipping tea when Gerson said, "I haven't told you what happened to me in the late seventies. I was outspoken. A political activist. One night the South Africans came to my home, covered my head with a cloth and drugged me. I never knew where I spent the next two years." He put down his cup, and his hands twisted the hem of his bright green shirt. "All I had in that room was a bed, a toilet and two Bibles, one in Afrikaans and one in English. My food was delivered on a conveyor belt of some sort. I never saw a person those entire two years. Then they drugged me again, put me in a car and deposited me in front of the Windhoek hospital. I was nearly naked because I had been wearing the same tattered clothes the whole time."

He said no more, and none of us seemed to know what to say either. Finally, uncomfortable with the silence, I said I thought it was remarkable that he had been able to accomplish so much since then, and without appearing bitter. It seemed like a stupid thing to say, and I hoped Gerson wouldn't find my words patronizing. His eyes were still sad, but he smiled broadly. "What good would it do to be bitter? We Namibians must be busy now with nation-building."

It was a relief to leave the campus for our weekend missionary retreat at the coast. The morning drive from Windhoek was pleasant enough, a well-paved highway with very little traffic. After two hours, the small bushes and acacia trees became fewer and the mountains rough and rocky. This was mining country: gold, uranium, and semi-precious gemstones. After we passed through the tiny town of Uis, we noticed vendors by the side of the road selling stones and rock crystals in the shadow of the Brandberg, Namibia's highest mountain. Old women, their heads tightly wrapped in colorful scarves, were sitting at rickety wooden tables while small children shouted and waved to passing motorists. We stopped. The women spoke no English, so we transacted our purchases with the children. As we were getting ready to leave with our handfuls of colorful stones, one of the women said something to the little boy who had sold us the rocks.

"My grandma, she says, do you have any bread or shoes?" All we had was a packet of cookies, some hard candies, and the shoes on our feet. The little boy was happy with his candy and cookies, and the old lady waved as we drove away.

Half an hour later, the bushes and trees had vanished. We were entering the Namib Desert, what some call the Gravel Desert. It was easy to see why the guidebooks referred to this barren area as a moonscape, a vast craggy expanse of gravelly plains, mountains and canyons. It takes its name from the Nama word for "enormous," and geologists estimate that the Namib is eighty million years old, the oldest desert in the world. This was our third trip through the Namib, and I still experienced the same feelings of desolation I'd had the first time we drove through. It was a relief, an hour later, to see fog on the horizon, the sign that we were approaching the coast.

Swakopmund resembles a Bavarian village—with date palm trees. Founded in the late 1800s when Namibia was still a German colony, the main street still retained its original name, Kaiser Wilhelm Strasse. Sausage and sauerkraut is as popular a menu item in the local restaurants as local seafood or Namibian game.

It felt good to be among our small gathering of Americans for the weekend, to unload some of the emotional baggage we'd been toting around for the past three months. Despite the unusual circumstances at the seminary, I had the sense that we were coping as well as any of our other colleagues.

Since no group activities were scheduled for Saturday afternoon, Lou and I decided to walk about a mile through the beachside neighborhoods. Were we still in Africa? This could have been any affluent American or European seaside resort, with its tastefully landscaped stucco homes and modern condominiums, but it was impossible to ignore the gardeners in their royal blue jumpsuits trimming the bougainvilleas, weeding the flowerbeds, and watering the lawns. Or the maids who stepped outside to shake a rug, or remove some thick, fluffy towels from a clothesline. I had seen the tin-roofed townships where they lived on the edge of the city. Had seen them trudging home at the end of their workdays. What must they think, these workers who lived in three-room shacks where the towels were thin, who lived in neighborhoods where there were no sidewalks and lawns? Those were the neighborhoods where some of our students lived.

We had a destination that afternoon: the church guesthouse. Several weeks earlier, I had phoned to make reservations for the Christmas holiday time. Our children would be visiting us, and since the game park had been fully booked, we had planned to bring them to Swakopmund, to visit the seal colony at Cape Cross, and even do a little camping in the Namib. Since we were here in Swakopmund anyway, it seemed prudent to confirm our guesthouse booking. We found Sister Katrina in the little dining room of the guesthouse compound. Speaking slowly and distinctly—I could tell she wasn't very fluent in English—I explained who we were and that we had just come to make sure everything was in order for our December visit. She asked us to follow her into her office where she would look at the guest register.

"No, I sorry. No Bauer for those days."

"There must be a mistake." Now I was speaking even more slowly and clearly.

"No, no," she insisted. "No Bauer in December. See?" She pushed the register toward me.

"Well, can we please make a booking now?"

"Oh, no. Everything fully booked for whole month."

I had thought I'd made progress adjusting to African inefficiency, had thought I'd learned how to take screw-ups in stride, but now I felt my frustration turning to anger. I knew the entire month of December was peak holiday time throughout the country, not just for tourists, but also for the locals. Many companies, even government offices, closed for most of the month and it was unlikely we would be able to find any place available to stay along the coast when Jason and Megan came to visit.

That evening our group gathered for a seafood dinner at The Tug, a popular beachside restaurant where patrons watch the sun slipping into the Atlantic Ocean. Mark Beukes, a student whom we'd met two years earlier in Otjimbingwe and who was now the pastor of a thriving Lutheran congregation in nearby Walvis Bay, joined our missionary group. During dinner, we mentioned to Mark our problem with Sister Katrina. He shook his head sadly. "She's becoming too old for this post. The Church is in the process of replacing her with a trained business manager." I wished they had done so before I'd phoned in our reservation.

The next morning we all gathered for morning worship at Mark's church. The service was in Afrikaans, but we could follow the liturgy and Mark translated his sermon for our group. As we were leaving the church and were being welcomed by parishioners, a middle-aged gentleman approached me and said hello. I replied in Afrikaans, "*Goeiemôre*" (Good morning). When he began chattering away in Afrikaans, I laughed, held up my hand, and admitted that he had just heard my entire repertoire of Afrikaans. He switched to English, and the first thing he said was that our family was most welcome to stay in his house when we returned at Christmastime. Mark must have told him about our plight. I grabbed Lou's sleeve and pulled him into the conversation. The man told us he was a retired primary school principal. He said he might be away during the holiday season, but we should feel free to stay in his house nonetheless. "I will just leave the key with Pastor Beukes," he said. "I will be disappointed if you and your children don't stay in my home." These Namibians kept surprising me, and I offered up a quick apology for being so quick to judge them based upon the Sister Katrina episode.

The school year was quickly drawing to a close. Classes had ended, and the students were completing their common assignments and studying for their final examinations. Soon they would be leaving the campus for their three-month summer holiday.

By the middle of November, the campus was deserted. The students and staff were gone, and half the lecturers had returned to their permanent homes in other parts of the country. We had long since packed away our space heaters and were using electric fans day and night. We doubted that our flat had any insulation, and being on the top floor, afternoons were becoming increasingly uncomfortable. Even closing the curtains against the sun offered little relief from the heat. Several afternoons a week, Lou and I would drive downtown to Wernhill Mall, just to enjoy the opportunity of walking through air-conditioned shops or sipping milkshakes in one of the cafés.

Two days before Thanksgiving, we loaded our vehicle with food, water, and two small suitcases in preparation for our visit with Ray and Lois. We had begun taking our anti-malarial medication the previous week, a precaution we always observed when traveling to the North. I had told Lois I'd make my favorite sweet potato casserole, but when I'd gone shopping for ingredients in Windhoek, I realized I'd have to substitute white sweet potatoes for the yellow ones I was used to, and replace the pecans in the recipe with hazelnuts. After visiting three grocery stores, I finally found cranberry sauce, imported from the United States, and I bought two cans.

In Namibia, when you say you are "Going North," the listener immediately knows the eight-hour trip will transport you to a geography and a culture totally different from Windhoek's metropolis. Ovamboland is Namibia's most densely populated region, and its inhabitants are governed by local headmen and chiefs. After driving north for several hours, the first thing you notice is that the hills and mountains of central Namibia begin to disappear. You start seeing rust-colored termite monoliths along the road, some of them over six feet tall. As you approach the government checkpoint, actually a veterinary control post, you're aware that the termite mounds are now white, from the soft, sandy soil of this region. You are entering Ovamboland.

Although you're still driving on a good tarred road, you reduce your speed. Herds of cattle and goats have the right of way. You start to notice structures that resemble forts from cowboy movies. These are Ovambo homesteads, surrounded by tall fences made from sticks. Inside each homestead is a cluster of small dwellings made from mud, sticks, and thatch, each with its own purpose—huts for sleeping, cooking, pounding mahangu (millet), and storage.

The hungry summer sun sucked the cool air from our vehicle, and I struggled to stay awake. Barefoot women, their muumuu style dresses swinging gracefully around their ankles, walked beside the road bearing ten-liter containers of water on their heads. Every so often we'd overtake a donkey cart full of kindling driven by a young boy or an old man. Schoolchildren in their uniforms waved to us, the boys' clean white shirttails flapping beneath their backpacks. We drove past tidy, unattended displays of hand-woven baskets and clay pots. From a previous trip, we knew if we were to stop, several women and children would suddenly appear from the bush and offer to sell them to us.

After we passed the town of Oniipa, I took a scrap of paper from my tote bag and read the directions to Lou. We turned left onto a gravel road at a green-roofed building that called itself a music shop and bounced along for about a kilometer until we saw the Oshigambo High School campus, a collection of sturdy-looking single story buildings. Ray and Lois's home on the campus was a well-built structure from the missionary times. Its thick concrete walls and fifteen-foot tall ceilings offered protection from the heat, as did the location of the kitchen in a separate building from the living and sleeping quarters.

Thanksgiving dinner was an international gathering—Americans, Namibians, and a flamboyant Nigerian traditional healer who was a guest teacher at the school. Two plump chickens replaced the traditional turkey. Adam, a young American missionary teacher, told us his mother had sent a fruitcake, and he happily shared it with everyone. It was a real feast of fellowship, our first Thanksgiving in the Namibian summertime.

The next day we bade our friends farewell and drove to the Etosha National Game Park where we had booked several nights in a two-bedroom bungalow, just behind the Okaukuejo water hole. Rainy season, which is usually from November through February, had not yet begun that year, and it was crackly dry in the North. This made for good animal watching at the waterholes and along the white gravel roads that crisscrossed Etosha. All we had to do was sit quietly and watch the animals come to us: zebras, springbok, oryx, giraffe, an elephant here and there, steenbok, dik-dik, birds and more birds, black-faced impala, kudus, a red hartebeest, and a few warthogs.

One star-drenched evening we sat on a bench, a few yards from our bungalow, discussing the strife we had experienced on the seminary campus. A waist-high stone wall topped with a few lazy coils of razor wire separated us from the floodlit water hole. We grew silent and watched the steady procession of springbok, giraffes, and a family of rhinos approaching from the bush beyond. Their hooves clattered on the rocks. Lou whispered, "I love this place! It's strange, isn't it? Sitting here, watching these creatures, we feel such tranquility, but just beyond this wall is a world where fear preserves life." I thought about my husband's comment, and I wondered if fear also preserved life on our campus. The students' fear of not graduating. The faculty's fear of being dismissed. The next day, as we drove along the hundred miles of gravel road out of the park, a Land Cruiser approached. On the side of the vehicle we read, "The Discovery Channel." The driver hailed us, asking if we had seen any cheetahs.

Chapter 7
A Startling Decision

*J*ason and Megan arrived within a few days of each other, and after celebrating a slightly belated Christmas in our tiny flat, we loaded our suitcases into the Venture for New Year's weekend at the coast. True to his word, Mr. Strydom, the high school principal, had left the keys to his house with Pastor Beukes. Walvis Bay (we learned the Namibians usually pronounce this "Walfish Bay") is Namibia's major port. Mark Beukes and his congregants lived in the section called Narraville, the "coloured" part of town. The homes here lacked the high walls and neatly manicured lawns of the white section of town, but the roads were paved and the houses well maintained. The black part of town—always the farthest out in any of these apartheid-era cities—was little more than a jumble of tin-roofed shacks. In Walvis Bay, where the desert meets the sea, the roads in the black section were no more than tracks in the sand.

We would only be spending two nights in Mr. Strydom's house since we had planned a one-night desert camping trip with our children for December 29-30. As soon as we unlocked the back door, I wondered if we had been too quick to accept his offer of free lodging. The dishes in the draining rack had little bits of food still stuck on them, and the countertops were gritty-slimy. In one corner was a small, encroaching glacier of empty bottles and cans. On the kitchen table I found a note addressed to us: "Dear Bauers: I've gone to be with my sister for a few days. Please make yourselves at home, and help yourself to any food in the fridge." I didn't think so.

The bedrooms were a jumble of papers, books, and piles of clothes. I feared what I would find when I peeled back the bedspread, but the sheets were clean, even ironed. I noticed Jason and Megan exchanging grim glances.

"Okay, so it isn't the Holiday Inn," I said, "but at least we've got a place to sleep for two nights. We'll get some groceries for breakfast and lunch, and we'll eat dinner at restaurants, all right?" That's the night we discovered Crazy Mama's, the best pizza restaurant in Namibia.

We were up and out early the following morning to meet our camping guide. Several months earlier, on our previous visit to the coast, we had met Lutz LaBarré in a little coffee shop. He was distributing brochures offering his services as a guide for a variety of excursions: fishing trips, desert camping, and extended tours to Himbaland. He agreed to take us all on a one-night camping trip into the Namib Desert and said he would provide everything we needed: tents, beds, food and drink. He also told us he would do all the cooking, we would simply have to show up with our overnight bags. This was my idea of camping.

A thick layer of clouds hovered close overhead as we bounced our way across the rocks and sand in Lutz's well-worn Land Cruiser. After the initial bustle of introducing our children to Lutz and loading up the vehicle, the drive settled into an uncomfortable monotony. The expressions on Jason's and Megan's faces said, "*Bo-ring!*" I remembered only too well the discomfort of being a young adult trapped in a vehicle with parents. Lutz must have sensed my mood. He glanced at each of our children.

"I'll bet you think the desert is boring, right? Right?" They offered embarrassed grins. "Well, I am going to show you that this landscape changes every half hour. I know you don't believe me. We'll have to stop and take a look." He brought the vehicle to an abrupt halt and jumped out. "Come on!"

We examined lichen growing on boulders, and tiny desert flowers. "See this little beetle? He collects all the moisture he needs—about forty per cent of his body weight—from the fog that covers this desert every night."

By noon, we had made many such stops, all accompanied by Lutz's geography and climatology mini-lectures. Every so often, we would see an ostrich pecking for a pebbly lunch. Even Jason and Megan were looking interested. Lutz parked the Land Cruiser in front of a huge natural rock shelter that resembled the mouth of a cave. He set up a folding table, covered it with a white tablecloth, and was laying out our lunch beneath the rocky overhang when we began to feel drops of rain on our arms.

"Look at this!" shouted Lutz. "It's raining in the desert! You are in the middle of a miracle. This only happens every fifty years or so. Tomorrow you will see all the flowers blooming." He explained that many seeds lie dormant in the sand—sometimes for ten years or more—waiting for rain.

After lunch we took a short hike and Megan found a desiccated snake carcass. "Oh," said Lutz, "you want to be careful of snakes like those. It's a sand viper. Twenty-five minutes after it bites you, you're dead." We all looked nervously at our feet.

When we set up camp for the evening, Lutz refused our help. "You just sit here," he said, unfolding several chairs and opening cans of soda for us. "I'll do the rest." He pitched three tents, allowing Jason and Megan to help him. He even made the beds with pretty flowered sheets and warm blankets. "You'll be glad to have your blanket. It gets quite cold at night."

After dinner—Lutz even refused to let us help him wash the dishes—we sat quietly sipping coffee. The night wrapped us in its own glittering blanket of stars so close you wanted to reach out and touch them. Lutz told us about his German grandfather who had come to Namibia as an adventurer. "The country was pretty wild back then, but he loved it. Settled down and never returned to Germany. I love it, too. It's still so rugged and untamed, at least the parts I prefer. I lived in South Africa for a while, and my brother still does, but this is my home."

"How do you think Namibia is progressing since becoming independent?" I asked.

He gazed into the fire and didn't speak for a while. After a few moments, he stood up and scratched his ample belly. "Answering that will keep us up too late tonight. Let's talk about it tomorrow, okay?"

The aroma of bacon and good, strong coffee lingered in the chilly desert morning as Lutz loaded the last of our camping gear into the Land Cruiser. Once we were underway, I reminded him that I was interested in hearing his thoughts about how the country was faring, almost eight years since becoming independent. Once again, he became quiet. I waited.

"I don't want you to misunderstand what I say. Apartheid was terrible. It was more than terrible. I know how much the black people suffered during those years, but...just look around. Sammy (Namibia's President Sam Nujoma) is letting this country fall apart. He is spending one million Namibian dollars (about US$145,000) *every day* to support our army's presence in the civil war in the Democratic Republic of Congo. Why are we doing that? Meanwhile, Namibia's water pumps and roads fall into disrepair."

"Are you suggesting the majority black population in Namibia is unqualified to govern the country?" Even as I recoiled at the answer I was anticipating from Lutz, I sensed a shift in my ground of understanding. An ever-so-slight realignment of the mental tectonic plates that defined Africa for me.

"In a word? Yes. When they came into power, they refused to listen to

Choosing Africa

people who had more experience in governing, even the whites who were sympathetic to their cause. Big mistake."

My entire frame of reference for Namibia was the black community. This was the first opportunity I'd had to talk about these things with a white Namibian. Although I am someone who avoids probing questions, my need to understand this environment kept propelling me forward.

"Surely you can understand why people who had been so cruelly oppressed might feel that way?" Oh, God, was I sounding sanctimonious? I really liked this charming, funny, passionate third-generation Namibian who obviously cared so deeply for his country. I didn't want to learn that he was a racist. Or maybe my understanding of racism was too simplistic.

"Yes, I do understand. We have a brand-new country, and we all have to pull together. Try to put that shameful past behind us. Use all our resources. Here we have a president who left school at age sixteen." Lutz sighed. "He doesn't know what he doesn't know."

"I've heard that redistribution of land is one of the top priorities of this government. What do you think about the willing-seller, willing-buyer initiative?"

"Oh, it sounds fine in theory. A farm comes on the market. The government pays a fair price for it and sells it to the blacks at a price they can afford. But let me tell you what is happening all over the country. I think you know that farming in Namibia is difficult because we're a desert country." He waved his arm across the rocky moonscape all around our vehicle. "And when I say 'farming,' it's not what you Americans think of as farming, crops and such. It's really cattle raising."

"Right. What you call farms, we call ranches."

"Yes. Well, it takes a lot of know-how to manage these farms. At the very least, you've got to know how to keep the water pumps repaired because if you don't, you'll lose your livestock. And you need to know about vaccinating the cattle. So what happens when people without this knowledge take over a productive farm? Their pumps break down, and no one repairs them. The cattle start dying. Hell, I've even seen them move onto farms and build little shanty houses like they're used to living in. They tear the roofs off perfectly good farmhouses, and put pieces of those roofs on their huts. It just makes no sense."

"So what's needed is education, along with the willing-seller, willing buyer program. I can understand that. But it's more complicated, isn't it? I mean, what if the blacks don't have money to get their pumps repaired or to vaccinate their cattle?"

75

"Ah, now you're beginning to understand why I say this isn't so easy."

Lutz's words remained with me after he returned us to Walvis Bay. I could understand his point of view, but even so I felt somehow disloyal to my African friends at the seminary. A knock on Mr. Strydom's front door interrupted my thoughts. It was Pastor Mark, our former student, inviting us to attend the evening service at his church. I had completely forgotten it was New Year's Eve—Mark called it Old Year's Eve—a time when many Namibian Christians gathered together to worship.

We left Mr. Strydom's house when we heard the *bong-bong* of the church bell. Mark's church was just up the road one block and around the corner. The parishioners remembered Lou and me from our previous visit to their church three months earlier and welcomed us with hugs and handshakes when we arrived at the church a few minutes before ten o'clock. While everyone was singing the opening hymn in Afrikaans, I glanced around at the congregation, at all these people who called themselves coloured, like our faculty colleagues, Dirk Cloete and Johan van Wyk. I wondered what life had been like for them during apartheid. Not easy, of course, but not nearly as tough as it was for those black Namibians in the townships.

Halfway through the service, Mark explained, in English, for our benefit, that at this service it was customary to honor those who had died during the past year. He invited representatives from families of deceased parishioners to come forward to the chancel area. About thirty or forty people left their pews and walked forward. Mark handed a candle to one person from each family. When he offered prayers for the departed, the people holding the candles raised their arms above their heads. I wondered if the flickering shadows on the church wall were the ancestors bidding a final farewell to their loved ones.

We drove Jason and Megan to the airport the next day. Namibia's month-long Festive Season was drawing to a close, and people were returning to Windhoek from their summer holidays. Lou and I were happy to turn our attention to our lesson plans for the new academic year. This year we welcomed to the campus seventeen new students. During the weeklong orientation, I interviewed each new student individually to assess their oral English abilities. When I asked Cereline Tsauses what was unusual or surprising to her about Paulinum, she said, "I was surprised to see the soccer field and the volley ball court. I thought that the only things theological students did was study and pray." Later in the week, in a small group, she said that she had given away all her trousers because she assumed the women always had to wear dresses here. Fortunately, she'd given them to her sisters and thought she could ask for them back.

During our first midday meal in the dining hall, I asked another young student how she liked the food. She paused, gave me a puzzled look, and said, "My name is Selma." I decided that either Selma needed to work on listening skills or I had to enunciate better.

When I asked Gert Beukes, a plump, anxious fellow, if he knew how to use a computer, he said, "Yes, I do! You just type in the name of a course and the computer will write your assignment for you." He wasn't joking.

Othusitse Morekwa from Botswana commented on the racism he noticed here, and we talked about tribalism in Namibia and the legacy of apartheid. He told me he was grateful Botswana had never had to endure apartheid. It would be several more years before he would tell me about some of the horrors of his own home country, tribal customs much more gruesome than racial segregation and classification.

Josephina Mulongeni, a fourth-year student, was thirty-two years old, a tall, gentle woman whose face and body bore signs of scars. When she was a girl, during Namibia's War for Independence, she and her five siblings had been victims of a bomb explosion. Only Josephina and one sister survived. Josephina had remained in the hospital for four months and then convalesced at home for another three months. She said that during the first two months of her hospitalization, she could neither move nor see.

Some of these students had never been away from their rural homesteads. When I asked Alina what surprised her most on her nine-hour journey to Windhoek, she simply said, "Mountains! I have never seen any before." One morning during orientation week we took seven students into town. Four were from the rural North and the other three from the Windhoek area. The latter group offered to be guides to those who had never seen their capital city. We gave them two hours to shop and sightsee. When we met them back at the car, the Ovambo students from the North were chattering to us excitedly in their broken English. They couldn't believe what they had seen, especially Wernhill, the modern, two-story shopping mall. What excited them the most were escalators. "The stairs moved! I was so afraid getting on and off!"

Unlike students in most colleges in the United States, our students each had a single room in the dormitories. This was a frightening experience for some of them, and they would say to us, "I have never slept alone before. I always sleep with my sisters/brothers." During those first few weeks, many of the young women carried their blankets and pillows into the room of a friend every night. They didn't mind sleeping on the floor.

Most of our students had never interacted with people from a tribe different from their own, and now suddenly they were living in dormitories with other students whose cultures were strange and perplexing. The only way they could communicate with the strangers was in their second or third language, English. Naturally, they clustered together with others who shared their own background and language.

At the end of February there was a traditional welcoming dinner party for the first-year students. Early in the morning on the day of the party, the mother of Johannes, a first-year student, had come to the campus to deliver some meat to her son because it was his birthday. Since Johannes was in class at the time, she gave it to Daphne, a fourth-year student, who put it in the refrigerator in Johannes's dormitory. Johannes and Daphne were Damaras, students from one of the Southern tribes. Matti and Elijah, Ovambos from the predominant Northern tribe, misinterpreted what they saw and accused Johannes and Daphne of stealing meat that had been purchased for the party. Unhappily, this was the first of many episodes of tribal conflict we were to witness on campus.

English classes continued to supply opportunities for intercultural learning. One morning, with ten extra minutes at the end of a class period, I asked my students if they'd like to learn some American idioms and slang. Joel couldn't stop giggling when I explained the word "wishy-washy."

The students seemed surprised that their American lecturers took such an interest in their welfare, and they told us they wished more faculty members would spend this much time with them. At the next faculty meeting, Lou and I invited our colleagues to consider offering the students opportunities to meet in small groups every week to talk about our lives together within this community. Our proposal called for each faculty member to meet once a week with a group of six or eight students, preferably in the faculty member's home. This was a new idea for our Namibian colleagues, most of whom had been trained in much more formal, European universities. Dirk said he would place our proposal on the agenda for the next meeting.

As we grew to know and trust one another, these young Africans started coming to our home on their own. The young men told stories of their lonely boyhood summers when, for months at a time, they were sent far from their home to tend the family's cattle. They were all by themselves at these cattle posts, sleeping at night in tiny makeshift tents. Kleopas told of the time a lion suddenly appeared in the tall grass. "I had my rifle," he said, "but I was afraid I would miss, so I just sat very, very, still. The wind was favorable and he never caught my scent." He grinned with delight when we started calling him Lion King.

Hainane was also sent to tend the cattle as a young boy. "My father was an uneducated man who did not believe in sending his children to school." When Hainane was eighteen years old, he was hospitalized for a serious medical condition. "A kind nurse began to teach me to read and write. I was very determined." He remained hospitalized for about a year, and when he was finally discharged, he chose not to return home, but to live with some friends who helped him get into school.

One afternoon Joel and Josephina came to our flat to visit. After they admired the framed photos of Jason and Megan and consumed the first round of juice and cookies, I asked them if they would be willing to share with me what it was like for them during the War for Independence. They fell silent, and I wondered if I had lurched into a place where such audacity was unseemly. I bit my lip and tried to think of safer spaces when Joel began to speak.

"It was eleven years ago. I was fifteen." He looked down at his hands and avoided my eyes. "The Namibian soldiers came to our village and talked to my parents. They ordered my friend and me to plant bombs along a certain road, about ten kilometers from our village. They wanted to blow up the telephone lines so the South Africans couldn't communicate with each other."

Joel said he and his friend set off on their bicycles, riding along the dusty path toward the location where they'd been instructed to plant their explosive devices. As the boys were placing these bombs by the telephone poles, one exploded, severely wounding the arm of Joel's friend. The boys tried, without success, to staunch the blood flow and staggered back home to their village. Joel said they left a trail of blood behind them. Eventually, his friend's arm stopped bleeding, but the boy died soon after he reached his homestead. The family panicked. They knew there was a trail of blood leading to the village and that the South African soldiers would soon find out what had happened. The villagers quickly buried Joel's friend. Then they dug another hole a short distance from the village and ordered Joel to hide himself in that hole in the ground.

"I stayed there all night, not knowing what would happen to me. I was afraid the soldiers would find me and kill me." The South African soldiers discovered Joel in the morning. "I thought they would shoot me and I would just die in my own grave, but they released me because I was so young."

Josephina nodded and slowly lifted her skirt to her knees, exposing the angry gash that marred her slim brown calf. "I got this in The Struggle," she said. "My sister—she died when the bomb exploded."

Lou and I had noticed that Josephina had returned to campus for her senior year limping painfully. "Last month I saw a doctor at the hospital near my village. I told him the pain was in my hip, but he said it was because of my leg injury. He gave me aspirins and vitamins."

"Did the doctor take an X-ray?" asked Lou.

She shook her head. Lou and I exchanged glances and small nods, and I knew we would soon follow up with Josephina and her medical care.

My students humbled me. I wondered if other expatriates initially made the same mistake I had made in assuming that these young Africans' halting English and unsophisticated ways implied simplemindedness. I was mortified to realize it was this kind of thinking that spawned the apartheid I openly despised. Not only that, it was the same sort of patronizing attitude that I believed characterized the missionary endeavors of the previous century. It was why I never identified myself as a missionary when talking with my Namibian friends and colleagues. I always referred to myself as a teacher or lecturer. When I considered the lives of my students and other Namibians, like our friend Gerson, I wondered what they must think of these well-off Americans who led lives of such ease.

Meanwhile, Lou and I kept asking our colleagues when the seminary's governing board would meet to select new leadership for the institution. We had thought this would happen before the students returned for the start of the new academic year, yet here it was March and Dirk Cloete was still the principal, even though we had heard that his church board had reassigned him to a parish. To maintain harmony between the two different Lutheran church bodies in the country, the positions of principal and dean of students rotated every three years between faculty members of the Northern and Southern churches. This year, the governing board would select a faculty member from the Northern Church to serve as principal.

When both bishops and the other members of the board finally came to the campus in the middle of March, there was little doubt that they would choose Dr. Michael Shangala as the seminary's next principal. This was an easy decision for the board, but the selection of a dean of students, who would also serve as vice principal, was troublesome. The dean of students had to be someone from the Southern Church, but the only faculty member from that church was Johan van Wyk, who had called the students baboons and goats. We all, faculty and students alike, seemed to tiptoe around the campus, hour after hour, not wishing to disturb the deliberations taking place in the conference room.

The governing board met all day long, and into the night. Toward dinner time, Lou joked with Hanns and Ute. "Maybe we will see a plume of white smoke when the board has made its choice." Finally, about ten o'clock, all the faculty members were called into the staff room. The chairman of the governing board was Kleopas Dumeni, the bishop from the North, that imposing gentleman with snow-white hair and booming voice. He announced the result of the board's election. No one was surprised when Dr. Michael Shangala was named principal.

Next, Bishop Dumeni announced the board's selection for dean of students. I gasped when I heard him pronounce my husband's name. I knew Lou would be the first non-African ever chosen for this position. Since Lou and I served the seminary through a partnership arrangement with the Southern Church, the board had determined this would be a way to uphold tradition while at the same time calming the fractiousness that had threatened to close the seminary the previous year. They could never have chosen Johan van Wyk, our cantankerous colleague. The bishop told Lou that his primary task would be relating to the students in matters spiritual, regulatory, and disciplinary. Another board member, Dr. Veikko Munyika, said Lou would be like "an elder brother" to the principal.

Across the table from us, van Wyk frowned and fumed, chagrined to learn that he had received no votes. He refused to look at either of us but scooped up his papers and stomped out of the staff room.

When the results were announced to the student body the following morning in the chapel, there was vigorous applause. One after another, the students approached Lou, shook his hand, and told him how happy they were that he was their dean. They said they knew he really cared about them. Lou was feeling less confident. He knew he and Michael could work well together, but he worried about van Wyk. What would he tell our own church officials in Chicago? As missionaries, we were forbidden to take up positions of leadership in the countries where we served, an acknowledgment that missionary roles today were different from what they had been a century ago. Fortunately, our Division for Global Mission understood the delicate situation of the seminary. Benyam and Harold both sent e-mails the same day saying that they would allow Lou to remain in place as dean of students.

Lou's early responsibilities included assigning students to be dining hall and cleaning prefects and laundry-room custodians. He was particularly concerned with matters involving the students' health as one after another approached him with complaints of colds, flu, or recurrences of malaria. The students soon learned they could come to our flat for ibuprofen and sore-throat lozenges. Within the first eight days of his tenure, Lou drove six students to and from doctors' visits. We wondered if we should put a red cross on the side of our vehicle and a flashing blue light on top. He also worried about campus security. Within a period of a few weeks, a bicycle and a pair of shoes were stolen from the balcony of one of our married student's flats. A student in the women's dormitory reported seeing a prowler peering in her window late one night.

Security walls surround almost all homes in Windhoek. Many residents have guard dogs. Burglar bars are standard features on windows, including those of our campus houses, flats, and dormitories. The seminary found funds within its strained budget to employ an armed security guard, but this proved to be a useless expense. Several times, when we returned to the campus at night after going out to dinner or visiting friends, we discovered the guard sound asleep behind the classroom buildings. Since there were small children living on campus, some of us worried about the rifle he carried. Pamela, an American colleague who worked downtown in the Southern Church office, told us about their newly hired guard. She started to giggle and tears were rolling down her cheeks when she said that the guard took his rifle with him into the men's restroom, set it upright on the floor, and accidentally shot a hole through the ceiling of the bathroom. The seminary eventually cancelled its arrangement with the security guard company and was able to find funding to install an electrified fence around the entire perimeter of the campus.

One day, Elijah, one of the third-year students, suggested to Lou that it would be nice if we American lecturers would eat with the students at lunch time rather than sitting by ourselves in the dining hall. We agreed, and Lou said that we had wanted to do so, but we had thought that tradition prevented faculty members from sitting at the students' tables. I told the matron that she did not need to set a separate table for us—we'd be joining the students at lunchtime. Her forehead crinkled into a frown. "Are you sure you want to do this?" I told her it was a way we could encourage the students to speak English.

Each day at lunchtime, Lou and I sat down at different students' tables. After a few moments of formal politeness, I found that most students were happy to talk with their English teacher about things other than prepositions and pronouns. But our foray into student territory was short-lived. A few days later, Fillemon, the student council president and a conservative Ovambo, told Lou that he and some of the other students did not think it was appropriate for us to eat at the students' tables. It seems we had offended their sense of propriety. It was not the way "elders" were supposed to behave. We went back to eating alone.

However, soon we had another opportunity to get to know our students better. The faculty decided to accept our earlier suggestion to set up what they called "tutorial groups" for our first-year students. These would be groups of six or seven students who would meet with faculty members in their homes once a week to discuss issues of concern to the students. During that year, two such groups of students came to our flat every week. We served juice and cookies. The discussions were usually open-ended. Sometimes we would read and discuss a book together. Through our conversations, we began to learn more about norms and traditions in Namibian culture. We learned that many young people lived with aunts and uncles rather than with their parents. I remembered what our friend, Veikko Munyika, had told us: "Here in Namibia, extended family is all-important. If I have plenty of children and you don't have any, I will send you one or two of mine." Many of our students grew up with cousins whom they would simply call their brothers and sisters.

Our students explained how their cultures dealt with death. Many people succumb to diseases such as malaria and AIDS, and many more die on Namibia's roads. Students frequently asked Lou for permission to leave the campus for a few days to attend the funeral of a family member. Most funerals in Namibia were held on Saturdays, allowing the family members enough time to travel to the event. An all-night wake is usually held on Friday evening. It is a time of reminiscing, hymn singing, and story-telling. Funeral services may last for several hours. The headstone is placed on the gravesite on the one-year anniversary of the death and is an occasion as important as the funeral itself, formally concluding the year of mourning.

Our students told us that in Namibia suicide victims are often not permitted church funerals. When they are, the casket is kept at the back of the church, and the deceased person is buried "backwards" in the cemetery, his feet in line with the heads of everyone else.

The high death rate from AIDS sometimes requires pastors to perform as many as five or six funerals a week. There are even collective funerals. When former students, those we had known in Otjimbingwe, came back to visit us, they told us that they had very little time to do any pastoral work in their congregations other than burying AIDS victims and caring for the bereaved. In the rural areas of the North, where most people have no cars, these young pastors had trouble visiting all the bereaved families because of the great distances they must walk from one family homestead to another.

On Palm Sunday, which was also my birthday, Lou was scheduled to lead the nine o'clock morning worship service in the seminary's chapel. At eight o'clock we heard loud pounding on our door. Dripping water from my shower, I grabbed a robe. Three students, trying to catch their breath, told me there was a major problem in the ladies' dormitory. Sewage was backing up through the shower drain, and two of the downstairs dorm rooms were already awash.

Lou grabbed a handful of wrenches from his toolbox and we hurried to the dormitory. Matheus, who lived in the small house across from the dormitory, met us there. Lou asked him to phone the plumber. While Lou attempted to staunch the flood, I drove to the grocery store to buy several gallons of bleach. When I returned, two male students were standing outside the dormitory having a heated argument about whose fault this was and how to fix it. After Lou had managed to stop the flow of raw sewage into the bedrooms, I organized a bucket brigade of half a dozen women. We found mops and started swabbing down the floors with bleach and water. They were unfamiliar with bleach. They liked the way it seemed to get rid of the odor, but I don't think they understood its disinfectant properties. One young lady asked me if she could use it to wash her hands. I suggested this would probably not be such a good idea. We relocated all the women with first-floor bedrooms into empty flats in our building. The Palm Sunday service was held in the chapel at four o'clock in the afternoon.

Since the plumber had not been able to locate the blockage, Lou contacted the builder and the engineer the next day and they corrected the problem. This was only one of several plumbing difficulties we encountered during that first year. About a month after the Palm Sunday episode, little puddles started appearing all over campus. Where were they coming from? There had been no rain for several months. Lou and Hanns thought these were the result of leaks from the underground water pipes. Again, the engineers and builders were called, and they started digging. The campus looked as if it were suffering an infestation of giant moles. Several days later, an angry engineer told the faculty what he had discovered. The builder had used wood glue to join the underground pipes.

Chapter 8
On the Road

*D*uring the five-day Easter weekend we traveled north to the town of Rundu in the Kavango Region, taking with us one of our favorite students, Paul Muha. His butterscotch-colored skin and almond-shaped eyes set him apart as a Kwangali, one of the country's minority tribes. Paul was every English teacher's dream student: he spoke the language fluently, turned in his assignments on time, and was reasonably competent in the mechanics of grammar and punctuation. During our twelve-hour drive to northeast Namibia, Paul told us about himself. He had been a high school teacher for five years in northern Namibia and had also worked as a translator for the Ministry of Justice and for the Peace Corps. Sandra, his wife, had a business-skills diploma, but she had been unable to find a secretarial job in Rundu so she was working as a clerk in a local grocery store. The couple had a three-year-old son, Princie.

We stopped for the night in the town of Otjiwarango, home of our favorite bakery and coffee shop where for lunch you could get the richest, creamiest chocolate milkshakes in all of Namibia. We always stayed at St. Theresa's Roman Catholic convent. Since the sisters could not afford to keep their adjacent hospital operational, they had turned it into a guesthouse, charging only seven dollars per person. Each small room, adorned with only a simple wood crucifix, had a small nightstand and one or two old-fashioned hospital beds. The sheets were crisp and white and smelled of sunlight. On the wall next to Lou's bed, at the same height as the pillow, was a tiny wood door. When we opened it, we saw a little shelf, recessed into the wall. We assumed it had been used for medications. In the evening, after we returned from supper at a local steak house, we sat with Paul in the courtyard and listened to the tolling of the convent's bell, summoning the sisters to vespers.

The following morning, several hours after we left the convent, we reached Rundu, the commercial center of the region. Cars and pedestrians clogged the pot-holed roads. I noticed several brand-new strip malls with familiar South African shops like Pep and Ackermans and Checkers, and a few smaller shops with Spanish-sounding names.

"Paul, what are those shops?"

"Oh, those are Portuguese shops. The Portuguese were the first to colonize this area, before the new borders separated us from Angola," he explained. "Many Portuguese people still live here and a lot of older Kwangali people still speak Portuguese."

Paul directed Lou onto a dusty track through a grassy field leading to the bank of the Kavango River. We bothered a small flock of chickens when we approached a tiny, cement structure painted pale green and surrounded by several tall, leafy trees. "When I was still a teacher, the government provided us with this house, free of charge. Luckily, Sandra and I were able to put some money aside from our jobs, and the government allowed us to purchase this house when I left teaching to enter the seminary." We climbed out of the Venture, stretched our legs, and began walking toward the river.

"This river is really the heart of the Kavango Region," said Paul. "The residents earn their living from fishing." He pointed to the horizon. "That's Angola over there, on the other side."

Several women in brightly colored sarongs were washing their clothes in the river and laying them out to dry on bushes. Bare-chested men in shorts and wide-brimmed straw hats were fishing from small canoes. Others had waded into the river with large, cornucopia-shaped fishing baskets. "During the dry season," said Paul, "when the threat of hippos and crocodiles is low, parents let their children play in the water." We noticed that the little ones were all playing on the riverbank. Did their mothers worry about sharing their washing water with crocs and hippos?

Paul told us that Sandra was working at the grocery store, so we arranged to meet him later, after we had checked into our room. The n'Gandu Lodge (*n'Gandu* means "crocodile") also overlooked the Kavango River, like Paul's house. Our small thatch-roofed bungalow had a tiny kitchen with a half-sized fridge, a two-burner hot plate, and an electric kettle. While Lou brought our suitcase and tote bags inside, I unpacked our cans of soda, packets of cookies, coffee, and tea. Unlike the Muha's tiny house, our lodging was air-conditioned and even had cable TV (two channels).

Later that afternoon, our Venture stirred up small clouds of dust as we bumped along the dirt road toward the tiny village of Mupini. The air conditioning seemed to have succumbed to the midday heat, and I wiped my neck with the navy blue bandana I always carried on such trips.

"Turn right," Paul said, and we drove into a compound where tall trees and gentle river breezes brought some relief from the scorching African sun. When Finnish Lutherans had established Mupini as a mission post in 1930, the village thrived with its school, clinic, and the little church where villagers came to be baptized, married, confirmed, and buried. The congregation had grown to 2,700 members. Many now worshipped at one of several outlying preaching points. Paul called these synagogues.

Budget constraints had forced the Finnish Church to withdraw its financial support in the 1990s, and Mupini had suffered. The marginal income of the congregants could not support a pastor, and the villagers struggled to keep the congregation intact. They sustained a Sunday school, several choirs, a youth group, and a seven-member church council. An elderly deacon led the Sunday service.

"Paul, how do people in Mupini make a living?" Lou asked.

"Some of them grow crops, and the villagers have started a few projects. A few of the educated ones have jobs in Rundu."

Lou parked the car under the leafy canopy of an old mopane tree. I was happy to stretch my legs and to breathe village scents again, the familiar pungent-sweet blend of wood smoke and animal dung. Paul hurried off, in search of the deacon who had the key to the church. A little girl in a ragged pink dress suddenly appeared from the nearby millet field. She giggled when I waved.

The mud-brick church wore a coat of fresh white paint. While we waited, I watched the birds swooping through the bell tower. It was easy to imagine this little church nestled in a grassy Alpine valley instead of a sandy African village. Paul returned accompanied by a slender old fellow with whiskery cheeks.

"This gentleman is the deacon." The old man smiled a toothless grin and we shook hands. I noticed that the previous owner of the deacon's formal black suit had been a shorter man. He took a key from his pocket and invited us to step inside. It took a few moments for our eyes to adjust to the darkness. Only a few sunbeams penetrated the narrow windows. Attached to the walls were empty Coke, Fanta, and Sprite cans, each holding a candle stub. Paul noticed my glance.

"The government has brought electric lines to Mupini, but the people cannot afford to pay for a connection."

I stared at the oversized framed painting of the white Jesus above the white altar.

"Come this way," Paul said as we stepped outside into the bright sunshine. I put my sunglasses back on, and we walked across the sand toward something that resembled a large mud beehive resting on a base of gray rocks.

"This is Mupini's bread-baking oven." There was a hole in the top of the beehive. The oven door was a piece of corrugated tin. The old man was saying something.

"He says the villagers hope their bread-baking project, as well as a brick-making project," he pointed to long, neat rows of mud bricks, "will help the congregation to raise enough money to support a full-time pastor."

We were driving away from the village when Paul mused, "I dream of coming back here to serve this congregation. I remember how it used to be. The missionaries had a big garden on the riverbank, and everyone had plenty of food. I would like to do that for my people."

When we approached Rundu, Paul said, "I would like you to meet Sandra's mother."

We turned off the highway onto a dirt road and entered a neighborhood of tiny cement-brick houses, each on a small plot of neatly raked sand. Paul directed us to park next to one of the houses.

"This is the home of my mother-in-law."

He led us into the back yard, and invited us to sit on the white plastic chairs while he went inside to summon Sandra's mother. The air was filled with the soft double cooing of African doves. Tiny yellow and pink flowers grew in a flowerbed directly behind the house. Soon Paul returned with a slender, elderly woman in a faded print dress. Her face, a much darker shade than Paul's, was a mass of wrinkles, her eyes wary. I'm sure we were the first Americans ever to visit her home. She shyly extended her hand. I was glad that Paul had taught us the traditional Rukwangali greetings, since she spoke no English:

Mwararapo? (Did you sleep well?)

Nhi! (Yes!)

Nawa? (Very well?)

Nhi. (Yes.)

Paul explained that we were his lecturers at the seminary and had brought him home for the Easter weekend. She nodded slowly, still looking wary, and then she suddenly got up and went into her house. I thought she was going to bring us some juice or soft drinks. Instead, she came out and thrust a Namibian ten-dollar bill (worth about $2.00) into Lou's hand. Paul translated: "She says this is so you can buy something cool to drink." Even in her obvious poverty, the old lady couldn't neglect this gesture of hospitality. To return the money would have been insulting, so later Lou slipped the bill to Paul and told him we wanted him to keep the money in the family.

On Saturday morning the lodge served a full English breakfast—fried eggs, thick rashers of bacon, grilled tomatoes, toast, juice, and coffee. Two kilometers away, Paul and his family were probably eating bowls of millet porridge and drinking cups of sweet, milky tea. Becoming a tourist troubled our heads and our hearts as it had years earlier in West Africa. And yet, tourism was Namibia's third most important industry, along with fishing and mining, providing employment to many who might otherwise be jobless. Although few Americans had even heard of the country, Europeans flocked to its lodges, guest farms, and game parks.

We stepped outside with our binoculars and walked to the end of the lush green lawn behind our bungalow. We could see villagers moving around on the other side of the river in Angola. That afternoon, we drove into town before the shops closed to buy some cans of soda for the next day's long drive to Windhoek. On our way back to the lodge, we noticed some Peace Corps volunteers walking along the road, distinguishable by their backpacks and jaunty, confident gait. I peered at one young woman with a blonde ponytail who looked familiar, and I realized it was Karen, a young woman we had known from our congregation in North Carolina. Of all places to meet someone from home! Lou reminded me that she had come to Namibia the previous year and was teaching at a school in the central part of the country. We pulled over to the side of the road and exclaimed over the coincidence of meeting each other. Karen and her friend needed a ride back to Windhoek on Sunday afternoon, so we arranged to pick them up from the backpackers' hostel where they were staying.

On Sunday morning when we entered the nave of the large Lutheran church in Rundu, we were surprised to see a huge, colorful mural on the wide wall behind the altar and extending to the walls on either side. The full-sized figures on this triptych depicted scenes from the life of Christ in rich hues and intricate detail. There were over five hundred people at that Easter service which was led by an elderly Finnish missionary. After the service Pastor Toivanen and his wife invited us to the parsonage next door for coffee. They were fluent in Rukwangali, and we learned they had been living and working here since 1958. Mrs. Toivanen, a cheerful, energetic lady in her seventies, wore a plain navy-blue dress and thin white ankle socks with flats. She poured coffee into dainty china cups and showed us a thick scrapbook filled with photos of Finland. "You must come to visit us when we retire and return to Finland next year!" Pastor Toivanen proudly told us that his wife was the artist who had painted the mural on the church wall.

Ascension Day and Africa Day, both national holidays, offered us another five-day weekend at the end of May. We decided to travel into the Kalahari Desert for two nights at the Intu Afrika Lodge. The brochure advertised a visit to a Bushman community.

The Kalahari Desert is vastly different from the Namib. Sturdy camel-thorn trees and small bushes stabilize its red sand dunes. The Kalahari's serenity was somehow more welcoming than the rocky Namib. Perhaps it was the trees. The bumpy gravel road to the lodge was adjacent to a large area called a pan: a flat depression of whiter sand that filled with water during the scarce rains, and where, because of the mineral salts, nothing grows.

At the lodge, an attractive collection of orange, adobe-style buildings, a porter carried our two small suitcases to our room. There was no television, telephone, or air conditioning, but we didn't miss these. The beds were comfortable and the bathroom was clean. The porter said that tea, coffee, and cake would be served in the dining room at three o'clock, and at four o'clock we could go on a walk with a Bushman tracker. We accepted both offers.

Our Bushman guide said his name was Alex. Later we learned that many Bushmen have two names: a Western name and their own, traditional name. Bushmen are short in stature. Their skin is a yellowish tan color, much lighter than people of the Bantu tribes. Their hair grows in a tufted pattern that has been called "peppercorn." Alex was barefooted and wearing a loincloth of animal hide. He carried a slender walking stick and had a small leather pouch slung over his chest. We had to hurry to keep up with him. Every so often he would stop and show us tracks of animals that inhabited this area: mouse, ground squirrel, rabbit, zebra, gemsbock, giraffe, and kudu. The wavy lines in the sand were, of course, snakes. We walked up and over the sand hills for over an hour. The sun had already disappeared behind the dunes, and tiny gray birds were roosting in the acacia trees. Worried, we saw the lights of the lodge about two long kilometers away. Lou and I whispered to each our fears that we would not reach it before dark, and my husband tried to explain to Alex, whose understanding of English was very limited, that we ought to turn back. But Alex just said, "No—a little more," and continued striding away from the lodge. And there, just over the next dune, we saw a long table spread with a white tablecloth. An elderly black gentleman was standing behind it. On the table were a bottle of wine, a pitcher of orange juice, a couple of bottles of beer, chips, dip, crackers, and peanuts. It was what the Namibians call a sundowner. Even more welcome was the sight of a large *bakkie* (pick-up truck) at the bottom of the dune. After enjoying our drinks and snacks, we gratefully climbed into the truck for the short ride back to the lodge.

Dinner was served in a *boma*, an open air dining area, the tables surrounding a cheery campfire. The desert night was chilly, and the warmth of the fire was welcome. A young Bushman woman welcomed us and invited us to sit at any of the several empty tables. The meal, served buffet style, was sumptuous: grilled pork chops, oxtails in gravy, crispy roast potatoes, broccoli in cream sauce, tiny sweet gem squash, and a tossed salad. For dessert, crème caramel. Afterwards, we enjoyed talking with Pat Gibbs, the managing director of the lodge, a 63-year-old gentleman from South Africa. Pat lived in Cape Town, and had been coaxed out of early retirement by a wealthy friend to act as interim managing director of the lodge. An outgoing, erudite gentleman, he told us the history of this lodge, which was only four years old, and he described the Bushman project that the lodge supports. He said tomorrow we'd meet the two young South African anthropologists, Michael and Betts Daiber, who had been working for about two years here at Intu Afrika assisting with a small *!Kung* (the "!" represents a vocal click) Bushman community of about forty adults and children.

When we returned to our room after dinner, I began reading a book, *Miscast: Negotiating the Presence of the Bushmen*, that Pat had lent me. The essays comprising the chapters were written by anthropologists who had studied the Bushmen communities throughout the past century. I felt chilled to read that the Bushmen had been hunted, murdered, and skinned, and that their embalmed or stuffed bodies were displayed as trophies. Sometimes recently buried bodies were dug up and boiled so the skeletons could be displayed. Because of their unusual anatomy—short stature, very large protruding buttocks, and unusual genitalia—young Bushmen of both genders had been captured and taken to Europe where they were exhibited in traveling museums.

On Saturday morning Betts Daiber told us about their work here. "As you probably know, Bushmen were the original inhabitants of southern

Africa. They have always been nomadic hunter-gatherers living in groups where leadership was undefined and tribal fights unknown. As the Bantu tribes moved down from the north and the early white settlers moved up from the Cape, they encountered the Bushmen. Because they weren't organized and could not combat the intruders, the Bushmen were displaced by those more dominant cultures."

"It seems that there are still a lot of Bushmen here in Namibia."

"Their numbers are decreasing. These hunter-gatherers have lost all rights to natural resources and access to land. The Bushmen here are dependent on government handouts. All their attempts to be self-supporting have failed due to lack of water, overgrazed land, and the absence of game. Bushmen are facing the dilemma of poverty, unemployment, abuse, and exploitation. And they are horribly discriminated against." Betts sighed. "Everyone seems to hate the Bushmen. During Namibia's struggle for independence, the South Africans conscripted many Bushmen into service to act as trackers to locate the blacks whom the South Africans fought and killed. Perhaps it's not surprising Namibia's black ruling party isn't working very hard to help the Bushmen."

"Is that what brought you here?" asked Lou.

"Yes. Pat has probably told you a bit about the Intu Afrika Corporation. This is a project that we hope will provide a role model for development projects with the Bushmen and other indigenous minority peoples. Pat and others thought it might be possible to build a reserve and lodge where eco-tourism could benefit both the investors and the Bushmen. Two years ago, a group of forty *!Kung* adults and children moved to a temporary camp here on the reserve. They built their own village, and today every family is staying in a house of their own on the reserve."

"How do they survive?" I asked. "It's not through those handouts, is it?"

"Oh, no. The objective of this project is really twofold. First, we wanted to empower the community to regain their dignity by creating employment and cultural activities that utilize traditional Bushman skills so they could earn an income. Things like game guiding, tracking, camp supervising, and craft making. We also want the Bushmen to become shareholders in the company."

Pat joined us, eager to explain. "We're getting ready to implement a new plan. We realized the Bushmen would not be happy simply staying on this reserve—they are still hunters and gatherers, you know. Besides, there were still so many of them in this area we weren't helping to become self-sufficient. So we developed a rotation plan. While we keep a core community of well-trained workers for the Reserve, other members of the community will rotate here to work for limited periods. When these people return to the desert, another group will take their place. This enables the larger community to benefit from work on the Reserve, and it satisfies the Bushmen's need to be on-the-move." The low rumble of a diesel-powered engine in the driveway interrupted Pat. "That's Michael. He's ready to take you to visit to the Bushmen community." Once we were seated in the open-sided Land Rover and bouncing along the sandy trail leading away from the lodge, Michael began to tell us what to expect.

"Some people prefer to use the word *Khoisan* or just *San* when speaking about these people, but the people you will meet call themselves Bushmen. They don't find the word derogatory. Here in Namibia, Bushmen had been slaves of the Herero (a black or Bantu) tribe for several generations. The children played together, but when the Herero children went to school, the Bushmen children stayed at home to do housekeeping and farming chores. Sometimes the young girls were used for the sexual enjoyment of the males in the household."

Michael explained that the peoples' homes were nearby, but we would not visit them so as to maintain their privacy. He said we would first see a pre-primary school and then a small communal area, a thatched hut where we could talk to the people and purchase the crafts they had for sale.

As we stepped down from our vehicle, we saw several small naked boys playing on the swings in a little playground next to the simple one-room school building. Michael ushered us inside. Colorful toys, books, and charts lined the walls, along with the children's artwork. I noticed some Montessori materials. The teacher, a short round lady wearing nothing but a thick grey blanket from her waist to her ankles, greeted us. She told us (through Michael who interpreted) that she was the music teacher and that she also taught the children traditional things they needed to know. While she was talking, two of the little boys scrambled onto Michael's lap. The teacher said she taught the children about the medicinal properties of certain leaves and roots and how to use the traditional digging stick to unearth edible roots and tubers. She told us she could neither read nor write. "If you send me a letter I will crumple it up and use it as toilet paper! But if you send me pictures, I will read those."

She abruptly concluded her talk: "That's all I have to say." We thanked her and walked around the little room. Alongside a shelf of simple readers was a chart of animal pictures and their tracks.

A few yards from the school a group of about ten adults was waiting for us next to a thatched hut. The men wore simple loincloths and the women either loincloths or blankets. All the adults were bare-chested (we tried not to stare), and all the children were naked. We were wearing sweaters in the cool morning air. We shook hands and exchanged names and greetings with everyone. Each person carefully repeated our names. One of the men invited us to sit down on the sand and ask them any questions we might have. Lou asked about their spiritual beliefs, but their answers were vague. It appeared that they did not observe any rites or rituals. An older woman asked us what "Happy Christmas" meant. She said a previous visitor to their community had told them about Santa Claus whom they saw as a demon. I told them about Jesus and his birthday. (I later found out that birthdays are meaningless to them. They do not measure time, so no one knows how old he or she is.) The teacher said she believed in God but she had never seen him. I told her that I hadn't either! Then she said that once a man came to them from Jerusalem carrying Bibles in a donkey cart. She said she wasn't sure whether Jerusalem was up there (she pointed upwards) or somewhere else.

We asked them about marriage and wedding customs. One pretty young woman said, "People just get together and kiss and talk mouth-to-mouth and then they are married." Apparently there was no marriage ceremony. She asked us about our marriage customs, and Lou offered a simple explanation. They all laughed when he said that the couple promises to love and to take care of each other.

"Don't you ever fight with each other and hit each other?" asked the younger lady. We said that sometimes this happens, but not very often. They laughed again. "We never see any scars on white people," she continued. "We get hit two or three times a week."

Michael later explained that years ago Bushmen used to abhor violence, and he wondered if the introduction of alcohol might have modified that behavior.

Before leaving, we asked permission to take a few photos. We also wanted to buy several items from their "shop," a fence made of sticks from which were hung the various crafts they had made to sell. Lou bought a walking stick, and I purchased a small white leather purse intricately decorated with leather fringe and tiny ostrich shell beads. I also bought a necklace and an ostrich shell etched with a drawing of a pregnant female figure. The sketch showed the fetus inside the woman.

Back at the lodge we enjoyed a hearty lunch and a short rest in our room. About three o'clock, we had tea in the dining room and were joined by an older couple from Germany. We all boarded the open-sided Land Rover for a late-afternoon game drive. Our guide and driver was Raymond, a young coloured man who had recently completed his studies in environmental science and conservation at the Polytechnic Institute in Windhoek. He warned us to hang onto the sides of the vehicle, and we careened up and over the dunes at break-neck speed. It felt like a carnival ride. We saw a few animals—gemsbok, kudu, zebra, wildebeest—but primarily we oohed and aahed over the rippled red sand and feathery-looking camel thorn trees, all bathed in the deep purple shadows of the early Kalahari evening.

After breakfast the next morning, we were paying our bill and buying souvenir postcards when Betts walked into the reception area and asked us if we could give some youngsters a ride as far as Rehoboth. They were the children of a black woman who worked at Intu Afrika. It was the end of their school holiday, and they were returning to their boarding school. We said we would be happy to do so, refusing her offer of payment. Along the way, I made little crocheted bracelets for each of the four children, and we gave them sweets when we dropped them off at the petrol station in Rehoboth, following the instruction we had received from the children's mother.

During July, the seminary's month-long winter holiday, we were traveling again throughout Namibia, this time on a journey of about 1,800 miles with Diane, Linda, and Natalie, friends from North Carolina. The three women, members of our Chapel Hill congregation, had been saving their money and planning this trip to visit their former pastor and his wife ever since we came to Namibia. What fun to see these familiar faces and to offer them a personalized tour. We felt like seasoned expatriates. Our first destination was a two-night visit to the rural home of our faculty colleague, Rev. Amaambo. Six hours after leaving Windhoek, we crossed the veterinary checkpoint into Ovamboland, the northern part of Namibia where seventy-five percent of the country's population lives. Ovamboland is about one hundred miles west of the Kavango area where we'd visited Paul several months earlier. We drove past thatched roofed huts scattered throughout the fields on either side of the road. Women in faded cotton dresses and barefoot children walked along the roadside, many of them bearing bundles of firewood on their heads. Occasionally we passed a donkey cart driven by young boys or old men and loaded with colorful plastic jugs for the water they drew from government water taps or community wells. Every so often, Lou would have to stop the car, yielding to herds of cattle chased by little boys with sticks.

We arrived at the town of Oniipa, a cluster of small shops and a Shell petrol station, which was also home to the headquarters of the Northern Church with more than half a million member—twenty-five percent of the country's population. Reluctant to burden the Amaambos with extra expenses, we stopped at the Punyu Grocery Store where we purchased cooking oil, tea, sugar, canned goods, toilet paper, and fresh vegetables. I remembered that Meme Esther liked Ricoffee, a blend of instant coffee and chicory, so we added two cans to our shopping cart. Linda and Diane located the toy section and bought a large ball and a Tonka truck for Rev. Amaambo's little grandson.

This was our second visit to the Amaambo home, and Lou was pleased he remembered where to turn off the paved road onto the dusty track through the fields that would take us to their house. Although many families in Ovamboland still lived in huts constructed from mud and sticks, the more prosperous families had cement or mud-brick houses. The Amaambo's home was constructed from mud bricks painted green, had running water, and used solar energy for lights.

When we arrived, about three o'clock, Meme Esther hurried outside to greet us. Wisps of gray hair escaped her head wrap, and a huge smile crinkled her face. "Welcome, welcome!" she cried, breaking into a little dance. She hugged each of us. "You will come inside and eat, yes?"

Our American friends were already charmed. Meme Esther was like everyone's favorite grandmother. You couldn't help liking her. I had seen the same reaction from the seminary students when Meme came to the campus. Close to seventy, she had more energy than most people half her age. She led us inside to a simple parlor. Like many such homes in Africa, this one had begun its life as a one or two-room dwelling, with other rooms and wings added on, as money was available. This made for an interesting configuration. The section containing the parlor and guest bedroom had its own outside entrance, but access to this wing from the main house meant walking through the bathroom which had a door on either end.

Meme said that we should help ourselves to the food arrayed on a table covered in a bright pink oilcloth. Rev. Amaambo offered a prayer of gratitude for our safe arrival, and we helped ourselves to a snack of cool drinks, slices of fresh papaya, and mashed potato salad with raisins in it. An hour later, we were still chatting when Meme said, "Now you will take a bath! Use the second bathroom—the one next to my bedroom."

I found her remark strange, but I obligingly walked back to the bathroom at the rear of the house. In this small room, painted a deep rose color, were a sink, shower, and toilet. A tiny cosmetic mirror hung from a nail on the wall. I shed my dusty traveling clothes. From our previous visit, I knew the showerhead and faucets were merely decorative. Meme had placed a fresh bar of soap, a bucket of steaming hot water, and another bucket of cold water in the shower stall. I lathered myself, and used an enamel cup to douse the suds with a mixture of water from the two buckets. Finding no towels, I drip-dried, which fortunately didn't take long in the arid climate. Natalie, Linda, and Diane took their turns after me. "Take your towels with you," I whispered.

After we had all bathed, the Amaambos said they wanted to show our guests the rest of their home, and they ushered us outside. Behind the house in the large sandy yard was a cluster of four traditional Ovambo-style huts made of baked clay and grass-thatched roofs.

Meme said, "This is our small traditional homestead. Our older relatives prefer to stay here when they come to visit." In addition to the sleeping huts, where one of Meme's brothers lived year-round, were several smaller huts that were used for storage and another one with a hard clay floor that was used for pounding the *mahangu*. Just outside this hut, in the leafy shade of a mopane tree, Meme proudly showed us her kitchen—a gleaming stainless steel double sink, anchored in the sand. "There is even running water," she said, turning on the tap. The water ran through the drain into the sand under the sink.

Rev. Amaambo introduced us to five-year-old Ndakalapo. He was a wide-eyed boy, skinny and very shy, but at his grandpa's urging, he solemnly shook hands with each of us. Linda handed him the ball and trunk and his face broke into a happy grin.

"We call him our grandson, but he is really the child of our niece who died. The boy's name means 'the one who was left behind.'" I wondered what it would be like to carry that name through life.

Also living with the Amaambos was a young man named Jonas who had come to Namibia from Angola as a child refugee. His father had been killed during Angola's ongoing civil war, and the Amaambos had raised him as one of their own. Two young women also lived at the homestead to help Meme with household chores as well as planting and harvesting their sizable crops during the nine months of each year her husband was teaching at the seminary.

The next morning the roosters awakened me at five o'clock. I lay in bed and listened to Meme singing quietly to herself in the kitchen across the hall while she began boiling pots of water on her propane stove. I knew she would pour the scalding hot water into large buckets, and carry them into the bathroom for our morning ablutions, just as she had done the previous afternoon.

During our two-day visit various relatives and friends came to visit. Meme Esther enthusiastically welcomed them all and somehow stretched the food to make sure no one left without having a meal. One of the visitors was Rev. Amaambo's younger brother, who was a physician at the nearby hospital. We learned that education was vitally important to this family. Rev. Amaambo himself had studied in the United States for several years. One of the subjects he taught at the seminary was Greek, and he told us he was the first translator of the New Testament from Greek into Oshiwambo. Years before, Meme Esther had started a primary school here in Oniipa where she had been a teacher and later the principal. One of their daughters was currently in the United States earning a master's degree that would enable her to teach at the University of Namibia.

Our last evening at the Amaambo homestead, we were all sitting outside under the tree while Rev. Amaambo told us stories of life in Ovamboland many years ago. The goats and chickens had already fallen asleep, and the huge orange sun was slipping down behind the crusty millet stalks, releasing its grip on the day. Johanna and Nangula, Meme's helpers, finished washing the dinner dishes and joined us. Ndakalapo was making soft vroom-vroom sounds and pushing his truck back and forth in the sand. My students had taught me that this evening story-telling time, previously such an important aspect of Ovambo culture, was starting to disappear because so many rural families were moving away from the North in search of employment in the towns, a pattern of urbanization happening throughout Africa.

Soon the mosquitoes chased us indoors. Our American friends thought this would be a good time to present their gifts to the members of the household, University of North Carolina T-shirts and hats. Meme was delighted. She hurried out of the sitting room, taking with her Johanna and Nangula. A few minutes later, the three women returned wearing their T-shirts. They danced their appreciation for us, stamping their feet, ululating, and blowing shrill metal whistles.

Before we left the Amaambo homestead the next morning, the household gathered outside for a formal farewell. We all stood in a circle while Rev. Amaambo offered a prayer for our safe travel. He and Meme Esther opened their hymnals and sang two hymns for us.

On the dusty shelf of *What I Wish I Had Done with My Life*, the package labeled Cultural Anthropologist was the biggest. What would it be like, I used to wonder, to live among people whose customs and beliefs were alien from my own? Would they seem exotic? What might we have in common? Now, within just a few months, I'd had this opportunity three times. And I would have more. What a gift! How could the value of my teaching English to the young adults at the seminary possibly compare to what I'd already been given?

Chapter 9
Caught Between Cultures

*B*efore our American guests returned to the United States, we wanted to introduce them to the von Seydlitz family who owned a 250,000-acre hunting and guest farm a half-day's drive from Windhoek. We drove onto the grounds of a whitewashed fortress anchored by a three-story tower. The Schonfeld complex, built in 1913, comprised eight luxurious guest suites, the family's spacious home, and a series of outbuildings: garages, a tannery, and a small slaughterhouse.

A young black maid welcomed us into the main house, where we met an older German woman, the mother of Elke, our hostess. She invited us to deposit our luggage in our rooms and join the family for lunch. The lounge and adjoining dining room were furnished with sturdy leather chairs and sofas and solid mahogany sideboards. African artifacts, mostly Bushman hunting tools, adorned the walls. It was easy to imagine hunters and adventurers from a hundred years earlier relaxing in these rooms after a good hunt, enjoying their cigars and glasses of ale.

"Susan! Lou!"

We turned around, and saw our host, a brawny fellow with a trim gray beard. Hartwig, wearing a safari shirt and khaki shorts, greeted us with big bear hugs. We introduced him to Diane, Natalie and Linda. Elke joined us—more hugs—and told us that lunch was ready.

Guest farms are popular with hunters and tourists in Namibia. Although visitors have their own rooms and bathrooms, everyone eats together. It's an opportunity to meet local Namibians and international tourists in an informal atmosphere. The long table was spread with platters of thinly sliced ham, a variety of smoked sausages, cheeses, breads, and three kinds of salad. There were half a dozen glass pitchers of fresh lemonade. A middle-aged German couple were the only other guests that day. Several members of the von Seydlitz family and their German helpers also joined us. Elke and her mother supervised the kitchen crew of five young black women. Seated at the head of the table, his little granddaughter on his lap, Hartwig said grace. The dinner conversation alternated between German and English.

"Why don't you have a little rest, and then join us for tea and cake on the verandah in about two hours?" said Elke.

"And how about a sundowner after that?" asked Hartwig.

We agreed. While Diane, Linda, and Natalie decided to hike the surrounding area, Lou and I retrieved our books from our room and made ourselves comfortable in the chaise lounges beside the pool.

An hour later our friends returned from their walk. They hadn't encountered any game, but they told us about the cheetahs they had seen in a large fenced enclosure on the grounds. Hartwig assisted the government, and his own financial position, by participating in a cheetah conservation project. The number of wild cheetahs in Namibia was diminishing, and their population suffered from inbreeding. Farmers whose livestock and game were threatened by cheetahs were encouraged not to shoot them but to contact the Cheetah Conservancy, which would capture them and send them to farms such as Schonfeld. Hartwig and others participated in genetically controlled breeding programs to strengthen the population. All the animals were later released into the wild.

Just before sunset, Hartwig reappeared and invited the five of us, along with the German couple, to join him for a sundowner. We climbed aboard Schonfeld's safari vehicle, an open-topped, modified Land Cruiser, and Hartwig tore off at breakneck speed. We made a brief stop at a pile of rocks alongside the trail to examine some ancient Bushman rock carvings. Then we lurched along the rough trails, heading toward a steep granite mountain on the edge of the farm. Hartwig stopped at the base of the mountain to shift into a lower gear and began roaring up, bouncing over boulders. Our butts flew off the seats, and Linda was so frightened she cowered on the floor. When we reached the precipice, our limbs were tingling. Hartwig jumped out and hauled a cooler from the back of the vehicle. He offered us wine, sodas, and an assortment of chips and crackers. Drinks in hand, we clambered to the top of the mountain just as the sun was setting. In the valley below a male kudu, sunlight glistening on its mighty rack of horns, stepped out from behind a tree. No one said a word.

After dinner, Hartwig said, "Come with me to the den. I have something you might like to see." The den, a separate building on the far side of the swimming pool, was really a bar, decorated with skins of zebras and lions and trophy heads of the kudus and wildebeests that had been hunted on the farm.

"Many of our guests are hunters from Germany," he told us. He bent down and fumbled with something. "Look, this is want I want to show you."

From beneath the bar, Hartwig produced an old red leather photo album, its edges soft and worn. "This is how the farm looked in 1945." He slowly turned the pages. There was the white tower that we'd seen upon our arrival. Flying from the turret was a Nazi flag. None of us could think of anything to say.

Sensing our discomfort, Hartwig said, "This is not a part of our family history I am especially proud of. During the war, all the Germans in Namibia and South Africa were rounded up and placed in internment camps. My grandfather was expelled to Germany, and my father was sent to a camp in South Africa."

Elke insisted we take with us packets of sandwiches and grapes when we left Schonfeld the following morning. Hartwig threw his arm around Lou's shoulder and extracted a promise that we'd return soon. As we drove toward home, our three guests tried to process this piece of Namibian history and culture. After their immersion into black village life with the Amaambo family, I knew they must have felt confused about their visit with a third-generation white Namibian family who were so rooted to this place. "What is hard for me to understand," said Natalie, "is how these descendents of Nazis continue to thrive in the country. I mean, look at the luxury of that farm, compared with the Amaambo's homestead, or those awful, urban squatter areas we visited outside Windhoek."

"It's the legacy of colonialism and apartheid," Lou replied. "Here you have a country in which the population is ninety-eight percent black, but almost all the economic wealth is in the hands of the two percent white minority. People call that economic colonialism."

"The Namibian government is seeking to redress that inequality by land redistribution," I said. "They have instituted a program that they call 'willing seller-willing buyer.' If a farm comes on the market, the government has the right of first refusal. When the government buys a farm, that farm is offered to members of the black population."

We talked some more about the feelings our visit to Schonfeld had stirred. "I like Hartwig and Elke very much," I said. "I think they are sensitive to the condition of the black majority. And yet, the longer I am here, the more comfortable I feel among the black people, even though I know that some of them look at my white skin and remember their colonial past."

On the last day of our friends' visit, I took them into downtown Windhoek for some final souvenir shopping. We joined the throng of tourists in the area called Post Street Mall, where street vendors peddled their crafts. I watched while my guests bought their woodcarvings, batiks, beaded jewelry, and African prints. Their shopping bags bulged.

The school year and our normal routine resumed. After our first morning of classes, we were walking home from the dining hall and our lunch of chewy goat and bouncy porridge. I told Lou to go on ahead to our flat because I had to take my laundry off the clothesline. I was folding our clothes and placing them in the basket when I heard the rumble of a *bakkie* pulling into the carport. Andreas Nowaseb, the married student who lived two doors down from us, was returning from a visit to his parents' home. Crowded into the back of the truck were two of his three children, an elderly couple I recognized as his parents, and a black and white goat.

The children jumped out and hauled the goat into the field just behind the carport. Andreas tethered the goat to an acacia tree, and all afternoon we listened to its plaintive bleating. Toward evening, when the noise ceased, I opened the front door of our flat. The carport roof blocked my view of the field, but the pungent stench confirmed that the goat had been slaughtered. For the next six weeks, the goatskin hung in the carport, curing. I was impressed by the efficiency of the African way: enough meat for a feast plus a rug, all in one package.

Soon thereafter, Hafeni and Nambala, two male students, approached my husband as he was walking to the dining hall for lunch. He told me later they were agitated and insistent, and that they'd taken him aside so no one could overhear their conversation.

"Pastor Lou," said Nambala, "because you are the dean of students, there is something you need to know about Nandi. Something we learned when we were at home during the holidays."

Nandi, a second-year student, was a great beauty—almond eyes, high cheekbones, lustrous ebony skin. She spoke softly and dressed modestly. When she strolled across the campus, her shoulder-length braids—dozens of them—followed the rhythm of her swaying hips. I could imagine Nandi in her village homestead, bearing an impossibly heavy water jug on her head or hoeing the family's millet field with the same graceful ease. She was a young woman wholly without guile. She turned in her assignments on time and tried to answer my class questions, but her

English was weak and I always had to listen carefully to understand what she was saying. At first, I had trouble breaking through her shyness, but once she and her classmates began visiting our small apartment in groups of two or three, she had relaxed into a trusting relationship with Lou and me.

"We had gone to Oshakati to do some shopping, and we met an old woman we knew from Nandi's village," said Hafeni. "She told us that Nandi had been pregnant."

"But she is no more pregnant," added Nambala.

"So…what exactly are you telling me?" asked Lou.

"That she had an abortion last month during the holiday! People in the villages have been talking about this," said Hafeni.

"What evidence do you have to support what you're saying?" asked Lou.

He told me the two young men had looked at each other, apparently surprised that he was unwilling to accept the veracity of their claims.

Lou phoned Michael Shangala, the principal, and arranged to meet him and the students that evening. "We need to find out from Nandi herself what, if anything, happened. We certainly don't need students spreading gossip about other students."

I couldn't believe that this lovely young woman had really had an abortion. The conservative traditions of her culture and her religion would cast the procedure as both a taboo and a sin.

Dr. Shangala phoned back an hour later and spoke with Lou. When Lou hung up, I knew from the scowl on his face the news wasn't good.

"Shangala's cancelled our meeting. He told me he believes Hafeni and Nambala." Lou's fists were clenched and he was pacing around our little living room. "He also said that he had talked to Nandi. He's calling a special faculty meeting for four o'clock this afternoon to determine her punishment. He's not even asking her to appear before the faculty. Do you believe this?"

I was truly alarmed about the potential fissure in our relationship with Dr. Shangala. Never before had he and Lou seriously disagreed over a matter of student conduct. What would happen if *all* our African colleagues tugged on these loose threads of rumor and innuendo? How could we oppose them without sacrificing the credibility and congeniality we'd worked so hard to establish? I could feel the fragile fabric of our acceptance beginning to unravel.

Abortion is illegal in Namibia, and the long arm of Namibian law also grasps those who assist, or even suggest, the procedure. Our seminary had never dealt with an abortion, but the seminary's code of conduct was clear in matters of out-of-wedlock pregnancy: immediate suspension. Within the past year, the faculty had engaged in three painful confrontations and confessions, with the result that one female and two male ex-students were now learning how to be parents back home in their villages.

"Of course, she denied that she'd been pregnant or had had an abortion," Dr. Shangala told the eight of us faculty members gathered around the conference table in the staff room, "but I am sure she did." He looked intently at the four Namibian men seated across the table from me, and I had the strangest feeling that his eyes were speaking a language I didn't understand.

Shouts and cheers from the volleyball court floated through the open window. Dust motes hovered in the late afternoon sunbeams above the table. Dr. Shangala told us Nandi had returned to the campus pregnant after the summer holidays and had seen a doctor in the city who had "taken care of things." Namibians love story-telling, and their descriptions are always filled with rich detail, but when Hans and Ute, our German colleagues, pressed him for more information, Dr. Shangala became uncharacteristically evasive.

Lou asked if we could phone her doctor, but was told no doctor in Namibia would confess to breaking the law.

Since I was the faculty secretary, I was quickly scribbling as much dialogue as I could capture, most of it from van Wyk:

Unacceptable!

Illegal!

What would the churches say if they learned we were harboring a criminal?

She must leave immediately!

Further discussion seemed fruitless. The Namibians' minds were made up, and we four expatriates seemed to be the only ones worried that these were unsubstantiated rumors. Was I imagining things, or did some of my African colleagues seated around the table even seem titillated by the apparent revelation? Why were they so eager to believe these rumors? What did everyone have against Nandi? I was careful to insert the word "alleged" into the minutes.

Dr. Shangala concluded the meeting two hours later. He told the faculty he would announce Nandi's suspension during the announcements at tomorrow morning's chapel service. Lou and I pushed back our chairs and hurried through the door into the inky African night, refusing to linger afterwards for the usual faculty banter. I felt as if I'd been caught in a cultural riptide. I knew that swimming with the current was the way to escape riptides, but not here. Not now. Outrage made my arms and legs feel stiff and clumsy. As we trudged across the moonlit campus toward our flat, we met several female students talking quietly amongst themselves. Lou put his hand on my arm and told me to wait.

"Good evening, ladies," he said. "Would you please go back to your dormitory and tell Nandi to come to my flat?" They assured him they would.

Furrows of fear and disbelief creased Nandi's forehead when she sat down in her usual place on our sofa. She reached for a throw pillow, wrapped her arms around it, and slowly rocked back and forth. Her braids fell forward and covered her face. Her voice was barely a whisper.

"I have a lot of pain and no menstruation," she murmured, "so when I went home for the term holiday, my mother she take me to the hospital. The doctor examined me, and I had a pregnancy test. It was negative."

Now I had to lean forward to hear her.

"Yes, I did break the seventh commandment with my boyfriend." (Our students referred to any sexual activity outside marriage this way.) "When I return to Windhoek, the pain it was still there and I still wasn't having any period, so I saw another doctor and had another pregnancy test. It was also negative, but still I have pain. My boyfriend take me to another doctor. He gave me some tablets. My period start and the pain is no more."

"Nandi, do you know what an abortion is?" Lou asked. She nodded. "Do you think you had one?"

She raised her head, lifted her shoulders, and opened her palms. The pillow slipped off her lap and fell onto the floor. I saw her eyes fill with tears.

"I don't think so. Wouldn't I know?"

After she left, Lou and I talked until midnight, but our conversation seemed to keep going in circles. Why did the faculty seem so quick to believe these rumors? Had Nandi told Dr. Shangala the same story she had told us? Was the faculty afraid of running afoul of the law, or was there something in the culture we simply didn't understand? We were certain RU-486 was not available in Namibia, and we were convinced Nandi had not had an abortion.

I slept fitfully. The sky was still dark at six-thirty the following morning when I phoned Dr. Shangala at home. I had hoped he would talk with us before giving Nandi the ultimatum and before making his announcement at the seven-thirty chapel service.

"It has already been taken care of," he said. "She's gone." He heard my silence and continued, his voice softening, "You mustn't worry about this, Susan. You may put your conscience at rest. The faculty did the right thing. You must trust me. I know my people."

What did *that* mean? Did Namibian women use potions to dispel unwanted pregnancies? Surely, women everywhere had always done so, but when I remembered Nandi's tears and her wide-eyed fear, I remained convinced she had not been one of them. What didn't I know?

Half an hour later, Dr. Shangala called back to remind Lou that abortion is illegal in Namibia and that the seminary was protecting Nandi from criminal investigation. Was he afraid of us? What did he think we would do? Lou and I believed the faculty was inflicting a horrible injustice upon this young woman, but we could go no further with our concerns. We were guests in Namibia, and could not undermine the authority of our hosts.

Storms and maelstroms in this arid country subsided as swiftly as they arose. Puddles leached into the sand and disappeared. Wind smoothed, and soon erased, the gullies. No one, other than Hans and Ute, would discuss Nandi with me. Mentioning her name made my students and Namibian colleagues uncomfortable. After a few months, it was as if she hadn't existed. In time, our relationship with Dr. Shangala healed but it never felt quite the same. He seemed evasive, and I heard a briskness in his voice that hadn't been there before.

Chapter 10
Being Ground Very Small

*T*he only salve for the sting of the Nandi episode was immersion in the routine tasks of teaching and living. Less thinking, more doing. One such task was laundry. I awakened early each Friday morning while it was still dark and carried my basket of clothes downstairs and across the lane that separated our building from the dining hall and workers' rooms. Here in Windhoek I enjoyed the luxury of a real laundry room with token-operated washing machines, ever so much nicer than washing clothes in the bathtub. I would load our clothes into the machines at six-thirty, before morning chapel. After chapel, I hung them on the clotheslines outside our flat. Jockeying for space on the communal clothesline was my biggest worry, and one reason for my early start. Although there were four lines, I always needed two of them for my weekly washing. If I had waited even an hour, I knew there would be no space available until sunset.

One day Peter, another early riser, joined me at the clothesline with his basket of wet laundry. This was the same Peter who, with his wife Solveig, had been with us in Otjimbingwe. The Iowa seminary where he taught had granted him a sabbatical leave for one semester, and Peter had returned, this time by himself, to teach New Testament. As he haphazardly tossed his shirts, socks, and shorts on the line, he said, "You know, Susan, my great-aunt used to say that you can tell a lot about people by the way they hang up clothes."

I guess he was right. Ritualized organization was such a part of who I was, and I had found it a useful defense against the unpredictability of African life. I always hung our underwear on the line in the back and quickly hung the bigger stuff—shirts and towels—on the second line in front of the underpants and bras. My concession to modesty. One day it occurred to me that I never saw any students hanging underwear on the clotheslines. Didn't they wear any? Didn't they ever wash it? Had I violated their sense of decency by hanging ours out in plain view, even hidden by shirts and towels? A few nights later, I was washing our dinner dishes when I happened to glance outside my kitchen window. There was

Ruusa, who lived in one of the downstairs flats, hanging about fifteen pairs of lacy underpants on the line. So the students did wear—and wash—their undies. I had just missed the timing.

The members of the Paulinum Governing Board—the bishops, treasurers, and other delegates from both Lutheran church bodies—came to town for their annual meeting. Because he was the dean of students, Lou was required to attend the twelve-hour meeting. The Board responded favorably to our faculty proposals to pursue steps that would accredit Paulinum to confer the Bachelor of Theology degree, instead of its current four-year diploma. They also approved our proposal to build a multi-purpose conference hall. The seminary was already realizing real financial gains from renting out vacant flats to Windhoek visitors and tourists. Greater rental and conference revenue could substantially reduce the costs to the churches of sending seminarians here.

The most exciting news to emerge from the Board meeting was Bishop Diergaardt's announcement that Dirk Cloete would be reassigned to a parish before the start of the next school year. The bishop said the Southern Church Council was unequivocal in its decision. We had hoped to hear about the reassignment of Dr. van Wyk, too, but Bishop Diergaardt told us, in a private moment, that he still could not convince any congregation to take him. The Board discussed proposals for other faculty changes, including the appointment to the faculty of two young Namibian pastors with newly minted doctoral degrees. Informally, everyone also knew that our dear colleague, Tomas Shivute, was the leading candidate to become bishop of the Northern Church when Bishop Dumeni retired the following year. We would deeply miss Tomas's wise and gentle ways. I wondered how the new faculty configuration would affect life on the campus. We could only hope the appointment of the new Namibian faculty members would diffuse the destructive power of Dr. van Wyk.

Meanwhile, Namibia was having its own internal troubles. More than five hundred ex-combatants from the North, unhappy for years that the government had done nothing to secure jobs for them, began a 770-kilometer march to Windhoek, demanding to see President Nujoma. *The Namibian* newspaper reported that village headmen were providing them with food and money since the marchers had nothing more than dried bread to eat. Many of them were women, some pregnant and some with children. They all camped out in front of the State House awaiting an audience with the President.

Recompense for these veterans had been a festering issue since Namibia's independence, almost ten years earlier. The ex-freedom fighters felt they were entitled to remuneration and/or jobs for their service during the war. Complicating the issue was disagreement about the inclusion of those people who had left the country as refugees and other patriots who had traveled overseas to broadcast Namibia's concerns to the world community, especially at the United Nations.

Their presence on the trimmed, green lawns of the State House must have been a source of utmost embarrassment and shame to Namibia's political leaders, many of whom had fought shoulder-to-shoulder in the trenches with these ragged, hungry veterans. Namibia's weak economy was hard-pressed to provide for the needs of these people, but to appease their demands the government allowed them to enlist in Namibia's army, even though critics of the policy claimed that many were unfit for military service.

One evening after dinner, we turned on the TV news broadcast and heard that Fidel Castro would be visiting Namibia. The government was urging all citizens to support Namibia's "friend and hero." Special buses would transport people to the airport to greet Castro's arrival at five-thirty the next morning. During the complicated cold war policy of the 1970s and 1980s, when the United States had shied away from supporting Namibia, Castro had supplied soldiers and ammunition so Namibia could defeat its South African oppressors. Namibia remembered who its friends were.

Not long after the hoopla of Castro's visit, Angela phoned and asked if I would like to meet her for coffee. I had missed seeing my German friend since she no longer taught at the seminary, and when she walked up to my table at the little coffee shop, I hardly recognized her. She had gained weight—about thirty pounds—and her eyes were sad and worried. She told me she had been traveling a lot as coordinator of the branch of the Lutheran World Federation devoted to bringing together the three Lutheran church bodies in Namibia toward the aim of creating one unified Lutheran Church. She loved her new job, but life at home was less salutary.

"Gerson was in hospital last month. He is having trouble controlling his diabetes, and he is very anxious because his business is not going well. He keeps doing work for relatives and other people who don't have the money to pay him. I have just started keeping his books, and I really got scared when I saw how much debt he has. He has agreed to take on a government contract for a large building project in Rundu. This would mean he'd be living up there for months at a time. If his health permits. His daughter—the one with the three children and no husband—lost her job, so now her seven-year-old is living with us. I think he has some serious emotional or psychological problems."

I had often wondered how she coped with the challenges of her cross-cultural marriage. I hadn't realized they were so severe. Even a pastor like Angela must feel as if her faith were being tested to the limits of her endurance. She must have read my mind.

"Oh, I do feel like Job sometimes! Let's talk about other things. How is life at the seminary?"

I told her about the upcoming faculty changes and about the strange, sad circumstances of Nandi's dismissal. When the waitress refilled our coffee cups, our conversation turned to our shared concerns for Namibia's future in these early years of independence.

"I see such contrasts, Angela, when we travel about the country. And even on our own campus. So many of our students come from villages that lack plumbing and electricity and, suddenly, here they are attending a school that has ten computers in the library. I don't think they even knew what a computer was before they arrived on campus, and now they're required to use them for their courses. The few students who do know how to use them often make fun of the ones who don't. I know those poorer students feel embarrassed and humiliated."

"You're right, Susan. Now imagine this feeling magnified throughout the country. I think the sociologists call it threshold anxiety. Here in Namibia it's also tied to the apartheid history. Black people who had previously been denied access to shops, restaurants, and magistrates' offices, suddenly find themselves free to enter those forbidden arenas, many of them still run by whites. How does a person who has always been told that he is nothing manage to find a voice?"

"Do you see this a lot in your work?"

"All the time! Many pastors avoid this anxiety by hiding within their parishes. Even when they see injustices, they are too timid to engage with the municipality or to confront other authority structures or persons."

"Do you think there are things we can do, either as individual missionaries, or as representatives of our larger churches?"

My friend looked thoughtful and appeared to choose her words carefully. "Being a missionary in a country like this is not so easy. We have gotten away from the terrible, old missionary models, but there is a lot of paternalism in the relationships between the northern and southern hemispheres. I have heard some people outside the church say that what we are doing is simply encouraging donor dependency."

"But we'd been taught that the current basis for relationship is the accompaniment model, a relationship based on mutuality."

"Oh, I know. It's the same with my church in Germany. Realistically speaking, though, how can you have such equality when there is such economic disparity? Some of my more cynical friends say that churches in Europe and America even encourage African churches not to establish reserve funds for current maintenance or future needs. In order for northern churches to feel good about their donations, the African church institutions must not become too autonomous or 'too responsible.' I know that sounds ridiculous, but when I go around to different churches these days, I am starting to examine their budgets."

I laughed. "Angela, that's exactly what Lou advocated at Paulinum. He finally convinced Matheus to add a maintenance line item to the seminary's budget when he presented it to the Governing Board. There wasn't even money available to buy replacement light bulbs."

Sighing about the situation, we parted with hugs and promises to meet again soon.

A week later, Paulinum hosted a five-day Conference of Lutheran Bishops, a high-powered gathering of church dignitaries from South Africa, Malawi, Angola, Mozambique, Namibia, and Botswana. Monday opened with a chapel service at seven-thirty, led by the bishop from Malawi. At the conclusion of the service, the executive director expressed his gratitude to this bishop who had been called to fill in at the last minute. He said the pastor who was supposed to lead worship was locked in his bedroom in a flat on the ground floor of our building!

The elderly pastor had gotten up around five o'clock to go to the bathroom. Returning to his room, he locked his bedroom door. The lock was defective, and he was stuck inside. No one was staying in the flat's second bedroom, so he called for help out the window and two of the students on their way to chapel heard him. He could not crawl out through the window because it was protected with iron burglar bars. After the chapel service, we hurried back to the apartment building. Lou brought his toolbox and started passing tools through the window to him, suggesting he try to remove the hinges from the door. Someone went to fetch Michael, one of the seminary's grounds workers. Michael was a diminutive chap, but very handy. He entered the flat and climbed into the bedroom through the tiny window at the top of the bedroom door that opened into the hallway. Once inside, he removed the door from its hinges. It took over an hour to free the poor fellow from his room. This pastor would surely remember the conference at our seminary.

The school year was almost over. I assigned essays to my English students and was startled by some of the sentences I read in their compositions. One defined "glacier" as "something without emotion." Another wrote, "The reason many Jews did not follow Jesus was because Jesus was smaller than Abraham." And "Sunday school teachers should teach the children songs, stories from the Bible, dramas and church conception." Perhaps this explained the high rate of illegitimate births in Namibia—children learned it in Sunday School!

Unfortunately, the academic year was concluding horribly for half of our first-year students, those who were members of the Southern Church. These eleven students were summoned to their church's headquarters in downtown Windhoek for their first meeting with the Church Council. The students were nervous, and asked Lou what to expect. Drawing upon his own experience, Lou suggested it was probably just an opportunity for the Council to get to know them and to answer any questions they might have. Wrong. The president of the Council scolded them about their disappointing academic performance, and told them they were not permitted to preach in their congregations or lead Bible studies during the upcoming summer holiday. One Council member said if they wanted to help their pastors during the holiday, they could "ride with him in order to open the gates and chase the goats." Another clergyman told them they were "nothing" and that the only reason they were at the seminary was for a free education since they couldn't find anything else to do with their lives.

When the students came to our flat in groups of three or four to tell us what had happened, we were speechless. Lou was embarrassed he had told them to expect a pleasant, encouraging meeting with the board members. If the intent of the board was to break our student's spirits, they succeeded. This was the same treatment our students had received from their two Southern Church lecturers, Dirk Cloete and Johan van Wyk. Later, Lou and I wondered if our two faculty colleagues, as well as these church board members, were perpetuating the way they themselves had been treated by the South Africans under apartheid. Or was there another operative dynamic we Americans didn't understand? Was this an example of a shame-based culture?

The sad expressions on the faces of our students brought back to us the difficulties of the year. We had expected, by now, to feel more, rather than less, integrated into our Namibian community. We knew our learning curve would not be a steady one, but in this community Lou and I sensed that we were, at best, irrelevant and, at worst, either meddlesome or culturally insensitive.

And then there was the social disintegration within the seminary. The uneasy truce established after the student strike had begun to fray. Faculty sniping still erupted along ethnic lines. Dirk and his uncle, van Wyk, seemed particularly offended by our presence and resented our input at faculty meetings. At one such meeting, Lou made an observation and Dirk lost his temper. He glared at Lou, jumped up and turned to Michael. "I refuse to attend any more faculty meetings at which those two Americans are present!" He began gathering up his notebooks and papers, preparing to leave the staff room.

"Dirk, please sit down," said Michael, "Lou is entitled to express his opinions. You know this is the only way we can all reach consensus."

What had happened? Dirk was the man who, in 1995, had told us he was eager for us to return to Namibia on a long-term basis. Although we knew that Dirk was an emotionally troubled man, and that he'd had similar problems with our German colleagues on the faculty, his comments felt like the thrust of a knife, piercing the thin shell of self-confidence we'd begun to acquire.

Lou said to me later, "Can you imagine an American university professor saying something like that to a visiting African?"

Michael and Dirk were from different tribal groups, and it was becoming clear that Michael's primary objective throughout his three-year term as principal was to keep the peace and to avoid a recurrence of the student strikes of the previous year. Throughout the school year Lou had attempted to perform his duties as the dean of students, making himself available to students and attempting to resolve problems. Yet, more often than not, Michael dismissed or ignored Lou's suggestions. The students had kept coming to our flat with their confusion, anger, and indignation. What could we do? We felt that our own integrity was compromised, but we seemed to be helpless to effect any action. The direct American approach to problem resolution didn't seem to work. We could only listen to the students, share their frustration, and affirm them.

Several months earlier, the United States State Department had issued a worldwide alert, warning American citizens living abroad that some thug named Osama bin Laden had threatened terrorist action against American military or civilian targets. Because I was a volunteer warden for the U.S. Embassy in Windhoek, I had received this travel alert and had notified the dozen or so Americans on my phone list to be "vigilant." None of us knew, really, what that meant. On August 8, we learned about the bombings of the embassies in Kenya and Tanzania. More than eighty people were reported dead, and sixteen hundred were injured. We gathered around the television in the recreation room with our students and watched the CNN coverage of the carnage. Later that night on the local TV news we saw a large display of armed guards surrounding the U.S. Embassy in Windhoek.

All this local and international strife was eroding our spirits and making us cynical. All we could seem to do was grumble and complain, so Lou suggested a long weekend off campus, to obtain a different perspective. At the Anib Lodge, on the edge of the Kalahari Desert, we joined our hosts and the other guests for dinner: a newlywed couple from Holland, two dapper young men from Italy, and an elderly German couple. When we were all seated around her large, round table, Olga, the assistant manager, passed around steaming bowls of sweet, stewed squash, oryx stew, rice, and grated beetroot salad. She filled everyone's wine glass with a fruity, South African merlot.

Olga's husband, a large, bewhiskered fellow who reminded me of our desert guide, Lutz, told us that Namibia was trying to be environmentally friendly by not building big hotels in the country. "Tourism is second only to mining as a source of income, but you can see how fragile our environment is. That's why you will find so many guest farms and lodges, like this one, which place a smaller burden on the land than do multi-million dollar hotels."

One of the Italians remarked that he hadn't seen any black lodge owners in Namibia. "The Namibian government," said Olga, "recently passed a law that fifty-one percent of these establishments must be Namibian-owned. It will be a long time before many of the black population can accumulate anywhere near the capital required to own and manage these lodges." (A prospect that seemed to please her.) "Of course, they will need to be educated, won't they? Lodge owners must have management skills or their businesses will fail." Olga didn't seem to think this would happen anytime soon, either. She sounded relieved.

Leaving the Kalahari the next morning, we drove into Namibia's other desert, the Namib, for two days in the Namib Naukluft Lodge. The weather turned dramatically warmer, and by the time we arrived we had shed our sweaters and jackets. When we checked in, we informed the receptionist that we would like to sign up for the lodge's trip to Sossusvlei. "Wonderful!" she said. "Someone will knock on your door at four forty-five tomorrow morning. You can come to the dining room for juice and coffee and our driver will leave at five-thirty. He will serve you breakfast when you get there."

We turned out to be the only guests on this tour. Our driver, Apollo, was a young Ovambo man who told us he had been working for the lodge for four years. He loaded several coolers into the back of an open-sided Land Rover, helped us into our seats, and we were off, our headlights slicing through the thick African night. Every so often, as we bumped and bounced along the chunky dirt roads, Apollo would slow to a crawl, yielding to a kudu or a hartebeest seeking an early breakfast. The dirt road turned into pot-holed tarmac and then deep sand as we approached Sossusvlei. The sun was beginning to rise, and Apollo parked the vehicle next to a picnic table under a surprisingly tall, green acacia tree. Three other identical Land Rovers and one battered Jeep were parked under other acacias.

Photographers seeking the world's most perfect sand dune will eventually find their way to this remote part of this mostly unknown African country. Thrusting one thousand feet into the brilliant cerulean sky, this red-ridged, knife-sharp swirl of sand is reported to be, at over one thousand feet, among the world's tallest dunes. The rich orange hue comes from slow iron oxidization and tiny grains of garnets.

Apollo said we could walk around for an hour or so, and when we'd finished our walk he would serve us breakfast. At the base of the dunes was a whiteish, cracked earth pan—an ephemeral oasis—hence, the beautiful large trees and other vegetation. Rarely had I experienced a place of such startling beauty. This felt like holy ground. I could feel serenity seeping into my bones. Lou grasped my hand, and we explored the dunes, preferring the view from below rather than the single-file hike to the top some of the younger visitors were attempting.

A white linen tablecloth covered the picnic table. Apollo had set out real china plates and glasses of chilled guava juice. There was a basket of crusty brochen and platters of salami and cheese. Another basket was filled with bananas, grapes, and oranges. He poured us steaming cups of coffee from the thermos. We could have been on the set for "Out of Africa." All that was missing was the Mozart clarinet concerto.

That night, after dinner, Lou switched off the lights in our room and joined me outside on the patio. We were sipping mugs of fragrant Rooibos tea and marveling at the overturned bowl of stars that occasionally spilled its shimmering contents onto the desert floor. Although we had promised each other we wouldn't dwell on our seminary worries, we couldn't help reviewing the school year that was almost over.

"Lou, do you ever think about Steve's comment to you before we came here? What he said to you about taking yourself out of your professional track?"

"I think about it all the time."

"Do you think we made a mistake?"

"Why do you ask?"

"Well, I think about everything we've been through—the strike last year, the business with Nandi, Dirk's hostility—and I keep asking myself if it's worth it."

"We gave up so much." Lou sipped his tea and gazed into the darkness. "I suppose I keep thinking about something we heard in Chicago. We were told the experience of being strangers in a strange land would grind us very small."

"Yes—like chalk dust."

"Well, no, actually like wheat to make the flour for the loaf. Or maybe, in a small way, we could be the leaven in the loaf here. I'm not sure our value in Namibia lies in what we teach these students as much as it is from making ourselves available to them, as we have been. Listening to them and showing them we care about them. That might have to be enough."

The next morning we decided to travel the gravel road through the desert to Walvis Bay, the busy coastal town where we had spent New Year's Eve with our children. This had to be absolutely the worst road in Namibia—four teeth-rattling hours of corrugated sand and gravel. After about two hours, we came upon a small airplane and several cars in the middle of the road! The pilot had run out of oil and was stopping passersby to ask if they had any to spare. We told him we were sorry, but we didn't. Two young women who looked like European backpackers got out of one of the cars and walked over to our car. They told us they were aid workers from Australia and that they'd been hitchhiking to the coast. When their driver had stopped to help the airplane, his immobilizer locked up, and he couldn't get the car started. So here were a stalled plane and a dead car in the middle of the desert. We agreed to take the young women to Walvis Bay and told the pilot and the driver that we would inform the police about their plight. That evening Lou and I were sharing a pizza at Crazy Mama's when we heard someone calling, "Hello! We meet again." We looked up to see the two young Australians, considerably cleaner and happier than when we'd first met each other in the middle of the desert.

The students finished their examinations, and the academic year ended. At the conclusion of the final service in the chapel, one of the third-year students, Festus Shiimi, walked to the lectern and said that he wanted to deliver a small speech. Festus had been diagnosed with severe glaucoma earlier in the school year, and Lou had visited him in the hospital many times. He also drove groups of students to the hospital to visit Festus. In his speech, Festus expressed gratitude to God for His care of him during what was a very frightening time, and appreciation for the support of the lecturers and students. "I would like to express words of special thankfulness to a man who actually sacrificed his energy as well as part of his property, filling petrol in his car, but only because of me. And this is Pastor Bauer. Rev. Bauer, what you did for me is something which I cannot forget and I promise to keep it in my remembrance as long as I live."

When everyone applauded, Lou blushed and looked down at his hands. What he had done was no different from what he used to do almost every week as a parish pastor. When I looked around, I noticed that neither Dirk nor van Wyk was applauding or smiling.

Chapter 11
Tending the Flock, Avoiding the Tigers

*M*abuku was lanky and loose-limbed, like the other young Namibian men and women on campus, but he lacked the easy, fluid grace of his colleagues. They were gazelles. Mabuku was a rough-hewn marionette whose parts didn't quite fit together properly. There was a kind of sweetness in his shy, lopsided smile that endeared him to me. I worried about Mabuku more than I did the other students who seemed tougher, more resilient. No one else on campus spoke Lozi, Mabuku's language, and in the months he had been a seminarian, the young man appeared to have few, if any, close friends. I was surprised that Mabuku's English was almost flawless, far better than that of the other students. "I had an American teacher for English in my senior secondary school," he said.

Our faculty colleagues from the Northern Church were pleased to have their first ever seminary student from the Caprivi, one of the more remote sections of the country. The Caprivi Strip, Namibia's long, skinny handle thrusting east into Zambia, Zimbabwe, and Bosnia, was a creation of colonial gerrymandering between the British and the Germans in 1890. Katima Mulilo, Mabuku's hometown, is the capital of the region. People in the more developed parts of Namibia considered the Caprivi a rough-and-tumble frontier, fertile ground for future development, commercial farming, and mission work. Caprivians were disinclined for that to happen, and there were rumors of a secessionist movement by these outliers.

Mabuku had arrived on campus at the start of the school year wearing dark sunglasses. He wore them constantly to all his classes, meals in the dining hall, and chapel services. Dr. van Wyk complained. "He looks like a gangster. He should be ordered to take off the glasses." Mabuku told everyone he had been in an accident, and the glare of sunlight and airborne dust bothered his eyes. What he never told anyone until the very end of the school year—perhaps because he feared he'd be sent home—was that he was blind in one eye.

During final exams Mabuku was hospitalized for malaria. The treating physician noted the blindness on his discharge orders and said Mabuku must return for an eye examination. The following week the ophthalmologist at the government clinic told Mabuku his blind eye had to come out as soon as possible. Mabuku came to our flat that afternoon and brought the doctor's orders to Lou. "Tatekulu, I do not have money for this surgery. Can the seminary's medical fund can help me?"

We could not imagine removing an eye without a second opinion, so Lou arranged to have Mabuku seen by a private ophthalmologist. We quietly paid the forty-dollar doctor's fee with money we had received from a sponsoring congregation. The doctor confirmed that the risk of infection and damage to the remaining eye required removing the blind eye—the sooner, the better. The ophthalmologist also discovered that Mabuku had glaucoma in his good eye and gave him eye drops. Lou told Mabuku he would take his financial request to the lecturers' council.

Mabuku scheduled his surgery for early November, just two weeks hence, and we suggested he stay in Windhoek because it would be too exhausting and expensive to make the one-thousand-kilometer round trip to Katima. Michael agreed and told Mabuku he could remain in his dormitory room until he was able to travel home after the surgery.

Michael had come to our flat for a mid-morning cup of tea and to discuss this and some other administrative matters with Lou. I filled their teacups and joined them in the living room. Lou congratulated his colleague for having averted another student strike during his first year as principal.

"Removing Dirk from being the principal has calmed the students," said Michael, "but having him and van Wyk still on the faculty hasn't been easy, has it?"

Lou shook his head. "No, and we seem to be stuck with van Wyk. But at least Dirk will soon be off the campus. I just wish the bishop had acted sooner when he saw what was happening. Sometimes church folk, even bishops and other leaders, are too timid. They are afraid to control people whose behavior damages the church at large, and then everyone suffers."

"That happens a lot in our Namibian churches."

"It happens in American churches, too. Clergy think being assertive is unchristian, so bishops and pastors are reluctant to make hard choices. A long time ago I learned a fable that has been useful to me in my ministry.

"Once a week, a hungry tiger left the forest and went into the pasture where he killed one lamb. The rest of the sheep didn't know what to do, so they called a council and decided to sit down and talk with the tiger.

The tiger said he would try to control his hungry habit, but it didn't work. Every week, he would prowl through the night and devour another lamb. The sheep, worried and afraid, sought counsel from a wise old ram who told them, 'Haven't you learned anything? Negotiating with the tiger is never going to work. You've got to cage the tiger.'"

Michael laughed. "You should use that illustration in your church administration course. That's what Bishop Diergaardt did when he assigned Dr. van Wyk to the seminary."

"Yes, he wanted van Wyk in a place where his behavior would be under closer scrutiny. But now van Wyk is doing the same thing here that he apparently did before, and we faculty members [I knew Lou meant Michael] are afraid to challenge him."

Michael nodded and continued, "I am also afraid that Dirk is not going leave the campus without a fight. He's angry because the reassignment means he will have a much lower salary and a much smaller house for his family. I told Dirk I had received the formal notification from the church board and Dirk said the only way he would leave the seminary would be if the Southern Church suspended him as a pastor. We know the Church won't do that."

We all wondered how Bishop Diergaardt would resolve the inevitable standoff. He could not afford to lose face before the seminary's governing board and Bishop Dumeni of the Northern Church.

"Getting back to the problem of van Wyk," continued Michael, "I'm really afraid of that man and his manipulative ways."

Lou agreed, "He is not just malicious, he breaks the students' spirits. And have you seen how he grabs hold of leadership positions and fails to follow through? I remember that extracurricular theology course he said he wanted to offer to community clergy. He placed an advertisement in the newspaper, but then the entire project disappeared and we never heard anymore about it."

"Don't forget about how he volunteered to chair the seminary's worship committee," said Michael. Van Wyk had told us he had plans to write a new African liturgy that our seminary would showcase for churches all over the country. The committee had one meeting the whole year, and nothing happened.

"And what about the development office?" I asked. The seminary's development office had been established ten years earlier by a visiting American missionary. The task of the office was to send newsletters twice a year to supporters in Germany, Finland, and the United States, with the aim of raising funds for things the seminary could not afford. These donations had provided a minivan, a photocopier, and six computers for the library as well as eye examinations and prescription eyeglasses for the students. "Do you know that hundreds of copies of our newsletter have been collecting dust in the copy room for three months? Why haven't they been mailed? The faculty has never seen a budget for this office since van Wyk took it over."

Michael said, "You're right. I will ask him to give us that budget. I think we all remember those rumors about the missing financial records at Michael Luther High School when he was the principal there."

Before he left, Michael agreed to place Mabuku's request for financial assistance on the agenda of the next faculty meeting.

The weather was changing. Deep purple blossoms from the jacaranda trees swirled through the air and piled up along the curbs like lavender snowdrifts. One afternoon when a hot wind whistled through our windows and blew loose papers and magazines off our two small coffee tables, I stepped outside onto our balcony and saw a huge brown cloud of sand and dust swirling though the air. The sand tornado was heading our way. I hurried back inside to close all the windows on the south side of our flat, but not before all our furniture was coated with a thin layer of soft, brown dust. Matheus told me these sand cyclones were typical of springtime weather. We were approaching our second summer in Namibia, but somehow I didn't remember summer being this hot the year before. Even though I was careful to keep the curtains closed against the sun, the cement and plaster walls of our flat absorbed heat throughout the day. I had never handled heat very well, and I was realizing that if I hoped to accomplish any productive work, I'd best do it before eleven o'clock in the morning. Lou and I took sweaty afternoon naps or went into town where we'd find brief respite in some of the air-conditioned shops.

Life on campus had become boring with the students gone, and I looked forward to seeing my colleagues at the faculty meeting where we would discuss plans for the next academic year.

"I don't think the seminary ought to give Mabuku any money for this surgery," said Dirk when this agenda item came up for discussion.

Matheus, who had brought with him copies of the budget and cash flow reports, disagreed. "Rev. Cloete, the year is almost over, and there's plenty of unspent money available in the medical account. You know that if we don't use this money, it will not be available next year. We cannot carry over unspent balances."

"It isn't the money," said Dirk. "What if something goes wrong with the surgery? The family will blame the seminary."

"Dirk," said Lou, "this boy must have surgery, whether or not the seminary pays for it. I'm sure Mabuku's widowed mother would be grateful for our assistance. I can't imagine she would find the seminary at fault if there were medical complications."

"You don't understand how Africans behave, Lou."

Van Wyk nodded. "Besides, if we paid for this surgery, how many other students will come to us with similar requests? This is a bad idea."

Lou sought support from the others around the table. Tomas, Michael, and the two Germans were sympathetic to his request. Amaambo, who had served for three years as the previous dean of students, wasn't so sure. This discussion, like so many others we'd endured, circled the staff room, uncertain where to settle. One thing was becoming clear. The faculty was used to a dean of students who functioned as either a cop or a tattle-tale. They were not accustomed to, nor did they seem pleased with, a dean who was an advocate for the students. They also misjudged the limits of my husband's patience.

"Never mind!" said Lou, slicing through the long-winded debate. "Susan and I will find the money to pay for the surgery." This seemed to satisfy our colleagues, and we moved on to the next agenda item.

The discussion about Mabuku must have set van Wyk on edge. For the remainder of the meeting he peppered the staff room with sarcastic innuendoes and angry staccato outbursts against his Ovambo, German and American colleagues. He said the students had complained to him about the lack of spirituality they experienced on the campus. As if on script, Dirk proposed an accredited course on spirituality, a course that required a 1500-word paper and numerous written assignments. Lou suggested that spirituality was more than simply an academic concern, and proposed the alternative of small group experiences. He described the two student groups that had met in our home weekly throughout the year. Lou told me later he felt he might as well have been invisible. The faculty decided to add this highly structured course to an already overburdened curriculum—and agreed to allow van Wyk to teach it! These two—van Wyk and Dirk—had most likely staged this plan well before the meeting. Hanns and Ute, seated across the table, sent us "What were they thinking?" looks of disbelief. So much for caging the tiger.

The faculty overturned its earlier decision to offer a course on pastoral counseling to the second-year students, thereby defeating another of Lou's proposals. The discussion of Lou's revision of the code of conduct, which he had done at the request of the Governing Board, was aborted because the faculty could not reach consensus about disciplinary policies and procedures.

In the final item of business van Wyk proposed that I temporarily take over Ute's task as accommodations manager during the upcoming three months when Hanns and Ute would be in Germany for their extended home leave. The previous year, the seminary had begun renting flats and dormitory rooms to guests. Some were overnight visitors and others stayed several months. Paulinum had also begun hosting conferences, using the large chapel as a meeting place and the dining hall for meals. Becoming a rental agent and a landlady was not a task I really wanted, but Matheus supported the proposal, reminding me how valuable this rental revenue was to the seminary's financial condition. "Please, Meme Susan, you have so much business and management experience. It is only for three months, and you are the most qualified." I relented, knowing that missionaries needed to help where they were asked, but not without wondering if van Wyk had an ulterior motive in asking me to do this. Ute said she would show me how to make reservations, handle billing, and find people to clean the flats and wash the bedding. She said I would be working closely with Sophie, the kitchen manager, and her staff of five workers who cooked the students' meals and cleaned the campus.

At the end of the meeting I lingered to help clean up the leftover food and dishes. Michael had suggested earlier that when I bought the food for the meeting I should also pick up some brochen for sandwiches. To accompany these crusty rolls, I'd bought a very small container of soft margarine. I gave the two remaining brochen and the leftover margarine to Dirk to take home to his family. Amaambo said how nice it was to have soft margarine, and Tomas replied, "Yes, but that margarine is very expensive. We always buy Rama (a cheaper, hard margarine)."

Our friend's offhand remark pushed me outside the perimeter of the community I'd been trying so hard to join. I knew Lou felt the same, as one after another of his suggestions to the faculty had been either ignored or disapproved. Thick cords of homesickness tightened around my chest. Why had I thought being a missionary in Africa was a good idea? Leaving my home, my children, and my friends, as well as a job where I had been respected and supported, seemed like an incredibly stupid thing to have done. Never had I lived in an environment as confusing as this

125

campus.

It really hadn't taken very long to learn and adopt most of the social conventions. Taking the time to properly greet a person, remembering to avoid American clichés, and learning how to drive a backwards-feeling car on the left side of the road were easily mastered. Even the seven-hour-long faculty meetings had begun to seem normal.

What was more difficult was adapting to African methods of decision-making and conflict resolution. The direct approach and frank, open conversation made these Namibians uncomfortable. Perhaps Dirk and van Wyk were right when they said we didn't understand Africans, but I couldn't find the underlying value in so many of their actions. I thought of the two students last year whose low marks had disqualified them for a diploma, a requisite for ordination. The Church ignored their academic failure, and ordained both young men. Where were the standards? Was this whole seminary a sham?

Neither Lou nor I could discern God's purpose for our life and our work on this campus other than our personal contact with our students. And yet, were they, really, anything more than surrogate sons and daughters? My earlier thoughts about the romantic life of a cultural anthropologist felt embarrassingly naïve, and I told Lou I was glad I hadn't mentioned them to people who knew more than I did about such things. Talking with other missionaries might have helped, but our friends Ray and Lois had retired, and complaining to our program director in Chicago felt too much like whining. I kept trying to remind myself that I was still a green expatriate—the Psalmist's stranger in a strange land—and that erecting walls of bitterness between myself and the Africans would only keep me on a lonely perimeter.

Fortunately, the arrival of a new missionary from the States, along with the request from Chicago that we orient her to the country, offered a positive redirection of our energy. Heather had just graduated from a Midwestern Lutheran college. She was a tall, cheerful young woman, bright and eager to learn as much as she could about Namibia. She would be replacing Ray, teaching English for two years at Oshigambo High School. Heather remained in Windhoek for a week, staying on campus in one of the guest flats just downstairs from ours. I drove her to the embassy and showed her the best places to stock up on household and school supplies since there weren't many shops in the rural area where she would be living. Heather was self-confident, but not at all arrogant. She was excited about moving to Oshigambo and had already spoken with some of the teachers at the high school who were in town for the long school holiday. She had grown up on a farm and she wanted to initiate a garden project with the students. We went to my favorite garden shop in Windhoek, and she left town with seventeen packets of seeds.

Soon after Heather left for Oshigambo, Mabuku had his surgery. Windhoek's Central Hospital served the city's indigent population. Whenever we'd driven past the five-story cement block structure, we had seen women squatting over cast iron cooking pots on the trampled dirt around the hospital and in the large dusty parking area across the road. The air was filled with the appetizing scent of grilled meat and smoke from the charcoal fires. Hospital visitors would buy food for the patients from these street vendors because otherwise the patients might not have anything to eat. A large red and yellow billboard in front of the hospital shouted, "HIV Kills!" At the bottom of the sign was a numerical ticker showing how many Namibians had died from AIDS so far that year.

Two uniformed, armed guards, one male and one female, were posted at the entrance. Even though Lou was wearing his clerical collar, which usually smoothed his way through such places, the guards patted us down and searched my handbag before allowing us to enter. The lobby was strangely empty. There was no one at the reception desk, just a collection of signs with arrows on the dirty tan walls. We turned left at the first corridor and followed the arrow for the elevators. Something on the floor attracted my attention. "Lou, those are blood splatters!"

A hand-lettered sign taped to the elevator door said the lifts were out of service, so we found the stairwell, dank and reeking of urine, and climbed the four flights as fast as we could.

Mabuku's bed was next to the window in this twenty-bed ward. I noticed the variety of colored and patterned sheets. In state hospitals patients had to bring their own bed linens. There were no privacy curtains between the beds, and I tried to avert my eyes from the faces of the men in the other beds. Visitors were lying on pallets beside several beds, apparently there for the duration of their loved one's hospitalization, offering comfort and helping to meet patient needs the overworked nurses couldn't handle. I saw enamel basins of mealie-meal porridge and plastic platters of chicken bones.

Mabuku broke into a grin as soon as he saw us. "Tatekulu! Meme! I did not think you would come!" He told us the surgery had gone well, and, no, he was not in too much pain. He gingerly touched the thick, white gauze bandage.

Mabuku was released from the hospital two days later, and after his one week follow-up visit with the surgeon, we gave him the twenty dollars for bus fare to return home. We told him we would try to visit him when we passed through Katima the following month on our way to Victoria Falls in Zimbabwe. Our future encounters with Mabuku would take us far beyond the Caprivi Strip. They would lead us into the strange land of witchcraft and sorcery and, ultimately, into the dark cave of betrayal.

Chapter 12
Witchcraft and Wedding Bells

*L*ou and I had just returned from a two-week road trip to South Africa when we learned that both Heather and Mabuku were also back in Windhoek. Mabuku was here to get his artificial eye. Heather had driven down with David, a retired American pastor and missionary colleague who was returning to the States after teaching in the North for the past year. Heather had said she'd come to our flat for dinner after she took David to the airport. She was fifteen minutes late. Then thirty. Had she forgotten? I phoned the guesthouse, but the manager told me he hadn't seen her since early that morning. Perhaps she had been delayed at the airport. Another half hour passed, and I was wondering whether to go ahead and serve dinner or continue to wait for her when the phone rang. Heather's voice was quivering.

"Heather, where are you? Is something wrong?"

"I'm at MediClinic. I was in an accident driving back from the airport."

"Oh, my God, Heather! Are you okay?"

"I am…but the car had to be towed. And the guy in the other car looked as if he was in pretty bad shape."

"Sit tight. Lou and I will be there in fifteen minutes."

MediClinic, on the other side of town, was Namibia's best hospital. Private, clean, efficient, and well staffed, it in no way resembled the government hospital where we had visited Mabuku just a few weeks earlier.

A custodian was polishing the large, plate glass windows when we stepped into the air-conditioned lobby. Straight ahead, a young woman in a crisp navy blue uniform was typing at a computer behind the reception counter. I heard soft music playing. Heather was sitting alone on one of the dove-gray upholstered chairs to the left of the entrance. When she stood up, I noticed a bandage starting at the base of her neck and disappearing into the V-neck of her dress. She hugged each of us gently and I was surprised how calm she appeared.

"Are you okay? Tell us what happened."

"I've just got a few cuts and bruises, mostly from my seatbelt. I was coming down Robert Mugabe Avenue. You know where it makes that sharp turn to the left? The driver of a car in the opposite lane was speeding and weaving and he lost control and crossed the median. That's when he crashed into me."

"Did the police come?" asked Lou.

"Yes, they were there pretty fast, and so was the ambulance. The man in the other car wasn't wearing a seatbelt, and I think he was seriously hurt."

"And what about your car?"

"A tow truck came and took it to a garage. I think I've got the card in my purse." She began to fumble with the clasp of the handbag on her lap.

"Never mind about that now," I said. "Are you allowed to leave the hospital? Would you like to come back to our place?"

"The doctor said I was free to go. If it's okay with you, I think I'd like to go back to my room at the guesthouse. I guess I'd better try to phone DGM to let them know what happened. They will need to tell me what to do about the car. The police want me to come to the station tomorrow to give them a full statement."

We stayed in close contact with Heather. Four days after the accident, she phoned to tell us the driver of the other car had died. The police had said she might need to testify at a trial, but they told her she was allowed to go ahead with her plans to travel to Tanzania for a holiday with two other young missionary teachers. We suggested she come for dinner before she left, and told her we had also invited our student from Caprivi to join us.

Mabuku had little trouble adapting to his artificial eye. We told him it looked so natural, we wouldn't have been able to distinguish it from his real eye, and he rewarded us with the biggest grin we'd seen on his face in the entire year we'd known him. Lou took him to the clinic for one final checkup. I was chatting with Heather and cooking our favorite chicken curry recipe for dinner when Lou arrived back home with Mabuku. Another young man was with them. "It's his brother," Lou whispered to me. "There are some problems."

The brother's name was Kapia. He was rail-thin and trembling like a frightened puppy. I grasped his hand and told him how happy I was he could have dinner with us. Tears sprang into his eyes. "Thank you, Meme." While the curry simmered on the stove, I joined Heather and the men in our living room. Kapia said his wife was in the intensive care unit with severe complications from her pregnancy. "The doctors say she may die." Tears trickled down his cheeks.

"Kapia, what happened?" I asked.

"She is bewitched!" said Kapia. He grabbed the arms of his chair to quell the trembling in his hands and looked wildly around the room, as if checking for demons. Lou leaned forward. "What do you mean?"

"When I married my wife, I did not pay the bride price. I did not have the money for this, so we just came here to Windhoek. When her relatives saw that we were gone, they told the witch doctors. They became angry and now they chase me." Kapia looked at his brother who nodded in agreement. "I wake up here, in my room at my sister's house, and they are there. I see them in the corner. When the witch doctors decide to hurt you—or kill you—you cannot hide from them. Even if I go to America, they will chase me and find me." He clasped his arms in front of his stomach and rocked back and forth, moaning softly.

After Mabuku and his brother left our flat that evening, Heather looked worried. "Is belief in witchcraft common here?"

"More than you would think, for such a relatively developed country," said Lou. "Our students won't talk much about this with us because their churches condemn the practice, but several of them have told me that when the doctors can't heal them, they will visit witch doctors and traditional healers." He chuckled. "Our brightest student on campus, Michael, told me he had a lot of stomach problems so he visited a popular witch doctor here in Windhoek. She told him to lie down, and she made small cuts in his belly. She began pulling things out of him like small rocks and pieces of pantyhose. Michael said that's when he realized she was a fake, because he saw her taking those things from the sleeve of her dress."

A few days later, just before he returned home, Mabuku told us that his sister-in-law had died and that Kapia had gone into hiding, fearing retribution from her family. We told Mabuku we would try to see him at Christmastime when we drove through the Caprivi. December is the month for weddings in Namibia, and three of our students had invited us to their weddings in the North, so we would be combining that trip with a Christmas excursion to Victoria Falls in Zimbabwe.

The seven-foot-high termite mounds were casting long, purple shadows on the white sand. We had been traveling for eight hours, hoping to reach the Lutheran guesthouse before nightfall. We passed little clusters of schoolgirls in blue plaid skirts and white blouses. Women were chattering and gesturing around the ledge of a communal well set a few yards back from the road. Namibia's Directorate of Rural Water Supply had decreed that fresh water must be within 2.5 kilometers (one and one-half miles) of each Namibian's home. Sometimes communities dug deep, wide wells like this one. Other times, the water supply was simply a spigot stuck in the ground.

Someone had tied a sway-backed brown cow to the fence surrounding the well. Hobbled grey donkeys with sleepy eyes and furry black crosses on their backs limped past the cow, looking for a blade or two of grass in the sand. Two small boys hoisted blue plastic jerry cans full of water into their donkey cart and started leading the donkey down the road. The boys, their legs powdered white from the sand, were wearing T-shirts and shorts, not school uniforms. If your family can't afford the uniform and the fees, you can't attend school. The boys didn't look up as we drove by. Neither did the little girl in the short yellow dress with the water jug on her head. I've carried jugs of water that size and once I weighed one. It weighed seventeen pounds.

We left our suitcases at the church guesthouse in Oniipa. There was still plenty of daylight, so we drove the rutted, sandy track through the bush to the Amaambo's home for a short visit. Before we left, Meme Esther took me down the road to her sister's home. "We must get for you a horse's tail!" She laughed when she saw the puzzled look on my face. "At Ovambo weddings, women carry horse tails on a piece of wood. We shake them and dance. You are now Ovambo lady so you need a tail, too." She laughed and squeezed my arm, and I felt happier than I had in weeks.

Our room in the guesthouse was simply furnished: two narrow beds, a table by the window and a wardrobe. As promised, the room boasted an en suite bathroom with a shower and a sink, but the toilet didn't flush, and the bathroom light was burned out. That meant we had to use the communal toilets and showers across the courtyard. This was rainy season, but there was no screen on the window, just mosquito nets for each bed. We slathered ourselves with insect repellant and sprayed the window curtains with Doom. Lou turned on our short-wave radio, and when we found the band for Voice of America, we heard that the U.S. House of Representatives had just voted the first article of impeachment against President Clinton.

When we awoke, there was a doily of fifty dead mosquitoes on the little table in front of the window, and I had bites on my arms and legs. I was glad we were taking our anti-malarial tablets, a precaution we always observed when we traveled to the North.

After a quick breakfast of cereal and juice, we left the guesthouse to pick up the Amaambos and Meme Esther's sister who would accompany us to the wedding. Aina, the bride, would be a fourth-year student at Paulinum next year. Her fiancé, Peter, was a former seminarian who had been suspended because he had fathered a child. The baby wasn't Aina's. Before leaving Windhoek, we had made arrangements to meet our student, Rachel, who said she would be waiting for us at the third house on the left once we entered the village of Okahau. She would ride with us and direct us to Aina's homestead. She came out of the house to greet us holding a white headscarf. "Meme Susan, Aina wants you to wear this." I had been told it was an honor to be given such a scarf to wear at a wedding, and I immediately wrapped it around my head and tucked in loose strands of hair. Meme Esther smiled approvingly.

Rachel climbed into the back seat of the Venture and showed Lou which sandy trails to drive to Aina's homestead. I noticed that Lou was getting better at learning how to swerve the steering wheel back and forth to avoid getting stuck. Several older cars and three pick-up trucks were parked outside the homestead, a dozen small stick-and-thatch dwellings enclosed within a tall fence of thin, sturdy saplings. Aina emerged from one of the dwellings wearing an elegant white satin wedding gown with a long train and a fingertip veil that would have made any American bride proud. She beamed at us and gave me a small hug before introducing us to her older sister, Saara, who was a dwarf. Saara was the third little person we had seen in Namibia. I was pleased and, I confess, a little surprised that the culture did not stigmatize them. Saara spoke English well, and took us around the homestead, introducing us to elderly relatives. When she returned us to the entrance, we saw that many more guests had gathered. Judging from the lack of vehicles, we assumed most of them had walked. We squeezed five additional wedding guests into our vehicle and drove to the church, about three kilometers away.

The church looked like most of the other churches we had seen in rural Namibia, a large mud-brick structure painted white with a tall steeple and bell tower. Rev. Amaambo and Meme Esther were busy exchanging greetings with friends, and Rachel said Lou and I were invited to join the wedding party that was assembling in the pastor's office, another freestanding mud-brick structure adjacent to the church, for the signing of the certificate. The pastor, an elderly gentleman in a clerical collar and long black frockcoat, shook hands with us and sat down behind a simple wooden table. Aina and Peter were seated in front of him. Hovering in the background were ten bridesmaids and several groomsmen. No one was smiling. There were no windows in this office, and at ten o'clock in the morning, I was already discreetly dabbing at rivulets of sweat dripping down my face and between my breasts. After the pastor had obtained all the official signatures in his thick black leather church register, we all stepped outside. The sandy churchyard was filling with guests. The older women were wearing their muumuu-style Ovambo dresses. About half a dozen of these elderly ladies who must have been Aina's aunts wore matching deep blue dresses trimmed with white rickrack. Several of the ladies were dancing, waving their horses' tails and blowing on whistles or harmonicas. The bridesmaids wore simple cotton two-piece dresses in lime green. The men were wearing small ribbon boutonnieres in their breast pockets that matched the lavender, yellow and pale green colors of the ribbons that made up Aina's bridal bouquet. No fresh flowers here. It was too hot and too dry to grow them, and too expensive to buy them.

By eleven o'clock everyone had started moving toward the church doors. I had hoped to be seated toward the rear of the nave so I could discreetly take photos, but the ushers seemed to have other ideas. They seated Lou and me up front in the sanctuary, on a bench near the pastor. Between us was another clergyman who shook our hands and whispered to us that his name was Rev. Matti Emunyela. Rev. Emunyela translated the wedding service for us. Following a brief exchange of vows and rings, the pastor returned to his place on the wooden bench. Aina and Peter moved to a bench in front of the altar, facing the congregation. Festus Shiimi, another of our students, conducted the rest of the service. He seemed to be the master-of-ceremonies for many speeches by friends and relatives. The congregation applauded when Lou delivered his own six-minute speech in Oshiwambo. I knew he had been well coached by our friend, Rev. Amaambo. Several small choirs augmented the ceremony with hymns and traditional songs. The service concluded about one-thirty.

The bridal couple, followed by their wedding party and a group of joyously ululating elderly women, set out on their slow procession back to Aina's homestead. Walking next to them were two attendants, each carrying green umbrellas to protect the bride and groom from the scorching rays of the sun. Their procession was preceded by dancing young women and followed by men singing hymns—about fifty people, in all. Aina and Peter never smiled. We noticed that Rev. Emunyela wasn't joining the procession, so we invited him to accompany us in our (air-conditioned) Venture back to Aina's homestead for the reception. He said the reception would not begin for another couple of hours, and he offered to show us around the village, including his own homestead and a new clinic that was under construction. We learned that as well as being a Lutheran pastor, he was also Namibia's Minister of Foreign Affairs. Prior to that, he had been a diplomat to the United States. I asked him where he had received his theological education.

"I obtained my Master of Divinity degree from Trinity Seminary in Bexley, Ohio, near Columbus."

"Oh, my goodness," I said. "I used to live there when I was a little girl!"

"Really? Perhaps you have heard of Montrose Elementary School. That is where my two children went to school."

My mouth dropped open. "That's where I attended second and third grade!" I said. He told us he had also studied law for a year at Valparaiso University in Indiana. Now it was Lou's turn to be surprised. "I obtained my undergraduate degree from Valparaiso," he laughed. Before driving to Aina's homestead for the reception, we stopped at a small cuca shop for Cokes. Nothing could have been more welcome on this hot afternoon.

Thick gray clouds piled up in the sky while we stood in front of the fence watching the bridal procession approach the homestead. I kept thinking about poor Aina's feet. Clad in her delicate white satin high heels, she had trod through the sand for the past two hours. The tantalizing aroma of roasting meat filled the air. It had been a long time since our morning cereal. Suddenly, a rush of family members came running through the gate to greet the bridal couple. The women were ululating, dancing and waving their horses' tails. Aina's uncle was brandishing a spear decorated with a brush of animal fur. One of our students leaned over and shouted in my ear that this symbolized the cow that had been slaughtered for the feast. Another uncle strode through the gate wearing a lush magenta velour shirt and carrying a rifle. As the procession approached the homestead, he fired two shots into the air, knocking to the ground a big leafy tree limb.

A tight crowd of wedding guests clustered around Aina and Peter who were now seated on white plastic chairs under the canopy of the tree that was missing its lower bough. In front of them was a small table holding four carved wooden cups. On the ground next to the table was a calabash full of traditional beer. Thunder rumbled in the distance, and the sky began to darken. Rev. Emunyela, along with two elders from the congregation, faced the bridal couple and led the gathering in prayers, hymns and a brief homily. After the Lord's Prayer, Nangula, the maid of honor, poured some beer into the wooden cups and handed them to the bridal couple and two bridesmaids. Another bridesmaid took me aside and gave me a large, shallow basket. She told me to put our gift in the basket, place it on my head and join the offering procession—a long queue of women who were bearing on their heads brightly wrapped packages, handmade baskets, clay pots and money. I joined the slow-moving queue, feeling terribly self-conscious, and tried to ignore my husband who was grinning broadly. Unlike the African ladies, I had to steady my basket by holding it on my head with my hand. When I reached the wedding party, Aina motioned me to sit down next to her. After all the women had delivered their gifts, Aina told me it was time to move toward the house, where food was being served. Saara hurried to us, seated us on white plastic chairs outside the largest hut, and brought us our meal: roasted pieces of beef, goat and chicken, potato salad, macaroni salad, millet porridge, and coleslaw. She offered us a choice of traditional millet beer served with a gourd from a large clay pot, soft drinks, bottles of Windhoek Lager, or fruit juice. Nangula, who was one of my English students, told me all the food had been prepared by family and friends. She said a secretary had to be appointed to record the dishes brought by each guest because the bowls, pots and baskets could not be returned empty to the donors. That would be very rude, she said. Lou and I made sure we bade farewell to the parents of the bride and groom, and Aina's father told us that it was a great honor for him to have had two white people at the reception. That embarrassed me. I wondered if he believed me when I told him that the greater honor was indeed ours.

Before we had finished making our farewells, big drops of rain began to splash on our heads. We all squeezed back into the Venture, shaking the rain from our arms and hair. As we drove along the steamy tarred road through the large towns of Oshakati and Ondongwa, we saw the *oshonas* (lake beds) in the fields filling with water. These had been totally dry when we drove past them in the morning. Cows and goats were wading knee-deep in the puddles beside the road. Meme Esther and her sister conferred with each other, and Meme told Lou that when we reached Oniipa, he should drop them all off at a small shop on the main road. She said they did not want us to risk getting stuck in the sand driving back to their house. A few kilometers outside Oniipa, Meme Esther and her sister started to sing softly, in Oshiwambo, "Lo How a Rose E'er Blooming." Lou and I sang along in English. I suggested "Silent Night" and "Oh, Come All Ye Faithful." We continued singing carols all the way back to town, English in the front seat, Oshiwambo in the back. Christmas was coming. Before we parted, I handed Meme my horse's tail.

Chapter 13
The Smoke that Thunders

*W*e bade farewell to Rev. Amaambo and Meme Esther and set out for Victoria Falls, Zimbabwe, a journey that would take us farther into central Africa than we had traveled before. We began early in the morning, passing men and boys leading goats and cattle to wells or grazing land. At the Ovamboland veterinary checkpoint, we agreed to give a lift to a policeman who was traveling to Tsumeb, about an hour away. We arrived in Rundu in the mid-afternoon. The receptionist at the Ngandu Lodge told me she had no record of a reservation from our travel agent, but she managed to find us a room, and we went off in search of some good Portuguese bread. Next we stopped at the large Lutheran Church where we had worshipped last Easter to visit the new pastor, a recent Paulinum graduate named Moses Cilunda.

This tall, slender young man was something of a rabble-rouser. In a good sense. He was outspoken and quick to condemn injustice or unfairness of any sort. Several months after he graduated, he returned to Windhoek for a church meeting and had stopped at our flat for a visit. Moses' family had sent him away as a young boy to live with distant relatives who were financially better able to care for him. The language he learned to speak in that household was different from that of his parents. The relatives had also given him a different surname—Sirunda— and Moses told us he was trying to legally change his name back to its original form. Moses had one other distinguishing characteristic: a hearty, generous laugh that bubbled up from deep inside him and engulfed all who heard it. It was hard not to like Moses.

Moses told us he had been working very hard. One day last week he had two weddings and two funerals. When we asked him about his upcoming Christmas service, he told us that they would start ringing the bell at 3:00 a.m. and that worship would begin at 4:00 a.m. Moses said this was the custom passed on to them from the Finnish missionaries. "One year some of the elders tried to change the time of the Christmas Day service to six o'clock, but the people protested. They said it was too much like a regular Sunday service, and that the day was nearly over!"

Moses said he would perform another wedding the day after Christmas. He told us he was responsible for nine "preaching points" throughout the area, but with no car he either had to walk many kilometers every day or depend upon parishioners to drive him from one homestead to the next.

The next morning, we continued our eastward journey toward Mabuku's hometown of Katima Mulilo located in the Caprivi Strip, that skinny, gerrymandered piece of Namibia that thrusts eastward into central Africa, bumping into Botswana, Zambia, and Zimbabwe. Katima is at the very end of the strip. Most our day's drive took us through a game preserve, and we saw numerous road signs warning drivers to be watchful of elephants. Lou maneuvered our vehicle around impressive piles of dung in the road and we saw many uprooted trees, but no elephants. We laughed to see small brown monkeys solemnly peering at us through the leafy branches, the only monkeys we had seen in Namibia.

This seemed like a good time to pull off onto the shoulder of the road to have some lunch. While we were eating our sandwiches, we saw a small group of women and children walking slowly down the road. When they reached our car, we gave them the rest of our sandwiches, along with our cookies, grapes, four juice boxes, and half a loaf of bread we had in our cooler. Leftovers for us. Sustenance for them. The children grinned and shyly said, "Thank you." The three mothers briefly met my eyes, nodded, and gathered the little ones to them. They continued their journey along the dusty road.

The entire Caprivi was lush with tall grass, shrubs, and stretches of forestland. It was nothing like the desert and semi-arid land in the central part of the country that we had become accustomed to. Why, we asked each other, wasn't this the breadbasket for the rest of the country? Where were the large farms? We saw many small villages and thatched-roof homes. Men were plowing fields with oxen-drawn plows and women were busy hoeing the furrows. And yet, for all the natural vegetation, we saw nothing that resembled a commercial farm, and very few vegetable gardens.

We arrived at the Zambezi Lodge just ahead of a thunderstorm. Our spacious room overlooked the Zambezi River, which is the border with Zambia. A small sign nailed to a tree warned guests not to swim in the river because of crocodiles. After a brief rest, we decided to explore the town. Most of the roads were unpaved, and the little shops appeared to be jumbled together without any plan. It was as if a giant had squatted in the dust and haphazardly tossed a handful of shop-shaped pebbles. We fell asleep that night listening to crashes of thunder and the drumbeat of rain on the tin roof of our lodging.

The next morning we visited Katima's Art and Craft Center, a collection of half a dozen small booths containing stone and woodcarvings, baskets and drums. Most of the lovely, intricate carvings sold in Windhoek and Swakopmund came from Katima, but the few pieces offered for sale that morning were not very interesting. We supposed all the good stuff must have gone to those urban centers. Lou located a public telephone and tried to phone Mabuku but there was no answer.

After the fierce thunderstorm of the previous evening, the potholes in the dirt roads were filled with water. Walking toward a small, round building that advertised itself as an Internet café (it was closed), Lou slipped in the soft mud, and went down on one knee. An elderly woman hurried over to help him stand up. I tried to keep from giggling, and for the rest of the morning, I called him Mud Man. (He was not amused.) I was still smirking when we entered a small supermarket for a few supplies. The aisles were crowded with shoppers and young men stocking shelves with canned goods and paper products and many packets of cookies. Instead of skirts, many of the young women wore pagnes, brightly colored lengths of African cloth.

After lunch at the Zambezi Lodge, I smeared insect repellant cream on my arms and legs and took my journal and a new Henri Nouwen book to a wooden bench under a tree on the riverbank. Nouwen's book, a recent gift from a friend, drew my attention inward, toward things spiritual. In our seventeen months in Namibia, God had seemed so absent. I was aware that my journal, already several hundred pages, contained few references to issues of faith. How could this be? We were missionaries, for goodness sake! I realized how infrequently I had experienced grace-filled moments here in Namibia. I missed the joyous worship and the nurturing community that sustained and strengthened me at home. Without those, my faith faltered, but reading Nouwen's simple, honest account of his own struggles helped. I reached for my bandana and wiped the perspiration from my neck. It was hard to believe that tomorrow would be Christmas Eve. Lou and I would celebrate a quiet Eucharist, just the two of us, in our room tomorrow night.

We left Katima Mulilo at seven-thirty the following morning, hoping to arrive in Victoria Falls within a couple of hours. But this was Africa. Our journey to the Botswana border was an hour of driving through corrugated sand, mud, and potholes. A large tourist bus kept passing us, so we endured delays at each of the four border-crossing checkpoints when the European tourists from the bus jostled to get ahead of us in the queues. Once we entered Botswana, Lou allowed the bus to roar past us while we stopped to watch a small herd of elephants ambling along the road.

Unlike our experiences in West Africa, no officials hassled us or demanded bribes at these border crossings, but when we entered Zimbabwe, we had an unhappy surprise. After filling out the usual immigration documents and standing in line for about fifteen minutes, the immigration officer informed us that before he could process our applications we needed to go to the customs window to pay the entry visa fee of thirty American dollars per person. Suddenly our cash, which had seemed plentiful and certainly sufficient, was severely depleted, and we still had another week on the road. Ahead of us in the queue was a red-faced gentleman with fierce eyebrows. He turned around, and in a clipped British accent he told us that President Robert Mugabe had imposed this new fee at the beginning of December. "Bloody outrageous, is what it is!"

We arrived at the Ilala Lodge just after noon. The lodge was located within walking distance of Victoria Falls. Though a far more elegant place than those in which we usually stayed, the cost was surprisingly reasonable, given the dollar's favorable exchange rate. A porter in a starched white shirt and maroon jacket carried our luggage to our room. We walked briskly past two restaurants, a casino, a swimming pool, and lots of staff. Later we enjoyed lunch on the terrace: shepherd's pie and mango juice. In the little town we found an Internet café and sent Christmas greetings to Jason, Megan, and my parents. The café had a sign in its window stating that they would even be open tomorrow, so we could check for a response on Christmas. We wandered in and out of the shops. I couldn't resist the temptation to purchase several meters of brightly patterned African fabric. Adjacent to the row of shops was a sprawling, open-air craft center. "Madam! Sir! This way! Stop here! Best price!" The quality of the wood and stone carvings was superb: graceful human figures that captured the same wistful qualities I had seen on the faces of my students when they hadn't known I was watching them. Just then, the sky turned dark, the wind whistled through the stalls, and the vendors scrambled to secure their flapping plastic ground cloths. We hurried back to the lodge, as large raindrops splattered our heads and backs.

I stepped out onto the balcony of our room in the late afternoon, and saw that the sky had cleared and the sun was shining. On the glistening, manicured green lawn below, four frisky little warthogs frolicked under the watchful eye and menacing tusks of Mama warthog. They looked like little gray furry pigs with impossibly homely faces. The porter had told us that wildlife often appeared on the lawn, and he'd warned us to keep our terrace door closed so that monkeys wouldn't wander into our room.

We dressed in our best clothes for Christmas Eve dinner. Garlands of dried grasses plaited with magenta ribbons adorned the sideboards and tables of the main dining room. Near the entrance was a ten-foot-tall Christmas tree constructed from ropes of straw arranged in a spiral cone and decorated with magenta bows and twinkling lights. Each table had a small glittering oil candle. Lou ordered a small steak and I had the evening's special, Crocodile Crock. The waiter laughed when he placed the steaming dish in front of me, "Madam, you must eat the croc' before he eats you!" Such a delicacy: small pieces of tender crocodile meat in a wine and cream sauce enclosed in puff pastry. Dessert was ginger ice cream with mango sauce. As much as we enjoyed the food, the highlight of our Christmas Eve dinner was the jazz trio: a keyboardist, a guitarist, and a drummer. We lingered over our coffee, enjoying the trio's extensive repertoire including *Take Five, Never on a Sunday, Georgia on My Mind* and gentle jazz arrangements of *Für Elise* and *The Moonlight Sonata*. Sprinkled throughout the medley were jazz variations of favorite Christmas carols.

We returned to our room humming strains of *Hark, the Herald Angels* and began to prepare for our Christmas Eve Eucharist. I placed the white headscarf from Aina's wedding on the coffee table. This would be our altar cloth. I lit the candle we had brought with us, poured a bit of wine into the bathroom glass, and placed a small piece of bread on a saucer. I turned off the lights. Bending toward the candlelight, Lou read the familiar Scripture lessons from Isaiah and Luke and, in a soft voice, reflected that this story of a humble birth took on deeper meaning today as we remembered the small homesteads and villages we had seen that morning where the men were plowing the fields with oxen and the women were bent over at the waist hoeing, or rhythmically pounding millet. As a short meditation, I read a few paragraphs written by Henri Nouwen in 1995 on the last Christmas Eve of his life. The words of this gentle priest and teacher helped us remember why we were here. *God is where we are weak, vulnerable, small and dependent...I increasingly believe that our faithfulness will depend on our willingness to go where there is brokenness, loneliness, and human need. If the church has a future it is a future with the poor in whatever form.* Lou reminded me that the true value of our African endeavor would not be so much what we were teaching, but, in Nouwen's words, to remain close to those who were broken, lonely, and in need. People like Nandi and Mabuku.

My husband consecrated our communion elements and we communed each other in the glow of candlelight. I could not recall a more intimate experience. A Christmas Eucharist is both a reminder and a promise deeper than humans can fathom. Birth and death folded in upon each other and bathed in the light of a star. Or a candle. We sat and held each other's hands for long moments in that quiet African night.

After breakfast on Christmas morning we went exploring and drove along a road that paralleled the Zambezi River. Stopping at a small parking area, we locked the Venture and walked along a footpath through what felt like a dense jungle of trees, vines, and bushes. The path ended on the bank of a swiftly flowing stream, a tributary of the Zambezi, and we stood on huge flat rocks as the water rushed by. Trees obscured the mighty Victoria Falls, but we could see the great cloud of spray and mist arising from them. Because of the holiday, we would have to wait until tomorrow to go there.

We continued our drive and soon came upon a gigantic baobab tree. A skinny grey-haired man in a tattered coat—a badge on his coat identified him as a government guard—told us the tree was twenty meters in diameter, and was fifteen hundred years old. The guidebook simply called it The Big Tree. What sort of protector was this slight, seedy fellow for such an ancient, arboreal giant? The guard sidled up to us, and in a thin voice, with several quick glances over his shoulder, told us he was trying to sell some small woodcarvings to earn enough money to buy shoes for his child. Would we like to see them? We told him we would, and he told us to stay where we were. "My boss, he don't want me selling my things when I work here so I have to hide them." He scurried away and we watched him squat behind a large leafy bush several feet from the road. When he returned he was carrying two small, carved figurines, heads of a man and a woman, about inches tall. "My son carved them. Nice work, eh?" We paid ten dollars for the pair, and hoped that his story was true.

We had just returned to our room at the lodge when we heard African drumming and singing. From our terrace, we looked down and saw a group of about ten men and women in traditional Zulu clothing. The men's faces were painted with fierce white streaks. They wore animal skin loincloths around their waists and bands of white fur and feathers on their arms and legs. The women were adorned with elaborately beaded necklaces and headdresses. We hurried to the courtyard where a crowd had already gathered. Such leaping and singing! A young woman standing next to me translated the words of their songs. "They are telling stories about going on a great hunt," she said. Of course, this little show was choreographed for us tourists, but it was the first African chanting and dancing we had seen since we'd last visited West Africa five years ago, and I realized how much I had missed these joyful expressions. Namibia's early German and Finnish missionaries had outlawed such carryings-on, and the prohibition had stuck. We laughed and clapped and tapped our feet while we continued watching these Zulu dancers perform for the guests of the lodge.

Christmas lunch was another lavish buffet. All the diners' tables were adorned with Christmas crackers, hats, streamers, balloons and small favors. We gathered ours up to give to the village children we knew would see along the road on our return trip to Namibia. After a short rest in our room, we opened three small Christmas presents we had brought with us. Our favorite was a gift from Jason, a one-pound container of Kraft Parmesan Cheese—impossible to find in Namibia. We returned to the Internet café but were disappointed no one had responded to our Christmas Eve e-mails. We were browsing through a souvenir shop next door when Lou said, "Look at this!" There on a display table was a collection of small wooden carvings identical to those we had bought from the baobab tree guard. Lou turned one of the figurines upside-down and read the price tag: four dollars for the pair. "We got ripped off," he grumbled.

"Well, I don't suppose he earns much, standing around guarding a thousand-year-old tree."

"No, probably not. Now we know why the hotel staff tells its guests not to buy from street vendors. I hope he used the money to buy food for his family, not beer."

I bought some small gifts for our children. As I was paying for my purchases, I told the shop clerk, an ebony-skinned young man of about twenty, that I was surprised to see so many shops open on Christmas day. "In Namibia everything would be closed."

"Is Namibia a Christian country?"

"Well, not officially, but most Namibians seem to be Christians."

"This is really a pagan town—except for me! I am a Lutheran!" He was thrilled to learn that Lou was a Lutheran pastor. He said the Lutheran congregation here held Sunday services at the primary school in the "location." He said tomorrow's service would begin at ten o'clock, and he gave us directions. "I will tell all my friends that an American pastor will come to church!"

While we were shopping, there had been a tremendous thunderstorm, and we returned to our room just as the power went out. Fortunately, a very loud diesel generator provided back-up power. While I was trimming Lou's hair on the terrace, a hotel staff worker stopped by to turn down our beds and leave complimentary wine and chocolates. Earlier, the maid who cleaned our room had left us two small carvings of hippos—the hotel's gift to its guests.

Christmas dinner was another feast: a five-course meal ending with steamed Christmas pudding and mince tarts. Throughout the day, we kept reminding each other of Christmases past, sharing memories from thirty years of church and family-focused celebrations. We remembered fondly our last several years in Chapel Hill, where we would invite about a dozen guests to our home for our Christmas evening buffet dinner. We specifically invited those who had no family with whom to share the holiday, and our celebrations always included our special friends Alice and Lillian, two older ladies who were very dear to our family.

We awakened early the next morning, eager to tour Victoria Falls. At the car park across the road, young men were renting umbrellas and big yellow slickers. Carrying our raincoats and cameras, we paid the ten-dollar per person entrance fee. The gatekeepers said they preferred American dollars, and we worried again about our dwindling supply of cash. The park encompassed several square kilometers of paved walking trails through dense tropical jungle. Turning to the left, we came upon a large statue of David Livingstone, the Scottish missionary and explorer who "discovered" the Falls in 1855. The inscription said "The peoples of the Congo and Nyasaland" had erected the statue. Continuing our walk toward the Falls, we kept getting doused and were glad for the raincoats. The main display was an immense thundering torrent of white water and mist. The Makololo, who lived here in the mid-nineteenth century, called these Falls *Mosi oa Tunya* which means "The Smoke that Thunders." Livingstone renamed them after his sovereign, Queen Victoria.

The roar of the Falls was so loud Lou and I had to shout at each other. Although we knew that Victoria Falls was twice the size of Niagara Falls, we were unprepared for the overpowering feelings of majesty inspired by the tumbling torrents. Livingstone called them "columns of watery smoke" that "must have been gazed upon by angels in their flight." In addition, there were smaller falls from the Zambezi River's tributaries. Two of these were the Horseshoe Falls and the Rainbow Falls. Standing across from the latter, I saw a rainbow in the gorge below.

Later that afternoon we joined about twenty other people on a sunset cruise on the Zambezi River. Snacks and drinks were included. Along the way, the captain pointed out a variety of colorful birds flaunting their plumage in the trees on the banks. I kept scanning the water and finally saw the hippos and crocodiles gliding past our boat. A young black Zimbabwean couple was seated next to me and across from us was another black family with two little boys who squealed each time they spied a hippo's tiny ears break the surface of the river. Perhaps those little boys knew what I didn't know until later: more people are killed by hippos than by any other African animal.

We saw many more indigenous black tourists here in Zimbabwe than we had encountered on all our travels throughout Namibia, but that evidence of prosperity would be short-lived. Although Zimbabwe had been independent since 1980, it was easy to see that now, in 1998, this was a country in trouble. The past year had brought strikes and rioting to the streets of Harare; the currency was collapsing, and the inflation rate stood at forty percent. Robert Mugabe, the country's president, was reminiscent of the previous generation of Africa's dictators. The country could ill afford its present military engagement in the Democratic Republic of the Congo in support of Kabila's resistance against rebel groups backed by Rwanda and Uganda, a conflict that some international news commentators were predicting could become a pan-African war.

Early the next morning, just as the sun was rising from the misty clouds on the horizon, I stepped out onto our terrace and saw four mongooses frolicking on the lawn below where the little warthogs had played the day before. They were long, brown, sleek creatures with thick pointy tails and dark stripes on their backs. They prowled and pounced upon each other like frisky house cats.

After breakfast, we set out to find the Lutheran worship service in the primary school the shop worker had told us about. This was certainly a part of Victoria Falls the average tourist would never see: small, square, cement houses with corrugated tin roofs nestled next to each other, children playing in the sewage ditches. After stopping twice to ask directions from passersby dressed in their Sunday best, we found the school, a simple concrete structure with exposed beams supporting a tin roof. In the classroom were twenty rows of wooden benches, about half of them filled with worshippers, mostly women and children. In front was an array of musical instruments: guitar, keyboard, and drums. Two men and one woman were leading the congregation in singing. On the blackboard behind the singers, someone had painstakingly written the words of four verses of "Love Divine, All Loves Excelling," the hymn Lou and I had chosen for our wedding service thirty years ago. It was now ten o'clock. During the next thirty minutes, women continued to wander in and soon the benches were filled. There were no elderly people here. Almost everyone appeared to be in their twenties and thirties, and there were lots of infants and children.

The singing was energetic and continuous, from one hymn to the next, with lots of swaying, dancing, and hand clapping. This was followed by a cacophony of everyone at once praying his or her own prayer. It did not resemble any Lutheran service we'd ever attended. Lutherans tend to be more subdued, and this felt more like a Pentecostal experience. After about an hour, a young man stood up and began to preach in English. Another young man translated his sermon into an African language. This was stream-of-consciousness preaching, one theme flowing into another. The evangelist knew his scriptures well and there was a message here for everyone: repentance, being born in the spirit, and how to proclaim the Gospel in everyday life. Fifty-five minutes later, he returned to his opening theme. Lou whispered to me that his aching back couldn't endure any more sitting on the hard wooden bench, so a little after noon, when the congregation arose to sing another hymn, we slipped out the back door. As we drove past the Roman Catholic Church, we saw a man sitting outside playing African drums.

Moving between two worlds—the bare poverty of the "location" and the subtle, elegant comfort of our lodge—was an experience that had endlessly replayed itself in our lives these past seventeen months. Birth and circumstance had given us luxuries and advantages forever denied most of those we encountered in this other world. It was the discomfort of that reality that had brought us to Africa. Not from a sense of guilt, but from a desire to share in the lives of the poor. It was our attempt to live out the Gospel mandate. I was already beginning to understand, as Lou had suggested on Christmas Eve, that very little I would actually *do* here in Africa would make much difference over the long term, but maybe the person I was trying to *be* would matter. Surely our willingness to participate in our students' weddings, to be part of their lives and listen to their sorrows, to provide them with a welcoming space in our home was worth something. Was it worth enough? How does someone measure such things? It seemed so amorphous, so intangible. So lacking in results we could point to and say, "I did that!" which, of course, is The American Way.

I knew it was neither the poverty nor the inefficiencies that kept threatening to break our spirits at the seminary. It was Johan van Wyk. His bigotry and hatred had seeped like venom into the systems of the church at large and the seminary in particular. When Lou and I talked about him, we were astonished all over again to consider how many peoples' lives that man had actually destroyed in Namibia. No one had ever taught me how to live and work with someone like that. Somehow, I knew, I would have to learn.

After lunch, we walked back to the little shop where we had met the young man who had invited us to church. When we told him that we had been to the service at the primary school, and that it had seemed very Pentecostal to us, the young man told us that the *Lutheran* service had been in the *other* classroom! And that they had been expecting us! Oh, dear.

That evening the warthogs returned to the lawn: two adults and five little ones. The babies tussled and wrestled with each other. The smallest one kept running around in circles, chasing his tail. Suddenly, he stopped and looked around. He must have realized that the adults and his brothers and sisters have wandered away. *"Hey, guys, wait for me!"* He scampered off after them.

The next day we reversed our long journey back to Windhoek: a night in Katima Mulilo, one in Rundu and two nights in the Oniipa, where we would attend yet another wedding of this marrying season. In Oniipa we experienced a Parable of Grace. We had already decided to forego two nights in the sweltering, mosquito-riddled church guesthouse in favor of the Punyu Hotel. It wasn't much more expensive than the guesthouse, and a room in the hotel had one huge benefit over the guesthouse: air-conditioning. Our room was simple, but clean. After checking into the Punyu, we visited the Amaambos to finalize our plans for attending the wedding.

Lou and I enjoyed our dinner at the Punyu and shared a giggle about the name of our entrée, Chicken Gordon Blue. Lou decided to pay with his Visa card rather than putting the charge on our room bill. When he opened his wallet, he discovered that the card was gone. Panic! Where could it be, given all the distance we had covered during the past two weeks? Did we use his card when we bought petrol in Vic Falls? Our receipts, back in our room, would tell us. Meanwhile, what do we do? This was more than just losing a credit card. Our Visa card was our bank debit card and our ATM card. Our only easy access to cash in Africa. If we canceled it, how would we get cash? While frantically considering our alternatives, I offered the waitress my own Visa debit card to pay for the meal. She returned with two cards in her hand: the card I had just given her…and Lou's card! She said that when she processed the payment, she noticed that the surname on my card was the same as the one on a card that had been left on a table a week ago. Apparently, when we had brought the Amaambos here for dinner the previous week, Lou had neglected to pick up his card from the folder containing the bill. The honest waitress had kept it, hoping that we would return. She received a generous tip from us that evening, and Lou made a point of passing on our praise to her supervisor when we checked out on Friday morning. We were ready to begin the new school year with open minds and, I think, more generous hearts.

Chapter 14
Listening for the Drumbeat

*T*he students began returning to campus the third week in January, full of smiles and hugs and eager greetings for their friends. One of my duties as interim accommodations manager was to be the Key Lady, so each of the fifty-four students had to come to my flat to collect their dormitory room key from me. At the end of the last term, after the students had left the campus, I had visited each of the three dormitories, lugging the big, cluttered basket of untagged keys that Sophie had given me, and I had matched each key to its room. The week before the students returned I posted signs on the outer doors of each dormitory and in the dining hall, telling the students to come to my flat to obtain their keys. They were surprised to find each key attached to a colorful plastic key ring and tagged with the appropriate room number. As they were leaving, most of them said, "I will come to visit. I have many stories to share with you!"

At nine o'clock the next morning the faculty gathered in the staff room for its first meeting of the school year. Our primary task was to plan the class schedule. To our surprise and dismay, Dirk was there, in defiance of Bishop Diergaardt's orders removing him from the seminary faculty and reassigning him to a congregation. How would Michael handle this challenge? Lou and I shuffled the papers in front of us, and I noticed others around the table were doing the same, except for Dr. van Wyk who was chatting amiably with Dirk about the travels he'd taken during the long summer holiday. Michael called the meeting to order and offered an opening prayer. Then he turned to Dirk. "Rev. Cloete, most of us are surprised to see you here. We thought your Church Board had assigned you to the Khomasdal congregation."

"No, you are mistaken." Dirk spoke slowly, a half-smile teasing his audience. He leaned back in his chair and clasped his hands together in front of his ample belly. "I am still on this faculty and will still be teaching my usual subjects this term."

Michael simply shrugged and no one else said a word. I wondered what the Governing Board would do when they arrived the next day.

Would the students initiate another strike when they discovered Dirk had not left? I felt a familiar queasy feeling in my stomach. My enthusiasm for the new school year was evaporating.

That evening I was glad I'd already planned the first six weeks of English lessons because my tasks as accommodation manager were becoming a lot more complicated. Late-arriving students were still showing up to claim their keys, the bishops and other members of the Governing Board had begun checking into the vacant flats we had prepared for them, and twelve visiting students from an American seminary had also just arrived and needed to be settled into spare dormitory rooms. In the midst of all the confusion, somehow Bishop Kaulinga ended up in a flat that had neither sheets on the bed nor towels in the bathroom. When Michael phoned to tell me, I hurried to the supply room behind the dining hall, scooped up sheets, towels, pillows and a duvet, and took them straight to Bishop Kaulinga's flat. Of all people! He was the serious one who never smiled. I apologized profusely for the oversight and made his bed as quickly as possible.

Lou, because he was the vice principal and dean of students, attended the Governing Board meeting the next day. The meeting started at nine o'clock in the morning. When my weary husband dragged himself back to our flat at ten o'clock that evening, he told me that the Board members, especially Bishop Diergaardt and General Secretary Rev. Gurirab from the Southern Church, were very displeased about Dirk's rebellious behavior. His defiance made them look ineffective in front of their Northern Church colleagues on the Board. By the conclusion of the meeting, the Board decreed that Dirk must resign immediately, and they ordered Bishop Diergaardt to speak with him the next morning. "At that point, the Bishop looked relieved," said Lou. "He also said that he would make the announcement to the student body. I can't help thinking, though, that Dirk is not going to just slip quietly away."

Lou and I had planned to return to the States at the end of this academic year, completing two years of service. Now we were having second thoughts. Would Dirk's departure cause us to revisit our decision? Probably. Although Dirk could be very charming and engaging, we had discovered him to be a deeply troubled man. He told lies, stole money and seminary equipment, and stirred up dissension among the colored students against their peers of other tribal backgrounds. Although his uncle, Dr. van Wyk, was the more cunning and manipulative of the two, Lou and I wondered if his power would be weakened if he were the only troublemaker remaining.

I tried to put my mind on other things. At the end of the week I drove four of the American students to the bus stop in town to catch the bus for the airport. Our Namibian students seemed to have enjoyed the opportunity to interact with these American seminarians. I wondered if they were surprised to find out how much more rigorous the American theological curriculum was than their own. Perhaps they couldn't tell.

That night Lou was able to listen to the live radio broadcast of the University of North Carolina basketball game on our computer. He had connected speaker wire from the computer in our office to the little speakers in our living room so we could close our eyes and almost imagine we were back in Chapel Hill listening to the game. It was always the little things, like listening to the familiar voice of Woody Durham, the announcer, or hearing the radio commercials for Wendy's hamburgers that made me feel homesick.

The atmosphere on the campus seemed calm. There were no untoward surprises, the students seemed to be in good spirits, and Lou's and my classes were going well. Since we were both several weeks ahead in our lesson planning and neither of us had Friday classes, we decided to travel to the coast for a long weekend.

Fortunately, there was a vacancy at the church guesthouse. On Saturday we awakened early, had a quick breakfast in our little room, and drove north toward Henties Bay, a sparsely populated, remote portion of the Namibian coastline. To our left, we saw a wide, lonely beach strewn with boulders and rocks. I couldn't help imagining Jason and Megan on the other side of the Atlantic Ocean. What were they doing this Saturday morning? Here and there, surf fishermen had driven right up to the water's edge with their four-wheel-drive vehicles. We passed occasional clusters of tiny gray fishing shacks. A dense layer of fog hung over the water, adding to the feeling of desolation. To our right, the white sand and the lichen-encrusted rocks of the old Namib Desert extended as far as the eye could see. I wondered what it must have been like for early explorers who landed here, or on Namibia's remote Skeleton Coast a little to the north. Their relief at having found land must have quickly turned to despair when they realized they had arrived on the edge of this barren, unwelcoming desert. Many of those who did not perish when their ships wrecked on the perilous coastline surely lost their lives when they attempted to venture inland. We parked our vehicle on the hard-packed sand beside the road so we could go walking among the beach boulders. I grabbed my cardigan. Even though it was late January, the middle of summer, the damp air was chilly. We clambered up and over the rocks, but when Lou slipped, dousing his left shoe and sock in the frigid surf, we decided it might be better to do our sightseeing by car.

We were driving slowly along the coast road, on our way back to Swakopmund, when Lou spotted an old wreck offshore and decided to take a closer look. He started to drive across the sand toward the water, a distance that looked to me to be about the length of a football field.

"Lou, are you sure this is a good idea? That sign we just passed said 'No Off-Road Driving.'"

"Oh, it's okay. I know how to drive in sand, and the Venture has a high clearance." What our vehicle didn't have was four-wheel drive. We'd only traveled a few yards from the paved road before the engine started to groan and we could feel ourselves sinking. I knew better than to utter a word. When we climbed out of our vehicle, I was alarmed to see that all four wheels were buried deep in the soft sand, all the way up to the top of the tires. We didn't have a cell phone, and even if we had, I don't think we would have known whom to call. We didn't even have a shovel.

I looked around to see if there might be someone who could help us. Far off in the distance, we spied a pick-up truck. "Why don't you go ask them for help?" said Lou as he tried to shove the sand away from the wheels with his hands.

"Oh, no you don't! *I* didn't get us stuck. I'll stay here with the car while *you* go ask for help."

"Fine!" He tromped off, and returned about fifteen minutes later riding in the cab of the pick-up truck with a middle-aged man and woman. The fellow said he and his wife had come to Namibia from Johannesburg to enjoy a little fishing. He took a shovel from the back of his vehicle, dug the sand away from our tires, and ordered us all to put flat rocks in front of the wheels for traction. He attached a sturdy rope to our Venture's front bumper and looped the other end around the back of his truck. He started to drive while Lou slowly let out the clutch and we two women pushed from behind. Nothing. Our car couldn't gain any purchase, and the pick-up truck looked as if it might become mired in the soft sand, too. We dug out more sand from around our wheels and found more flat rocks to lay down a longer track. After several unsuccessful attempts, we finally got it out of the deep sand and onto the road, enormously grateful to our rescuers.

Before we began our trip back to town, I told Lou to take off his wet sock. The air at the coast was so humid, I doubted the sock would dry overnight in our room, but if I dangled it out the window as we drove back to Swakopmund, it would probably be dry by the time we reached the guesthouse. The sock-flag seemed to be drying nicely, but just as we reached the edge of town a gust of wind ripped the sock out of my grasp and sent it sailing across the road.

"Lou, pull over, and back up slowly! Your sock just blew away!"

When I climbed back into the Venture, Lou had regained his sense of humor. "Susan," he said solemnly, "we need to get back to the guesthouse and lock ourselves in our room, so we don't create any more damage today."

I was unpacking our suitcase at home on Sunday evening, and Lou was opening the windows of our stuffy flat when there was a knock at the door. I continued pulling dirty clothes from our suitcase, and a few minutes later my husband entered our bedroom, a wide grin on his face. "Susan, Michael has just asked if I would baptize Penna next Sunday at the Paulinum worship service!" What an honor. The Shangalas' little daughter was just a month old, and we knew there were many other pastors—Namibian pastors—whom Michael could have asked. After Michael left, we made plans to visit the Roman Catholic bookshop where we knew we'd be able to find a baptismal candle for the service.

The next morning I was walking past the seminary's office building after teaching my early morning English class when Christa, the secretary, hurried through the door and handed me a fax. It was a request from our friend, Dr. Veiko Munyika, asking me to proofread a paper he had written for a theological conference he would be attending next week in Helsinki. I faxed my corrections back to him that afternoon, just before Angela stopped by with a small booklet about women's rights in Namibia. "Susan, I know this is short notice, but can you edit this for me before I send it the publisher? I'll need it by Friday morning."

Before the week ended, I had a visit from Paul Muha. The knife-sharp creases in his trousers and heavy scent of aftershave told me Paul regarded this meeting as more than just a friendly student visit. He left his shoes at the door of our flat, common practice for most Namibians. I invited him to sit down on the sofa in our living room, and offered him the customary glass of cold mango juice. Earlier, I had closed the curtains against the midday heat, and I reached for my glasses. I noticed he was holding a sheaf of papers in his hand. Sometimes Namibians are reluctant to get to the point, so I gently prompted him.

"Paul, was there something you wanted to discuss with me?"

"Meme Susan, I would humbly like to ask you to help me with my project." He looked down at the stack of handwritten pages on his lap. "I have discovered that no one has written a history of our tribes, the Kwangali and the Mbunza people. The elders in the Kavango Region know these events, and I have talked with many of them. I am very afraid that when these old ones die, much of that history will be lost." Paul was right. African culture and history is oral, and without a written record, important details tend to vanish.

"How can I help you, Paul?"

I knew what was coming—a lot of editing and proofreading. I hadn't expected the typing. His manuscript was over seventy pages long, full of complicated names and a few charts. I wished I'd learned touch-typing. Several times each week, for the next three months, Paul and I exchanged portions of the manuscript. Despite the extra work, I was pleased I could use my editing skills for this task.

In the process, I learned about the two matriarchal tribes that had established themselves in this section of northern Namibia where kingdoms and royal families still rule. Paul had found a photograph of Kanuni, the chief of the Kwangali tribe from 1924 to 1941. In the photo, this beautiful serious-looking young woman is squatting outside a thatch-roofed hut, probably the Kwangali palace. Strings of beads from her elaborate headdress caress her shoulders. Her only garment is a short, leather skirt. Perched on her knee is a young child, wearing strips of animal hides and beaded anklets trimmed with leather fringe. I couldn't turn away from the serene self-assurance of Kanuni, the young chief-mother. That graceful, confident expression I'd seen on the faces of so many African women spoke of a rootedness to family, tribe and land. Such women had no need to question their purpose in life.

My favorite part of the manuscript was learning the legend of the Kapande Tree. It was said that Kapande was a famous drummer who lived around 1800. He was a prominent guest at all ceremonies: initiations, marriages, harvest festivals, and coronations. People said that Kapande's drum had the power to heal illness.

Paul wrote, "One only had to listen to his drum to be healed. When he sat down with his drum, everyone danced as if he were in a trance or hypnotized. When his day came to 'enter the tree,' it was like this:

A drum dance competition was arranged. It was the most esteemed ceremony in Mbunza. The people wanted to see whether Kapande was still the champion. His friends who were invited started to play the drum dance at eight o'clock in the evening, and played until five o'clock the next morning. As a result, the people fell asleep. They weren't happy and were not in the mood to dance. Kapande arrived around five o'clock—sunrise—with his assistants, beating his drum. When the people heard the sound of his drum, they awakened from their slumber, stood up, and ran frantically toward the sound of his drum. The friends who had been competing against him were shocked and stopped playing their drums. Some started singing and dancing. When Kapande beat his drum the people immediately knew what kind of song they must sing.

While he was still playing his drum, Kapande began to climb the Munyondo tree. The people did not realize that in the Munyondo tree there was a hole. Kapande entered into the Munyondo tree still playing his drum. All the people were dancing, young and old, male and female.
Suddenly they realized that he was gone! They could only hear the sound of his drum. When they tried to bring him out of the tree, they found that it was impossible to do so. For two days, the people could only hear the sound of the drum. So Kapande entered into the tree with his drum. The tree is still standing near the main road from Rundu to Nkurenkuru and to this day it is still known as the Kapande tree.

I hoped that one day Paul would show me his Kapande Tree. I wanted to listen to the drummer.

Not all African experiences were as sanguine. I was horrified to read what my student from Botswana, Morekwa, had written in his English composition about a custom in his home country. It was not uncommon, wrote Morekwa, when a shopkeeper opens a new shop, for him to hire someone to kill a person so that he may obtain the body organs. These organs are taken to a local witch doctor who grinds them and cooks them with special roots and bark to produce a charm—*muti*—that will guarantee the success of the shop. When I asked him if this still happened today, Morekwa nodded his head sadly and assured me that it did. He also said that politicians who are running for office sometimes use *muti*. Scotland Yard, according to Morekwa, was called in to investigate one such recent case involving the death of a child. He said university students in Gabaronne, Botswana's capital, had launched a protest demanding the release of Scotland Yard's findings. It wasn't clear to me why Scotland Yard had become involved.

Early one morning Lou and I stepped out onto the balcony of our flat with our cups of coffee. We often enjoyed having breakfast here. As we looked over the railing, we saw a large, open-top truck with wooden side rails parked in front of Dirk's house. The logo on the door of the truck identified it as belonging to the Southern Church, and we realized it was the Church's moving van, used to move the household belongings of pastors and their families from one parish to another. After these many months, was Dirk finally going to leave campus for his new congregation and parsonage? While we leaned over the railing watching the driver and his companion climb out of the truck, Dirk stormed out of the house, waved his arms, and sent the truck away! Later in the morning, Lou told me he'd heard rumors that Dirk had refused the salary of his new congregation. Since he was no longer drawing a salary from the seminary, he was, in effect, "squatting" in faculty housing while the seminary continued to pay his utilities.

"What do you think Bishop Diergardt will do?" I asked my husband. "He seems to be afraid of Dirk."

"If I were the bishop, I would advise Dirk that the moving truck would be returning on a certain date—along with a police car—and that if he did not vacate the premises, he would be arrested for unlawful occupation." That seemed a reasonable approach, but we both knew it would never happen.

I was finally feeling more comfortable with my accommodations manager tasks. People must have noticed, because at the February faculty meeting, Dr. van Wyk asked if I would continue with this job after Ute Lessing returned from Germany, in a few weeks. He said the kitchen staff enjoyed working with me, that I was "like a mother to them," and that Ute could sometimes be very bossy. I knew what he was saying was true, but I also knew van Wyk rarely acted without an ulterior motive. He and the Lessings had tangled more than once, and pushing Ute out of this position of responsibility sounded like vindictiveness. I told the faculty I did not actively seek the job, but I would do whatever they wished. They voted unanimously to appoint me to the post of permanent accommodations manager.

As I had feared, Ute was furious when she returned to find herself stripped of her responsibilities. After the next month's faculty meeting, I tried to tell her that I had not sought the job. "With your heavy course load and caring for your two small daughters, wouldn't you prefer to avoid dealing with tenants, overnight visitors, and conferences?" She just glared at me, lifted her chin, and stomped away. I had never considered Ute a close friend—she and Hanns seemed to dislike Americans, in general—but I was sorry for this rift.

Meanwhile, Lou was struggling with the difficult situation of a female student, Metumo, who was suspected of stealing money from another student—her best friend on campus. Metumo was a sullen, lumpish girl. Lou and I had both had occasion to speak with her about plagiarism, an academic offense not uncommon on the campus. Perhaps that's why we were not altogether surprised at the allegations of Metumo's theft. It fell to Lou, in his role as dean of students, to investigate the case against her, starting with bits of evidence he'd begun receiving from other students.

The following Saturday afternoon, the sky grew greenly dark. Streaks of lightning slashed through the clouds. The thunder was so loud it sent the little children, playing on the swing set below our balcony, running home screaming and crying. We slammed shut the balcony door and hurried to close our windows while outside the huge purple storm clouds chuffed across the sky. Suddenly we heard a faint, metallic "pop," like the sound a light bulb makes when it expires. The lights didn't flicker, so we couldn't figure out what might have happened. Until a bit later when we tried to go on-line to check our e-mail. We discovered that the sound we had heard was the dying gasp of our computer modem. Although the computer had not been turned on, a surge of current had flowed through the telephone line, frying the internal modem. It had not occurred to us to unplug the phone from the wall during an electrical storm. We contacted a computer technician the next day, and he told us he could sell us an external modem and help us try to reconfigure our system, but we might lose our e-mail address book in the process.

During the next few days, Lou sequestered himself in our little home office every afternoon and evening, painstakingly writing up the results of his investigation into Metumo's theft. He said he saw a behavioral pattern emerging that had apparently been going on for some time. At the end of the week, with all the lecturers assembled in the staff room, he distributed to each faculty member copies of his four-page report, her signed confession, the bank statement, and a report from her intern supervisor. Metumo was called in. Her appearance told us her story before she ever opened her mouth. Most Namibians I knew took great pride in their appearance. Unless they were working in the fields, their clothes were always clean, ironed and often starched. Metumo's yellow blouse, half tucked into her too-tight black stretch pants, was soiled with food stains and wrinkled. Michael invited her to sit next to him. She said nothing, slumped into her chair and refused to meet anyone's eye. When the faculty members asked her to explain what had happened, her responses were curt, almost defiant. Although she appeared frightened, and certainly depressed, she expressed no remorse at having stolen such a considerable sum of money from her best friend's bank account. After she was excused from the meeting, Rev. Amaambo and Dr. Shivute suggested that members of her congregation in the North must have known about her sociopathic and dishonest behavior.

"Why would the Church Board have recommended such a person for the ministry?" asked Lou.

Rev. Amaambo shrugged. "Perhaps they thought she would change."

"Hah!" replied Dr. van Wyk. "Leopards don't change their spots."

"The Church is in such need of pastors," said Tomas Shivute, "they don't always screen candidates as carefully as they should."

The faculty was unanimous in ruling to expel her from the seminary, effective immediately. The decision would be announced to the student body after Monday morning's chapel service.

Meanwhile, our own national church back in the States was beginning to nudge us for a decision about whether we would be renewing our contracts for another two years. With everything that had been happening on campus, Lou and I hadn't really discussed this, and when we'd tried, we couldn't seem to make a decision. Sometimes we wondered if our presence here was making a difference, and sometimes we found ourselves overwhelmed with frustration and homesickness. And yet…something more than sheer determination seemed to keep tugging at us, compelling us to remain in Namibia.

Minivans full of Namibian school teachers had begun to arrive on the campus. The national teachers' union was holding its annual conference in Windhoek during the weekend, and I had booked spaces for twenty-five teachers in our empty flats and dormitories. I had told Sophie about these guests and had assumed she'd told her cleaning staff to make sure the rooms were ready. Apparently, that hadn't happened because at least half of the rooms had unmade beds and no towels. The seminary's cleaning staff didn't work on weekends, so I hurried to the women's dormitory and recruited four students to accompany me to the storeroom behind the dining hall. We grabbed armloads of sheets, pillowcases, duvet covers, and towels and spent the next two hours making beds for our guests.

As word kept spreading about our having some flats and dormitory rooms available to paying guests, my accommodations manager job was becoming more complex. The staff situation was a delicate issue, too. These workers had originally been hired to simply clean the seminary, and having so many paying guests was putting an extra burden upon them. Often, they had to arrive earlier or stay later than usual. None of our workers lived on campus. Matheus, our treasurer, picked them up each morning in the seminary's minibus and drove them back home at night, not an uncommon practice in Namibia where employers often provided housing and/or transportation to their employees. In the long run, this arrangement was cheaper than providing our workers with taxi or bus fare. When breakfasts had to be prepared for our guests, it wasn't unusual for Matheus to leave the campus at four o'clock in the morning to collect Sophie and her crew of cooks. Everyone agreed that the income was critical for the ongoing survival of the seminary, and this group's three nights, including breakfasts, would provide a net revenue of nearly seven hundred dollars, not an insignificant amount for an African seminary.

The day after the group left I launched yet another new career track: piano teacher. One of our musically gifted students, Elijah, had been begging me to teach him how to play the piano. I'd visited a music shop and was surprised to find on the shelves copies of the old, red John Thompson books from which I had learned to play the piano as a child. Most Africans I had met couldn't read music, but they were very quick to observe and listen and try to play by ear. I met Elijah at the chapel at four o'clock, and for the next hour I explained notation and fingering and scales. I wasn't sure if Elijah, a rather impatient young man, would actually be learning to read music so much as he would be copying what I demonstrated, but it didn't matter.

In the midst of all our busyness, Lou and I sat down one evening, took a deep breath, and decided to renew our teaching contracts for another two-year period. When several of our American friends sent us e-mails asking us why we wouldn't be coming home, I told them that we were just now beginning to enjoy a degree of trust and confidence that allowed us to feel that we were useful and that our work was valuable. Strangely, some of the practical tasks that had nothing to do with our job descriptions were precisely the ones in which we seemed to be making our most constructive contributions: Lou, in property maintenance and repair and I, in managing the rental of flats and rooms to guests.

We tried to be as honest as we could with our American friends and family members, explaining that, as foreigners, we were always aware of being aliens, no matter how warm and welcoming the people we encountered. Our own culture would always set us apart from our colleagues, students, and friends in Namibia.

Even after decades of being a clergy spouse, Africans were teaching me a deeper meaning of hospitality. From Africans I was learning to shed some of my own need for autonomy, such an integral aspect of my personality, as well as my home culture. These days, rather than feeling startled or annoyed, I *expected* to be summoned half a dozen times each day by a knock on our front door. Often our callers had no particular reason for coming to our flat, other than to visit with us. Learning to relax into this more lingering lifestyle became easier when I remembered that Africans' sense of self is derived by knowing who they are *in community*. It's what they called *Ubuntu*: a person is only fully a person through other people.

And yet, I knew I would never become comfortable with the disparity of wealth between us and our Namibian friends. In a few weeks, Jason would be obtaining a master's degree from Cornell University, and Lou and I would be flying to Ithaca, New York, to join in the celebration. Our Paulinum faculty colleague, Rev. Hasheela, could not afford to attend his daughter's graduation in the bordering country of South Africa. The last time we had returned to Namibia from a trip to the States, we'd had to bring back an extra suitcase to hold all the books we'd bought. Our faculty colleagues were able to spend a maximum of sixty dollars a year on books for their professional libraries.

Some of my friends back home told me they felt trapped in their consumer-driven society. They said the seductive, skillfully manipulated imperative to buy more "stuff" even quashed feelings of gratitude for the abundance they already had. I knew what they meant. We seemed to have lost the sense of the word *enough*. Lou and I experienced it ourselves when we returned home for visits. I was ashamed at how gleeful—how avaricious—I felt the first time I shopped in an average, well-stocked American grocery store after having lived in Namibia for over a year.

Now that we'd chosen to remain two more years in Namibia, Lou and I told each other we wanted to continue to function as a bridge between the needs of the Africans with whom we lived and the generosity of our friends and church members back in the States. We now had a discretionary fund from which we could discreetly respond to some of the more urgent requests we seemed to get every week. Just this week, we had given Mabuku money so he could transport the body of his deceased sister back to the Caprivi for burial. Poor Mabuku. As if his loss of a sister, his partial blindness, and his bewitched brother were not enough, his problems at the seminary were really just beginning. And so were ours. Those problems would jeopardize my husband's credibility among his Namibian colleagues.

Chapter 15
Pulling Up My Socks

*F*or the past week, Lou and I had been buying packets of Easter candy whenever we'd seen some on sale. Unable to find any Easter grass in the shops, I'd bought sheets of colored crepe paper and had given myself a blister cutting these into thin strips. I filled four cloth bags and three plastic shopping bags with crepe paper grass. I awakened early on Easter Saturday, boiled five dozen eggs, and set out my little bottles of food colors. By lunchtime the countertop in our tiny galley kitchen was a crazy quilt of brightly dyed eggs. The next morning, after Lou and I returned home from the Easter service at the Inner-City Church in downtown Windhoek, we filled all our available shopping bags with the "grass," dyed eggs, chocolate candies, and jelly beans. Taking care not to be seen by the students, we carried our bags to the dining hall, closed the curtains, and locked the door from curious eyes. We divided our bounty among the eight long tables, sweet centerpieces for the students. When Theophilus, the kitchen worker, rang the bell for Sunday dinner, we stood in the corner of the dining hall watching the startled faces of these young men and women as they walked through the door. No Easter Bunny had ever visited any of these Namibians. They wasted no time picking through the Easter grass, and before they'd even said the table blessing, there was a small pile of eggs and candy in front of each dinner plate. When the students saw us, grinning in the corner, they applauded and cheered.

Our Easter dinner was the same Sunday dinner we had every week here in the seminary's dining hall: baked chicken legs, white rice, gravy made from a packaged mix, cubes of boiled pumpkin (what Americans would call winter squash) sweetened with brown sugar, cold sliced beets and vanilla pudding with canned fruit cocktail. We always enjoyed that nice dinner on Sunday, the best dinner of the week, but I was feeling a touch of holiday homesickness that day. I missed the Easter dinners I used to cook back home: roast leg of lamb and mint sauce, asparagus, new potatoes and coconut cake.

How closely we in the northern hemisphere associate Easter with springtime. The association is so deep within us that it's nearly impossible to think of Jesus' Resurrection without thinking of daffodils and fresh grass and redbud trees. Here, summer was ending. In the chilly evenings we were hearing the final songs of crickets and locusts. The green grass of the ebbing rainy season was already becoming brown. The sky was nearly dark by dinnertime.

Early one morning I was sitting on the balcony of our little flat, a steaming cup of freshly brewed coffee warming my hands, and my flannel robe pulled tightly around me. The air was so clear in the heart of the dry season, and I heard a symphony of birdsong. One of the birds had a call that sounded exactly like a wolf-whistle. It took me many weeks to realize that this really was a bird and not one of our students! Even here in the suburbs, I also heard roosters crowing, another type of birdsong.

Our students often sang, too, as they walked from place to place. So did the seminary's workers as they went about their tasks of peeling vegetables or hanging clothes on the clothesline or sweeping. Mostly what I heard were hymns—the tunes were recognizable, even if the words were not. Later in the day, I would hear the sounds of cue sticks hitting balls. The students' poolroom (they called the game snooker) was just across the road from our flat, in the same building as the dining hall. The cheers and good-natured insults were a gauge of the mood on campus. During tense times, like the strike, the poolroom was silent and dark. In the afternoons and well into the night, we could hear students calling one another's names across campus, yelling that someone had a phone call. There was one telephone for the students located in the dining hall/recreation room complex, so to call their friends to the phone, they would step outside and shout in the direction of the dormitories.

In June 1999, the U.S. Embassy in Windhoek closed, along with other U.S. embassies around the world, because of terrorists' threats against the United States. I received this message in a phone call directly from the embassy because I had agreed, upon our arrival in Namibia, to serve as a "warden." My task was to phone about fifteen other American citizens living in Windhoek to advise them that the embassy would be closed and to "exercise vigilance as you go about your daily activities." I knew no more about the specific nature of those threats than anyone else who watched CNN, and none of us quite knew what it meant to exercise any more vigilance than we already did. Oh, well. I was happy to help the embassy satisfy its care-taking requirements.

Just after the Fourth of July, Lou and I were once again caught up in a

Mabuku family tragedy. We had hoped life would become easier for our student with the artificial eye, but Mabuku came to our home one Sunday night, more distraught than I had ever seen him. He said that his cousin had just been transferred to a Windhoek hospital from the hospital in Katima. "He has the same sickness that took the life of my sister! He cannot move or talk." His older brother and another half-sister had died of the same affliction, and Mabuku was terrified that he would be next. "Would it be wrong for me to go to see the witch doctor?" We didn't know how to answer his question, but after he left, I e-mailed two doctor friends in North Carolina asking them if they had ever heard of anything like this. They hadn't. Lou wondered if this might be some sort of acute form of collective hysteria, a phenomenon we'd already heard about several times in Namibia, though usually occurring within groups of schoolgirls. We remained in close contact with Mabuku during the next few weeks. There seemed to be little change in the cousin's condition. We never asked him if he'd visited the witch doctor.

Although it was still several months away, we were beginning to plan for our November trip back to the States. This would be an official home leave, during which the national Lutheran Church expected us to visit as many of our sponsoring congregations as possible. Lou and I had enrolled in the frequent flyer program with South African Airways, and a few weeks later we received in the mail two items from the airline. The first envelope contained our membership number—a PIN number—with the admonition to keep this in a safe place. In the second envelope was an introductory "welcome" packet that contained a free plastic luggage tag. Printed prominently on the tag was...our secret PIN number!

One morning, while chatting with colleagues after the chapel service, I told Michael I would like permission to add a brief item to the agenda of the week's faculty meeting. I had exciting news. "Michael, I've just received a letter from our Division for Global Mission in Chicago. A large congregation in the Washington, D.C., area is donating *three thousand dollars* to our student book fund!" This latest donation would supplement the students' annual book allowance, adding twenty dollars a year to each student's account for four more years. I was surprised that Michael's response was a frown and a grunt.

Later in the morning, Michael stopped me between classes. "Susan, would you come to my office after tea break so we can discuss this?" I brought with me a copy of the e-mail I'd sent to DGM on Sunday advising them of the best way to transmit these funds. I had planned to give this to him right away, but it had slipped my mind. "Please, sit down, Susan." Michael remained standing and began to pace back and forth in front of his desk. It had been a long time since I'd been called into a principal's office. I thought he would be delighted, and I was bewildered by this reaction. He stopped his pacing and perched on the edge of his desk, staring straight through me.

"In the past, our colonial rulers, the white South Africans, and even the missionaries, would deny us Africans information. They would just tell us what they thought we needed to know. I know, from the years I spent in America, that other people often regard Africans as stupid or ignorant." Now he was gripping the edge of the desk with both hands, and he was almost shouting. "We can't help that our English is broken, or that we are poor. If we were not poor, I would just send gifts like this back to the donor."

He continued, lowering his voice, "I know, Susan, that you understand us. I just ask that you keep us informed, so that when we receive money like this, we are aware of it. That it doesn't come as a surprise."

I didn't know what to say. Humiliated, I mumbled an apology, and I assured Michael that I had intended to give this to him, but I had forgotten. I said I hoped he knew our national church did not hold those prejudicial views of Africans.

I walked across campus to our flat thinking about Lou's baptism of Michael's little daughter, just a few short months ago. Was Michael sorry he had asked Lou to do that? The ground of our acculturation that had begun to feel solid was crumbling and shifting again. Paulinum had, once more, become a lonely place. Why had we chosen to extend our contracts until 2000? As vulnerable as my encounter with the principal had made me feel, it didn't take much for me to dive headfirst into my pity pool. I was always giving so much to this seminary, receiving little, if any, thanks for my contributions. What really hurt was knowing how hard I tried to be polite, respectful and culturally sensitive. It seemed to make no difference. Michael's dressing down made me feel like a boorish American who didn't have a clue about how inappropriately she was behaving. Would we always be perceived as rich, know-it-all Americans? I couldn't wait to return to the States for our two months of home leave.

Lou suggested we follow the Austins' advice and leave the campus for a long weekend. Fortunately, we were able to book a bungalow for three nights at the Okaukuejo Rest Camp in the Etosha Game Park, our favorite Namibian retreat. Frustrations and irritants of the recent weeks melted away. Every morning and afternoon we filled our water bottles, collected our camera and binoculars, and drove the white gravel trails through the park's eight thousand square miles. We stopped the car to watch a small family of giraffes munching leaves from treetops. We parked beside a waterhole to watch dusty elephants splash themselves in the center of the pool while slender, white-tailed springboks took cautious sips from the edge. From the stand of trees in the distance emerged a stately procession of zebras. Back at the camp, we donned our bathing suits and enjoyed a quick swim in the pool. Afternoons were still warm here in the northern part of the country. From the camp store we purchased a small bundle of firewood, and after each day's game drives we cooked dinner on the grill outside our cabin. Sweet wood smoke filled the air.

The weather back in Windhoek was chilly. We hauled our suitcase and Coleman cooler up the steps to our flat, and I reminded myself to look in the top of the bedroom cupboard for extra blankets. After we had unloaded everything from the car, I turned on the little portable radiator in the front hall and walked into the office to ask Lou if he wanted to join me for a cup of tea before I finished unpacking. Suddenly I heard a loud "whooshing" sound. We looked around and saw that the radiator had sprung a leak. Hot oil was gushing out into the front hall and kitchen. The radiator held about eight gallons of oil. There was no way to staunch the flow without injuring ourselves, and nothing to do but wait until it had emptied itself. Then we got to work with paper towels, mops, and cleaner. The linoleum floor in the hallway and kitchen was slick as ice. The long red and orange carpet runner in the front hall was saturated with oil. We would need to replace it. Lou and I kept telling each other how lucky we were that one of us hadn't been standing next to the radiator when it sprang the leak. Luckily, we had another small heater.

During the next few weeks, I was immersed in what felt like hotel management. I was desperately trying to bribe, threaten, and cajole fifty-four students into keeping the campus super-clean because thirty-five professional musicians were coming from Johannesburg and would be staying in our several vacant flats and empty rooms in the student dormitories. My stomach turned inside out when I inspected the grimy, crusty bathrooms in those dormitories. I drove to Game, the large discount store about a mile away, and bought six scrub brushes, ten pairs of rubber gloves and a dozen one-liter bottles of bleach. That night at the vespers service I reminded the students that I expected this campus to shine! The next day I returned to Game with Sophie and a list of supplies.

Matheus had examined the seminary's budget and had given us permission to purchase a toaster, waffle maker, drip coffee maker and some more bed linens.

When I had looked at the calendar that morning, I was surprised to realize it was the two-year anniversary of our arrival in Namibia. Lou and I were feeling a little better about our decision to renew our contracts for another two years. Michael was behaving more cordially. Was he feeling embarrassed about his outburst two weeks ago? Staying busy seemed to help our spirits, too, but I was growing weary of my frequent mood swings. I was used to charting a course, making decisions, and moving forward.

This month I would be teaching bookkeeping to Lou's third-year church management class. Because of my background in banking and accounting, Lou thought my skills might be useful in showing these young adults how to manage money when they were pastors of congregations. Although most of them would be lucky to receive a few dollars every week in the offering basket—these were the students who would be paid in grain, goats, and chickens—a few of the bright ones would be responsible for thousands of dollars in monthly congregational income. I was planning to teach them about general ledgers and other basic record-keeping skills. I talked to some students and to our treasurer, and discovered that these students did not even know how to keep a checkbook. I decided to simplify my course. I would teach them how to write checks, make deposits, maintain a check register, and reconcile a bank statement. I bought each student a small pocket calculator. It took almost the entire first class period to make sure they all knew how to use them.

By Friday I was almost ready for our guests from South Africa who would be arriving that evening. Early in the morning I'd driven into town to buy ten liters of yogurt and five large bags of muesli for Saturday's breakfast. I withdrew our weekly housekeeping money from the ATM and stopped at the neighborhood Caltex station to fill up the car with petrol. When I got back I delivered the food to the kitchen staff and the car to Lou, who was waiting for me in the carport so he could take to the airport a group of Americans who had been conducting workshops throughout the country.

As Lou and I were sitting down to lunch in the dining hall, Hanns walked up to our table accompanied by six guests. He introduced them as the "advance guard" for the orchestra members, their various managers and support personnel. I left my fish and potato salad, and showed the managers around campus. Peter, the general manager for the orchestra, suggested that I give him the keys to all the rooms since the group would be arriving rather late that night. He said he would distribute the keys so he wouldn't need to disturb me. This required a trip to our flat and, for reasons I couldn't understand, a reassignment of rooms. I also gave Peter the thirty-five campus maps I had created and photocopied. A final verification with Sophie and the rest of the kitchen staff assured me that the rooms were all ready. I spent the afternoon quietly grading English papers.

At about nine o'clock I heard the rumbling diesel engine of the bus and hurried outside to greet our guests. I discovered that they had not been in touch with Peter, who was staying somewhere off campus. They were not pleased to learn they couldn't quickly check into their rooms and go to bed. I understood their grumpiness. They had been traveling from South Africa for two days and were very tired. One young lady sighed deeply and looked around the campus with a sneer on our face. "Are there any decent hotels in Windhoek that aren't too expensive?" I assured them we would soon have them settled, ran back to the flat, and called Peter on his cell phone which, I discovered, was a long distance phone call to South Africa. Very expensive.

"Peter, your group is here!"

"What?! Why didn't they phone me first?"

"I don't know, but they need their keys."

"All right. Tell them I'll be there in twenty minutes."

Half an hour later, Peter was handing out keys and maps, and all the musicians went off to their rooms. Peter asked me if we had an extra private room for Jocko, the bus driver. "No, we only have what you asked for. If he can sleep with the others tonight, we do have one empty room that our staff can make up for him tomorrow."

Peter left, and I returned to our flat and got ready for bed. Not the smoothest of arrivals, but at least everyone was settled for the night. I was reading in bed when the phone rang. It was Michael. "Susan, I just received a phone call from two more orchestra members. They're traveling by car and I gave them directions to the seminary. They should be here soon."

Another costly long-distance phone call. "Peter, two more members of your group will be arriving in a few minutes."

"Oh, that must be Fineas and Robert, our road manager and

technician."

"Peter, I do not have the list with the room assignments. I gave it to you."

Was I sounding less than professional? I paused and took a breath. "Where are they staying?"

"I'll have to call you back. The list is in my car."

I asked Lou to wait for Peter's call and pulled a sweat suit on over my pajamas. I hurried across campus to the front gate to meet our guests because I wasn't confident the night watchman would let them in. Actually, I wasn't even confident that he would wake up. By ten o'clock he was usually sound asleep in his little guardhouse adjacent to the front gate. By eleven o'clock the two latecomers were settled, and I climbed back into bed.

I was startled awake in the middle of the night by the jangling of the phone ringing again in our living room. I ran to answer it, assuming it would be Peter, my new best friend. I didn't want to awaken Lou who had been grumbling about my having taken this accommodations job. But it wasn't the outside phone, it was the inside line. I heard sobbing and shouting, and after a few moments I realized it was Mabuku, phoning from his dormitory. I implored him to slow down and tell me what had happened. "My mama has passed away! Oh, my mama! Ohhhh—she has passed away. Can I speak to Pastor Lou?"

I'd been a pastor's wife for enough years to know that there were times when only the voice of the pastor would calm a person, so I woke Lou up and he talked to Mabuku for a while and returned to bed. Half an hour later, the phone rang again. Mabuku was saying that he must go to Katima immediately. "If I can't find a ride, I'll walk!"

Lou slipped on some clothes and walked over to Mabuku's dorm room. Lou told me later that he had met Michael there. Mabuku told them his relatives, who lived in Windhoek, were planning to leave at four o'clock, so Lou and Michael agreed to drive him to their house. "It didn't take us very long to determine that Mabuku had been drinking. He had trouble giving us directions, and then he just passed out on the back seat. I brought us all back to campus, and when we pulled up in front of the men's dormitory, I had to shake him to wake him up. I told Mabuku I would speak with him again in the morning and see what arrangements could be made."

When the alarm buzzed at six-thirty, I felt as if I'd hardly had a wink of sleep. After taking a quick shower, I gathered up our laundry and carried my basket to the laundry room, adjacent to the kitchen. It was five minutes past seven, and there was no sign of the kitchen staff. Breakfast for the musicians was supposed to be ready at eight. I shoved my laundry into the washing machines and hurried back to our flat to phone Matheus. "Matheus! Where are the workers?"

He didn't know. But the Toyota pickup was also gone, which meant that one of our student drivers must have left to collect them. They arrived at seven-thirty, and my heart sank. I knew it would be impossible for our workers to prepare the "full English breakfast" we had promised the group. Matheus met me in the dining hall and we began putting the tablecloths, plates, and cutlery on the tables. We set out small pots of butter and jam. I asked Sophie how she was cooking the eggs. Perhaps boiled would be easiest.

"Oh, the meat market forgot to deliver the eggs yesterday." Of course, no one thought it might be a good idea to go out and get any. At least we had plenty of yogurt, cereal, and toast.

I went outside to tell the group that had begun assembling in the courtyard that breakfast would be about fifteen minutes late. Several of them started telling me their rooms were very cold, and that there was no hot water. I apologized, explained that the rooms were not heated, promised I would find out about the hot water, and hurried off to the staff room across campus to collect the extra coffee pots that the kitchen workers had forgotten to bring to the dining hall yesterday. When I reached the staff room, I realized I had brought the wrong bunch of keys with me, so I ran back to our flat to get the right ones. When I finally returned to the dining hall with the coffee pots, the guests were eating breakfast and Sophie was in the kitchen frantically slicing salami and cheese. I told Jocko, the bus driver, that after everyone was fed we would move him into a private room and give him his new key.

When I told Sophie that her workers would need to prepare a room for Jocko, she said, "We have sheets and towels, but no more blankets or duvets." Oh. I told her I would buy another duvet this morning and bring it to her. I went to the laundry room behind the kitchen, pulled my clothes from the washing machines, and quickly hung our laundry on the line behind the dining hall.

When I arrived back at our flat, an abject Mabuku was sitting on our living room sofa looking glumly at his shoes. Lou and I had a quick, private consultation and we agreed to give him the money he needed. Sixty dollars would cover his round-trip transportation to Katima, with a little extra money to buy food. We knew our sixty dollars might take a side trip to the local shabeen or liquor store, but we really didn't have time to think about that this morning. I put some oranges, cookies, peanuts, and juice boxes into a plastic bag for Mabuku. Then we drove him to the vacant lot north of town beside the B-1 highway where drivers park their minibuses to take paying passengers to the North. Next, we headed to the discount store. As usual, the store was crowded with Saturday morning shoppers because all the shops in the country closed at noon on Saturday.

When we arrived back home, Lou kept trying to reach Michael by phone to tell him about the resolution of the Mabuku situation. When Michael finally returned to campus from his own Saturday chores and phoned back, we heard some disturbing news. Michael told us he had been talking with Nambili, a second-year student, and one of our two student drivers.

Nambili, whose name meant Man of Peace, was an older student. He had been a teacher before entering the seminary, and he possessed a maturity that distinguished him from many of the other students. Nambili told Michael that he had driven Mabuku to his relatives' home the previous afternoon, and that his conversation with that family revealed that Mabuku's story was a complete fabrication. His mother had not died. Nambili further disclosed that most weekend nights Mabuku would come back to the campus drunk and aggressive. On Friday, the night had Mabuku phoned us, sobbing and upset, Nambili said a taxi had delivered him to campus. Mabuku had no money to pay the taxi fare, and the students he asked for money refused to lend it to him. A brawl nearly ensued. Mabuku finally gave the taxi driver his shirt as payment.

This would not have been the first time we'd been suckered by a student. Nambili said Mabuku's brother lived in a rough section of town. Hesitant to drive there alone, Lou made plans for the two of them to drive him to Mabuku's brother's house so that he could talk to the family directly.

After lunch, I received a phone call from Dr. Rohn. As well as being my personal physician here in Windhoek, he was the person in charge of the orchestra group's weeklong visit to Namibia. He was a gentle, reasonable man. Dr. Rohn told me, very apologetically, that the musicians had many complaints: the space was too cramped, there was insufficient hot water, and could a more substantial breakfast be provided?

I told him that we had no more empty rooms available, that we were checking to make sure the electrical back-up system for our solar water heaters was working properly, and that there had been an unfortunate problem with the breakfast that morning. I promised to try to make things better for the group.

Dr. Rohn assured me that most of the complaints were not our fault. "I know what the seminary's facilities are like and, really, I think they are very adequate. It's just that this orchestra is used to staying in three-star hotels, and our sponsoring organization simply can't afford that sort of accommodation for them here in Namibia. I, uh, hope you won't be offended if some of their soloists move to private homes."

I didn't know what more I could do. I hoped that breakfasts for the remainder of the week—the area over which we did have some control—were satisfactory. The breakfast the group received yesterday included two types of juice, coffee or tea, three kinds of cereal, yogurt, toast, butter and two kinds of jam, sliced cheese and salami. The only thing missing was the hot entree. Maybe I could wake up extra early to help the staff prepare eggs, bacon, waffles, and pancakes.

When I saw Michael in the staff room at tea break the next day, I told him about the group's complaints. He shook his head ruefully, patted my arm and said, "We will have to pull our socks up!" I was glad for his empathy, but I wondered if I would have any socks left by the end of the week.

Chapter 16
Mabuku's Struggle

*O*n Friday morning, I went to the dining hall at five o'clock to make coffee for the visiting musicians. Peter had told me they wanted to be on the road by six and would only need coffee, juice, and toast this morning. Before they boarded their bus, I distributed the sandwiches our kitchen staff had made the previous evening, a practice I'd noticed was prevalent in many lodges throughout the country. They were a happier group than when they arrived, perhaps because their concert performances had been so well received. Windhoek was a surprisingly international city, with many expatriate residents, so large audiences responded with enthusiasm.

We had neither seen nor heard from Mabuku all week, but Lou and Nambili went to the brother's house three times, looking for our errant student and seeking information. The brother told them Mabuku had been showing up at his house late at night seriously intoxicated. How did the seminary faculty and the Northern Church miss this problem when they screened him as an applicant? Lou told me that the Lutheran Church in the Caprivi, where Mabuku lives, is really only a mission. There was never a full time pastor there, so it appeared that no one from the Northern Church knew Mabuku very well. Lou said that, according to the brother, Mabuku had appeared to have his life under better control when he first arrived in Windhoek, but the loss of his eye and the deaths of close relatives had plunged him back into former ways. Lou left messages with the brother and also with an older sister, asking Mabuku to contact us.

Meanwhile, a special faculty meeting was scheduled to discuss an upcoming pastors' in-service course to be held on our campus. This two-week, continuing education opportunity for Namibian pastors was underwritten by the Lutheran Church in the United States. Although Ute and I rarely spoke to each other these days—she was still angry about being stripped of her accommodations manager duties—I was pleased when she raised the idea of having a workshop about AIDS during this refresher course. I was also grateful when she suggested that a Namibian should lead such a course. We had spoken often with Hanns and Ute about why this seminary hadn't been discussing the devastating impact of AIDS on the Namibian society, and how it might respond. Our Namibian colleagues did not oppose Ute's suggestion, but they really didn't support it very strongly, either.

The figures and projections, only now being published in 1999, were devastating. As the infection rate soared—about twenty-five percent of those between the ages of fifteen and forty-seven were affected—entire segments of the population were being eliminated. Teachers, lawyers, and even health care professionals were succumbing to the disease at an alarming rate, and all over the country grandparents were trying to care for AIDS orphans on their own meager social security allotments, sixty dollars a month. The cost of drugs, even AZT, was way beyond the means of Namibian citizens. Most of the pastors we knew were conducting funerals every Saturday, sometimes several in one day. Educational programs appeared to have little impact on behavioral changes. Sexual promiscuity and illegitimate births were out of control. The NGOs and Namibia's Ministry of Health were finally advocating condom use. And yet, the churches remained silent. Lou and I were astonished and ashamed that the Lutheran churches would not endorse, or even support, the use of condoms. The Church said this encouraged promiscuity, the same argument proffered by those in the Religious Right in the United States. We expatriates here on campus walked a narrow corridor, seeking to help the students grasp the magnitude of the AIDS pandemic, while trying to be careful not to condemn the Church. How many more deaths would have to occur before the Church decided to respond?

Mabuku finally returned to campus, and one evening Lou took him to an Alcoholics Anonymous meeting in downtown Windhoek. When he returned home, he said Mabuku had appeared interested and responsive. Mabuku had always been shy, but now he was also filled with shame and guilt. Perhaps these would be motivators for change. Michael had suspended him from attending classes yesterday and told him to stay in his room. Michael left the next morning for a trip to the North, and Lou, who became acting principal in Michael's absence, told Mabuku that he should attend classes. "He needs to stay connected and focused on his studies," Lou said, "especially since he is still battling loneliness and grief over the deaths in his family.

How would this turn out? We knew it was not possible to predict success in dealing with alcoholics, but we hoped Mabuku had the desire to turn his life around. Our great fear was that the principal and other faculty members would treat Mabuku's behavior harshly and would suspend him. Bishops, deans, and local pastors within the Namibian churches were very strict, even vindictive, or so it seemed to us. All Law and not much Gospel. Lou and I told each other we would continue to suggest a compassionate approach when the faculty met to discuss his situation the following week. We knew we risked being humiliated by being told (again) that we "do not understand the African way."

We were right. On Monday afternoon, the faculty met and the discussion revealed a clear and uncomfortable schism between the four white expatriates and the four black Namibians. Although I would have preferred a happier ground for reconciliation with Hanns and Ute, I was glad Lou and I were not alone in a stance that set us in opposition to our African colleagues. When we reached the agenda item dealing with Mabuku, Lou said, "I see two alternatives for dealing with the situation. The first is suspension. The second is a program I propose involving the following steps: Mabuku will attend two Alcoholics Anonymous meetings per week; he will have to show evidence of reading the AA "Big Book"; he must remain on campus during the weekends; he will receive counseling for the remainder of the school year; and, finally, the faculty will evaluate him again at the end of this school year, to determine if he should return for the next academic year at the seminary. Any violation of these requirements would result in immediate expulsion."

Serving as faculty secretary for the past two years had shown me how easy it was for certain individuals to misinterpret the content of the recorded minutes of our faculty meetings, especially when those meetings provoked deep divisions and controversies. My approach was to write a transcript of the discussion so there could be no subsequent truth twisting.

Michael: "I have grave concerns about this student's lying and the situation in general. This man will not be a pastor. I discussed the situation during the past weekend with Dr. Nambala when I was in Oniipa. The church leaders want Mabuku sent away. Let me also remind the faculty that other students are watching."

Dr. van Wyk: "I have respect for what Rev. Bauer has said, but will keeping an alcoholic on campus not have a negative effect on discipline?"

Hanns: "The students already know about what is going on. They have helped him cover up his behavior. I think Mabuku must make a public acknowledgment of his actions, and the students must also be involved in his rehabilitation and become a part of the therapeutic process. I also agree with the process spelled out by Rev. Bauer. No mercy should be shown for any violation of steps he has suggested, and there must be a final evaluation. If the impression arises within the student body that we are weak, we have lost our position with the students."

Michael: "In the past, Paulinum simply suspended students for episodes of alcohol abuse. The faculty cannot tolerate this behavior."

Dr. van Wyk: "We are running a Seminary, not an institution for alcohol treatment. We should ask his church to send him for treatment at an appropriate facility. Our image is being damaged."

Michael: "Do you know that one day last week, at about six-thirty in the morning, I saw Mabuku walking away from the dormitory with a woman? And let me remind you that I had even confronted Mabuku last year about his drinking."

Lou: "Clearly, the Churches must be more careful in screening whom they send to us. The Churches are wasting money if they send us candidates who are unfit for ministry."

Dr. Shivute: "I am also concerned about the larger problem of student drivers who return to campus at about eleven or twelve o'clock at night. I think there is the likelihood of more extensive drinking among the student population than we are aware of. I wonder if there are other students who should also be attending Alcoholics Anonymous. As for Mabuku, he is fragile, both physically and emotionally. I wonder how he could cope as pastor in a congregation."

Rev. Amaambo: "I really do not see much hope for improvement for Mabuku, but I think his Church should assist him in getting treatment. You know, Mabuku has many problems, besides alcoholism."

Finally, in an attempt to move the discussion to some sort of resolution, Hanns said, "I see, at this point, two questions that should be answered. First, do we react immediately or at the end of the term? Second—and I think this is the more important question—how do we deal with him as a person? What kind of institution are we? If we dismiss him, is there any pastoral care available?" He leaned forward and looked into the eyes of each of his colleagues seated around the large conference table. "I feel a responsibility to Mabuku. Our way of dealing with these kinds of situations is sometimes delayed, and often we think we have only one weapon, to send them away. Doing so may encourage students to engage in cover-up behavior to protect their colleagues against the lecturers' council."

Michael shuffled through a file of papers in front of him and produced a letter the faculty had recently received from Metumo, asking to be allowed to return to Paulinum. He reminded the faculty that she had been dismissed for lying and he asked, "What is the difference?"

I paused in my note taking and answered Michael. "Wasn't Metumo expelled for stealing, not just for lying? Mabuku's primary problem is alcoholism, not lying. A common characteristic of an alcoholic is lying and manipulative behavior. These symptoms can be dealt with during treatment and rehabilitation."

Hanns spoke again and urged the faculty to grant Mabuku eight weeks to demonstrate a change in his behavior.

"I strongly disagree!" said Dr. van Wyk. "We should release him now. Get him off this campus. He is infecting the student body!"

Dr. Shivute wondered if Mabuku could receive outpatient treatment by staying with a Windhoek relative, rather than at Paulinum.

Lou told the faculty about a three-week, residential treatment program in Windhoek.

"I think we need more information," said Michael. I suggest we postpone our decision for now. In the meantime, I ask the Dean of Students to investigate this rehabilitation center and find out if Social Services will pay for this."

At the conclusion of the meeting, which had begun at three o'clock, Lou and I hurried back to our flat. Now it was almost seven o'clock, and I had a group of six seminarians' wives scheduled to arrive for their first small group meeting with me.

The next morning, I was at home typing up the minutes of the faculty meeting when I received a phone call from Michael. He asked me if there were a young woman staying in one of the empty rooms in our women's dormitory.

"Yes, Michael. She is a guest of Elvin Nowaseb." Elvin was the son of one of our older students. The family lived in a flat in the same building we did. "Elvin came to me last week and said the young woman was coming to Windhoek for business reasons and needed a place to stay. He asked me if she could rent a room at the seminary, and I agreed." I wondered why Michael sounded so angry. What had I done wrong? I often rented out vacant dormitory rooms to Windhoek visitors.

"How does this look to our students? Even if there is no immoral behavior going on, it doesn't look good, does it? What will the students think about our staff supporting such behavior?"

"I'm sorry, Michael. This had seemed to be a legitimate request. What would you like me to do?" My heart was thumping, and I felt my jaw tightening.

"I cannot tell you what to do," he replied.

I responded, "Of course you can. You're the principal."

"Oh, just drop it," he said.

In my anger and humiliation, I composed a letter to Michael tendering my resignation as accommodations manger: *It has been made clear to me that, in the opinion of the leadership of this seminary, I have exercised poor judgment in this position. It would be better, for all concerned, for the duties of accommodations manager to be carried out by someone who better understands the system.* I couldn't decide whether or not to give the letter to the faculty. The change in Michael's attitude and behavior toward both Lou and me in the past six months surprised and hurt us. Why had all the goodwill started unraveling? I had never had to swallow so much humiliation as I had these past six months. My tolerance was stretched to the breaking point. Why should I continue to work so hard when all it yielded was misunderstanding and ill will? I cancelled this week's session of the TOEFL class I'd started teaching in the evenings. This was the class that prepared foreign students to take the English qualifying examination for study at an American university. I knew what I was feeling wasn't the students' fault, but I just didn't feel like facing them. I told myself I would stop seeking opportunities to contribute. This would be difficult because volunteering had become so much a part of who I was and how I functioned. I tucked the letter in my desk drawer and decided to wait a few days before making a decision. I knew my emotional state was too volatile.

A few days later I had a consultation with a plastic surgeon about removing a mole from my face. Dr. Rohn had told me the mole looked suspicious, and he recommended a second opinion. The South African doctor said that he wanted to excise the mole and he wanted to do the procedure before returning to Johannesburg at the end of the week. He told me to schedule the outpatient surgery at the Roman Catholic Hospital. The surgeon said that the biopsy results should be available within a week. He said that although the mole was dark with ragged edges, he did not think it was a melanoma. However, if the biopsy proved otherwise, he assured me that he followed the latest international protocols for melanoma. I'd had moles removed from my face before, and I wasn't worried about this one, but if the biopsy turned out to be malignant, I felt certain I would be on the first available flight to North

Carolina.

Lou and I arrived at the hospital at five-thirty on Friday evening. This was one of two private hospitals in Windhoek, and was so much better maintained than the State hospitals to which we had taken our students. The floors were scrubbed and shiny. The corridors had a fresh, clean smell. After filling out the paperwork and paying a fifty-dollar deposit, we were shown to the "waiting area" that was just the hallway outside the operating room. All the chairs were taken, so Lou and I sat in two empty wheelchairs. A nursing sister told me that there were three other patients ahead of me, so we opened our books, prepared for a long wait.

I was surprised when, twenty minutes later, I was called into the surgical "theatre." The entire procedure lasted fifteen minutes. All I felt was the sting of the anesthetic injections. I returned to our flat with a bandage covering the stitches beneath my eye. The nurse had told me to return to the "casualty" department to have them removed in one week, by which time I would likely have the biopsy results, too.

Meanwhile, as requested, Lou investigated treatment options available for Mabuku. He took him to see one of his Namibian friends, Ludwig Beukes, a Namibian social worker who worked with alcoholics. After the consultation, Ludwig determined that Mabuku did not seem to require inpatient detox. He suggested that regular attendance at AA meetings, combined with counseling, would be a reasonable plan, and Ludwig offered to counsel Mabuku free of charge.

At seven o'clock on Monday morning, the day before the faculty meeting to determine Mabuku's fate, the phone rang in our flat. It was Mabuku. He asked for Lou. "I'm at the Caltex station. I'm going to the taxi stand so I can go to the hospital to see my cousin." Lou told him to return to the campus immediately. The previous night, Lou had searched the campus for Mabuku three times. He concluded that Mabuku had likely not spent the night on campus, and that he had been gone all weekend, in defiance of the order he'd been given only a week ago not to leave campus without permission.

Lou and I had little time to discuss this because we both had a full day of classes and we had to get ready for our dinner guest, Dr. Nambala, the treasurer of the Northern Church. Lou had invited him to Windhoek to speak to his Church Administration class about budgeting and stewardship. Until recently, donations from German and Finnish churches had provided the main source of income for both the Northern and Southern Lutheran Churches in Namibia. Now, facing a dramatic decline in donor church funding, Namibian congregations had to find new methods of income generation. Dr. Nambala had been working with about thirty churches in the North, teaching congregational pastors and lay leaders ways to improve their financial situations. His stewardship efforts and guidance about budgeting doubled, and often tripled, those churches' incomes. Dr. Nambala had studied for six years in the United States, obtaining two Masters degrees from Luther Seminary. He also had a Ph.D. in history. His cloak of self-confidence made him seem more imposing than he actually was.

In the kitchen, I finished washing and tearing lettuce for our salads. While our stew finished simmering, I brought us all some juice, cheese, and crackers and I asked him about his experiences and impressions of the United States.

"Initially, I was reluctant to go to America. This was in the seventies, during the time of our war for independence from South Africa. I considered America an enemy of our country because the United States refused to support Namibia's struggle for independence. Your country, under Ronald Reagan, denied us help because we were getting soldiers and guns from Cuba. Namibia was a small pawn in the Cold War struggles that were playing themselves out in African and other countries throughout the world."

"When I settled in Minnesota," continued Dr. Nambala, "I discovered that there were two Americas. One was the America of those Cold War politicians. The other was the America of the common people. The individuals I met on campus and in churches were warm and outgoing. When I told them about Namibia, they were supportive of our struggle for independence."

But he had harsh comments for the way America treated its poor. "When I was in New York City, I was shocked to see people sleeping in cardboard boxes at the foot of the United Nations building. When I was studying in Minnesota, I also served as an associate pastor of a congregation in Minneapolis. On winter nights, some of us would help out in the homeless shelter the church sponsored. What sort of super power is America that it cannot even take care of its poor people?"

Listening to Dr. Nambala's comments made me feel uneasy, but since he was being so honest with us, I risked telling him that it was taking us a long time to feel that we were trusted by some Namibian people. I was unprepared for his reply.

"Mrs. Bauer, I understand what you are saying, but I must remind you that it is enormously difficult for Namibians of my generation to trust a white person."

How naïve I had been. I thought about our friend Gerson who had been imprisoned by white South Africans in a kind of dungeon for two years. Our black Namibian friends and colleagues must have horrific memories they were too proud or polite to share with us.

Early the next morning, Dr. Shivute phoned to tell us that Michael Shangala's mother had died during the night, and that Michael was preparing to travel to the North for the funeral. After Tuesday morning's chapel service, the faculty all gathered informally in front of Michael's house to offer condolences to him and his family. Michael paused in the midst of loading his truck and told Lou that he wanted the faculty to carry on with its plan to meet that afternoon. "I want this Mabuku situation resolved," he said to Lou. This meant that Lou, the acting principal, would need to chair the meeting. Given what we had learned the previous day about Mabuku's wanderings, the resolution seemed foregone.

The four-hour faculty meeting did indeed result in Mabuku's expulsion. After the meeting, Dr. Shivute accompanied Lou to Mabuku's dormitory room to give him the news. Later, Lou and I could only speculate on some of the "what ifs" surrounding this situation. Primarily, what if the faculty, last week, had endorsed an immediate treatment approach for Mabuku and what if he'd been able to attend several more AA meetings before the faculty meeting? On the other hand, perhaps Mabuku had not "hit his bottom," as people in AA say.

We would probably never know what would become of him, especially since the Caprivi Strip, where Mabuku lived, was now the site of recent armed uprisings against the government. The rebels were threatening to secede from the country, claiming that the government in Windhoek was unresponsive to their needs. We remembered our brief visit there during the Christmas holiday, and recalled the poverty of the area. The newspaper had recently reported that the Caprivi had about ninety percent unemployment. Mabuku's vocational prospects were slim.

Mabuku's expulsion brought to five the number of students in the current student body who had been "sent away"—suspended or expelled—in the two years we had been teaching at the seminary. That was about ten percent of the student body! Two students had been dismissed for impregnating women, Nandi for an alleged abortion, Metumo for stealing and lying, and now Mabuku for alcohol abuse.

That evening, at the end of the vespers service, Lou announced

Mabuku's expulsion to the student body. He tried to make his remarks instructive, as well as pastoral, and concluded by saying:

The parable of the Good Samaritan warns us about the religious ones who passed by a brother who was suffering. The parable also reminds us, in the example of the third passerby, what it means to care for our brothers and sisters. Let us serve one another in true Christian charity and love when we come upon someone who is wounded. Let us learn, from Mabuku's woundedness, about the perils of alcohol. Let us pray for him and for all who suffer from the disease of alcoholism, that they may know God's healing. Let us be courageous and compassionate, making ourselves instruments of that healing.

Lou concluded the vespers service with a hymn we had taught the students, one that had become a favorite. The lyrics were from the Prayer of St. Francis: "Lord, make us instruments of Thy peace."

When I climbed into bed that night, I set the alarm clock an hour earlier than usual. If Nandi's swift departure from the seminary after her expulsion was any indicator, I didn't have much time. After drinking a quick cup of coffee, I opened the refrigerator, and took out margarine, fruit, and packets of cheese and sliced lunchmeat. I made three sandwiches, wrapped them in waxed paper, and put them in a plastic bag, along with two oranges, a bunch of grapes, and a one-liter box of apple juice. I added a half-empty bag of chocolate chip cookies.

Mabuku's suitcase was open on his bed, which had already been stripped, the sheets neatly folded on top of the pillow. He had nearly finished his packing—his open closet was empty—but his tattered brown suitcase looked only half full. On the desk were his English grammar book and the green hymnal we issued to all students when they arrived. He didn't seem surprised to see me. We both began speaking at once.

"I've brought you some food."

"I want to give you my English book and the hymnal."

He handed me the books, I put my plastic bag on the desk, and we exchanged weak smiles. "Mabuku, I'm so sorry things have turned out this way." The time for lectures and admonitions was past.

"It's all right, Meme. I think I always knew this wasn't the place for me."

"What will you do now?"

He sat down on the bed, and his voice grew so soft. "I don't know, really. I think my English is not so bad, and my Grade Twelve results were actually quite good. Perhaps I can become a teacher. Or maybe I'll work for my uncle in his shop."

I nodded, suddenly unable to speak.

"Meme, I want to thank you for what you have done for me. I do not deserve your kindness. I have disappointed you and Pastor Lou." His eyes filled with tears. Both eyes. I couldn't tell which was the artificial one. I grasped his hand.

"May God bless you, Mabuku. I will think of you often, and I will pray for you and your family." I squeezed his hand and left the room before he could see the tears spilling from my own eyes.

Chapter 17
Hot Flashes

*T*he unsettling events of the past few weeks had one salutary consequence. They put us back in touch with Hanns and Ute. After Michael went north to attend his mother's funeral and poor Mabuku packed his bags for home, we sat down in our living room with our German colleagues to talk about what had been going on. Their two little girls played quietly at our feet. I poured us glasses of cold fruit juice and opened a couple of bags of chips.

"There is no sense of a unified community here," I said. "I guess that's been the biggest disappointment for me. The students and faculty don't support each another, do they? They're continuously engaged in conflict of one sort or another. Tribal tensions, hostility toward whites, students' distrust of the faculty, the faculty's scorn of the students."

"I think this seminary is really just a reflection of what's happening in the two major Lutheran churches," added Lou.

"It's broader than that," said Hanns. "We are seeing what decades of apartheid have done to Namibia. Even though apartheid was squashed, there is an underlying feeling of despair within the society at large."

"There seems to be real rage underneath that despair," said Lou.

"Oh, yes. The anger is always close to the surface," added Ute. "Have you noticed how many of our students have had close family members who have been murdered? It's frightening."

Hanns's comments reminded me of something I'd heard from our friend, Angela. As if reading my mind, he continued, "Colonialism and apartheid have stripped the Namibian people of their cultural roots and identity. Perhaps to a much greater degree than has happened within other African countries. Factor in the poverty, high unemployment, an out-of-control AIDS infection rate, an inadequate educational system, and this inexperienced black government, and you have a brush-fire waiting to happen."

"I don't think we can ignore the rapid infusion of new technology, either," said Lou. "Everyone wants TV's, cell phones and computers, but few people can afford them. I guess it isn't hard to see how that level of frustration can lead to alcoholism and violence."

The sun was setting. I switched on our table lamps and invited the Lessings to remain for a soup-and-sandwich supper. Hanns and Ute had been in Namibia slightly longer than we had, and they seemed to have a lot of friends in both the Namibian and German communities. None of us had been—nor planned to be—lifelong, career missionaries. Even as we shared our frustrations, we all acknowledged how much we had come to care about our adopted country. I was glad we had other missionaries with whom we could discuss our experiences and feelings. It helped knowing we weren't alone.

The next day, Lou and I returned to the hospital where I had the stitches on my face removed. The surgeon had done a good job. I didn't think the scar would be very disfiguring. The biopsy results were negative for any type of skin cancer. Before returning to campus, we went grocery shopping at the large supermarket in Wernhill Mall. We found Lou a pair of reading glasses at an optical shop nearby and had lunch at our favorite outdoor café on Independence Avenue.

One Friday night, Karen, the Peace Corps volunteer we had known back in North Carolina, came to visit us. We hadn't seen each other since our chance encounter in Rundu, over a year ago. Her parents were arriving the next morning from the States, and she needed a place to sleep before going to the airport. We had no guest room, but we told her she was welcome to sleep on a mattress on our living room floor. Karen was a sweet, energetic young woman who, the last time we met, had been ebullient and funny when she told us tales of her teaching experiences in a junior secondary school in a remote village in eastern Namibia. I admired her compassion for her students. Tonight, though, she seemed unusually quiet. After dinner she confessed to us that she was cutting short her Peace Corps service by a few months, and planning to return home early. She told us about recent episodes of violence at her school. "Learners are throwing rocks at teachers, teachers are routinely beating learners, and the faculty and administration are unwilling, or unable, to deal with it." Her eyes filled with tears. "I'm just so discouraged."

The next morning at breakfast she said, "I just don't like the kind of person I've become. A couple of weeks ago, I realized that many of my learners were failing the tests I gave them. My Namibian colleagues told me it was because I am the only teacher who refuses to beat them. I finally got so frustrated that I told my students I would beat any student who failed the next test. Three failed, and I called in another teacher to administer the beatings. I just stood by and watched. I felt nothing. What has happened to me? I know beating students is wrong."

When Karen first went to her school, about a year and a half ago, she was appalled to find teachers who railed against the Ministry of Education's decision to abolish corporal punishment in the schools. Now we talked about how easy it was to become tangled in cultural webs we couldn't fully understand. "What surprises me," said Karen, "is how close to the surface the violence is. The rock throwings, the beatings. When I arrived in Namibia, I was happy to be coming to a country that seemed so stable compared to, say, the Congo or Angola. But now, I'm just not so sure." I recalled Ute's comment about the high murder rate, and I reminded Karen about the horrifying accounts of domestic violence that were reported in the newspapers or on the evening news with alarming regularity. The previous week, a man had thrown boiling water in his wife's face and a color photograph of the scarred, blinded woman had appeared on the front page of *The Namibian*. I wondered how our young friend would remember her months in Namibia several years hence. Would bitterness and regret forever color those memories?

Every evening after supper Lou and I watched the eight o'clock news on TV. On Mondays, this was followed by a live panel discussion called "Talk of the Nation." One Monday evening, a panel of young people from the University of Namibia debated the issue of condom use in Namibia. Their widely divergent viewpoints reflected what we had heard around the country, as well as here on campus. Some students said that promoting condom use encouraged promiscuity. This was the predominant viewpoint of the Namibian Lutheran churches. A young man from the studio audience asserted that the society simply needed to return to the African values of faithfulness and to forget about using condoms. Another articulate young girl retorted, "If you want to return to African values, then get rid of the television and the computer! The reality is that we are living in a different age. Twenty percent of our young people are HIV positive. Our people are dying!" Lou and I wondered when the churches and the seminary would get the message.

"I think there's another below-the-surface issue here," said Lou. "A society's behavior cannot be separated from its values. I think the real objection to the use of condoms has to do with the deeply ingrained value of fertility."

A few weeks later we were entertaining another dinner guest, Vernon, a prominent South African pastor who was in Windhoek to teach a course about urban ministry. Lou and Hanns had taken his course last year, and the three of them would be team teaching the course to a group of Windhoek pastors. We were just starting to eat our dessert when there was a knock at our door. It was Franzina, the wife of one of our students. Their family lived in our building, three doors down from us. She told me that her husband, Andreas, was helping with a family wedding. "A cow has been slaughtered, and I need your help." I began to worry. What could she want from me that had anything to do with a slaughtered cow? She explained that in the Nama culture, it is traditional for the bride's family and the groom's family to exchange meat from each other's animals. The cow from the bride's family was being stored in the seminary's walk-in refrigerator and the staff had gone home for the day. Members of the groom's family were here with part of their cow to make the exchange, and they needed my help since I was the custodian of the kitchen keys once the staff left the campus each evening.

I unlocked the fridge and we stepped inside. There on the lower shelf were two huge, hairy, brown and white cow legs—hooves still attached. Franzina's two teenaged children hauled the legs outside and loaded them into the back of the family pickup truck. They brought in several large plastic trash bags filled with meat and stashed them in the refrigerator. The bovine exchange was completed, and Franzina and I wiped the drops of blood from the floor. We hurried back to our apartment building. I'd crossed the driveway to the seminary kitchen without a coat or even a sweater, and now I noticed that the air had turned bitterly cold. A frigid arctic front had arrived from the south, and outside our flat the students' laundry on the clothesline was blowing straight out.

During the last week in September, Lou and I boarded a small South Africa Airways jet with our five other American missionary colleagues, people like ourselves who were working and teaching throughout Namibia, for a two-hour flight to Cape Town. Our national church in the United States had selected this stunning, coastal location as the site for our annual retreat. It was just what we needed: a weekend in which we would meet with our directors from Chicago, laugh, and commiserate with one another, offer support to those among us who were struggling, and receive guidance. As we began our descent to the Cape Peninsula, diamonds of sunlight sparkled on the snow-capped mountains. We piled ourselves and our luggage into the cars provided by our hosts for the short drive to the retreat center, surprised by how much colder Cape Town was than Windhoek and wishing we'd packed warmer clothes.

The flat-roofed church retreat center was gunmetal gray and, except for the bougainvilleas of crimson and lavender filling the tiny courtyard, it resembled a military barracks. Like most buildings in southern Africa, the cinderblock rooms in this center were unheated. At four o'clock, when we all gathered in the common room for tea, half of us were wearing capes, the thin brown blankets we had hauled off our beds, in our attempt to stay warm. Each missionary had time for private conferences with Benyam and Will, our supervisors from America. Benyam, our immediate supervisor, was a tall, slender man with a gentle voice who had been born and raised in Ethiopia. Will, Benyam's former teacher and mentor, was a large, jolly fellow who used to be a bishop. His passion for global mission and for the interests of vulnerable, marginalized people was well known throughout the national church. Lou and I shared with these good men the reports of our work and our lives during the past few months. Were we still on track? Did they think our presence really made any difference?

After they listened carefully to our account of the past year, Will stood up and gave each of us big bear hugs. "Wow! You two have really been through a lot! I'm not surprised you're feeling discouraged. But don't forget that developing trust relationships takes a long time. I've seen too many people give up too soon, just when they were on the verge of establishing deep friendships and doing extraordinarily good work. I have great confidence this will happen for you." I hoped he was right.

The next morning we all boarded the spacious double-decker passenger ferry, along with about one hundred other passengers, for the thirty-minute trip to Robben Island. The sea was churning, but only one of us was seasick. (I was glad it wasn't me.) This mostly barren island of scrub growth and meandering, sandy trails leading nowhere had been, for almost four hundred years, a dumping ground for mentally disabled people, leprosy sufferers, convicts and others exiled for political reasons from the mainland of South Africa. These days, Robben Island was a very different place. Now there were even small farm plots here, and I remembered reading somewhere that ecologists were concerned that tilling the land would destroy this fragile ecology that supported a wide variety of endangered bird populations, including cormorants, herons and penguins. What a sad irony: human freedom equaled ornithological disaster. Inside the damp, stone walls of the prison we saw the cramped cell where Nelson Mandela had been incarcerated during the anti-apartheid struggle. Someone asked our tour guide, a former political prisoner who had been held here during the apartheid years, how he could stand to come back. He answered in a soft voice, "We must remember."

On our last evening in Cape Town, we were all huddled together in the frosty common room of the retreat center. By now, we were *all* wearing brown blankets. Big plastic buckets of fragrant hot popcorn were on the coffee table. Some of us sipped mugs of hot cocoa. Others had glasses of fruity South African cabernet sauvignon. Present at our retreat was Phillip Knutson, an American Lutheran pastor married to a South African, Lou-Marie, the daughter of a white pastor who had served a black congregation in the tinderbox of Sharpeville during the infamous massacre in 1960 when, it is reported, the South African police shot over sixty black people. Some say that event sparked the overthrow of white rule in the country. Phil was the son of lifetime American Lutheran missionaries in South Africa, and he considered himself more South African than American. He was a tall, slender, gentle man with sad gray eyes and a neatly trimmed beard. When I had first met Phil two years ago at our retreat in Namibia, I had two impressions. First, this was a man who would always tell you the truth. Second, here was a person who would never intentionally harm any other living being. He told us stories about the large Lutheran missionary retreats his family used to attend in the 1950s and 1960s. He and his wife remembered that in years past those retreats tended to be occasions when the white missionaries essentially set the agenda for their black colleagues. Lou-Marie said she remembered them as times for gossip! Phil said that at a recent conference he'd attended, one of his black clergy colleagues said, in exasperation, "Why don't all you white missionaries just go home and let us work things out for ourselves?" I remembered a recent comment of my husband's: "Many don't want our help. Sometimes our help is only propping things up, when failure or collapse might be the ashes and ruins out of which an African phoenix might take wing and rise."

One evening, soon after we returned to Windhoek, Jonah came to our flat wearing his favorite pink shirt. Jonah was now a third-year student at the seminary. He lowered his lanky frame onto our sofa, his back ramrod straight. Like some of his colleagues, he had begun referring to us as his parents.

"My mother and father, I have this trouble with my eyes. They pain me and I cannot do my assignments." Oh, no! Not another Mabuku.

"Jonah, I want you to visit the eye doctor at Katutura Hospital," Lou said. "Come back and tell me what the doctor says." Since Namibia's state-sponsored medical system was relatively inexpensive for its citizens, this was always the first-line treatment option.

Jonah returned a few days later and showed us his medical card. The doctor had written: "Patient needs surgery."

Surgery? How competent was this physician? Lou took Jonah to a private ophthalmologist who explained to Jonah that he had a pterygium. He said this was common in Namibia where people toil long hours in the glaring sunlight. Scar tissue begins to grow into the eye to protect it from the brightness. Jonah was at risk of losing his eyesight. Surgery was scheduled for the week after final exams.

At about this time, I began tutoring Ndiku Nakamhela. Ndiku, a slender woman in her mid-forties who always wore colorful African dresses and headscarves, was the wife of our newest faculty member, Ngno, and she had asked me if I'd give her English lessons. She came to our flat every Wednesday afternoon. What a charming new acquaintance she was—bright, eager to learn, and passionate about her volunteer work with abused women and children. One afternoon, after working on pronunciation, we began talking about funeral practices. Ndiku said she had accompanied Ngno when he went abroad to study for advanced degrees in Germany and Holland in the 1980s. When they returned to Namibia, Ngno became a parish pastor.

One day Ndiku learned that the president of the women's group was dying. "I was told that, as the pastor's wife, I was expected to keep vigil at the bedside of dying parishioners, especially when it was someone important, like this lady. I was scared, but the vice-president of the group said to watch her and do what she did. She told me to sit on one side of the dying lady's bed, and she sat across from me on the other side. For a number of hours, that lady, the vice-president, only talked with her eyes." After the woman had passed away, it was the task of those women in the house to wash the body and prepare it for viewing. The women took turns staying in the home for nearly a week. The family was never alone. The night before the funeral everyone came to pay their respects. They sang hymns all through the night.

Ndiku asked me about funeral practices in the United States. At several points, she stopped me and said, "And are the friends involved, too?" She meant at the funeral home, during the funeral itself, and with the family at home after the burial. I assured her that they were, but that they may not have stayed there every hour of every day. She said that while she was in Germany, she was shocked to discover that sometimes only the immediate family attended a funeral. "One of my African friends went to a German funeral. An old woman had died and my friend said that she and the old lady's son were the only ones there!"

Now that we were in exam period, I was counting the days until our two-month home leave. The anticipation of being back on our native soil helped me put the seminary's problems in better perspective. Or maybe I was in a sort of denial. I felt almost jubilant the day I picked up our airline tickets from our favorite travel agent at Trip Travel. I looked forward to savoring English muffins, using an oven that measured temperature in Fahrenheit, losing myself in a Barnes and Noble bookstore, driving on the right side of the road, replenishing my supply of underwear.

We would arrive in North Carolina on Halloween, spend a few days with our daughter, and rent a car. Home would be the cottage we had built in 1990 in the Blue Ridge Mountains. Our little two-story house, perched atop a hill in Fancy Gap, Virginia, had been designed for short weekend and summer retreats from our busy working lives. We had never imagined that it would, one day, be our only home in America. We had never installed a washer and dryer, but otherwise the house was adequately, if sparsely, furnished, and would be a comfortable place to relax in between traveling to our various speaking engagements, our visits to doctors and the dentist for routine examinations (for all the time we lived in Africa, I could never muster enough courage to schedule an examination with an African dentist), and our trip to Denver where our extended family would be gathering for Christmas. We were more fortunate than most of our missionary colleagues who, when they returned on home leave, were obliged to stay with relatives or in student housing on a Lutheran college campus in Minneapolis.

When they'd completed their exams, the students came to our flat to return their keys to me and to say good-by before they left for their summer holiday. One of these was Jomo Araeb, a short, jolly second-year student. He enjoyed telling us stories about the problems his family had with elephants attacking the family farm and tearing up all their crops, and Jomo said, "When I'd look out the window and see them approaching the house, I'd hide under the bed."

Jomo had told us that his mother was a spiritual healer who also had the gift of prophecy, and we invited him to bring his parents to our flat when they came to Windhoek to pick him up. His stepfather and mother spent about half an hour with us, long enough for a cup of tea and a little conversation. His stepfather spoke very little. I had the feeling he was a bit embarrassed by his broken English. Jomo's mother, a large, buxom woman with a generous smile and penetrating eyes, was much more gregarious. She said she was honored to meet Jomo's American lecturers and she hoped her son was a good student for us. Lou told them that next year he would be teaching Jomo in his Pastoral Counseling class. Mrs. Araeb looked intently at Lou and then turned to her son, "Listen to this man carefully. He has *The Power*!"

Lou caught my eye and smirked.

When his friends left the seminary for their three-month summer holiday, Jonah entered Katutura Hospital. The operation was successful, and he returned to campus the following day. Because the dining hall was closed, we told Jonah he should come to our flat each evening for dinner.

Namibians of Jonah's tribe were accustomed to simple fare. Their staple food was *oshifima*, a porridge made from millet. If the rains were sufficient, they would grow spinach, tomatoes, and groundnuts. For festive events, they might kill a goat or slaughter a cow. During the two weeks that he was our dinner guest, Jonah sampled pork chops and mashed potatoes, spaghetti, and meatloaf. One day I found Casa Fiesta Taco Dinners at the grocery store, and Jonah discovered that tacos were his new favorite food. He ate four of them.

Hoping that Jonah was feeling more comfortable with us, I risked teasing him a little. "Jonah, I see that many of your colleagues are becoming engaged. Is there some special lady in your life that you aren't telling us about?"

His face became serious, and I feared I had made a cultural blunder.

"Meme, Susan, it is not the right time for me to think about marriage."

"Why not?"

"You see, I still have a year to finish my studies and then I must do my six-month practicum. I must not be distracted by a marriage."

At the end of the two weeks, I bought him a pair of sunglasses and Lou gave him a few Namibian dollars for his nine-hour bus journey home.

I was relieved when Jonah left. His neediness had wearied me, and I was exhausted. I craved some time and space alone.

One more week, and I'd be luxuriating in the crisp clear autumn mornings in Virginia. This summer in Namibia felt hotter than our two previous summers in Windhoek. I couldn't seem to stop sweating, and would wake up drenched in the middle of the night. The little fans we had in every room simply swooshed hot waves around the flat. Heat oozed from the walls. I would ask my doctor if he thought I was entering menopause.

Lou had taken our suitcases down from the top of the clothes cupboards, and I was folding woolen skirts and sweaters when Michael phoned.

"I thought you and Lou would want to know that Dr. van Wyk in hospital. It seems that he has had a stroke."

When Lou and I visited the patient at the Roman Catholic Hospital, I was surprised how frail he appeared. Dr. van Wyk had always taken such care with his appearance. The thin, trimmed mustache, the slicked-down hair, the knife-creased trousers. Seeing him lying in bed looking disheveled, his speech slightly slurred, I wondered how such a diminutive being could have persecuted and tyrannized so many people. He grasped our hands and his mouth twisted into a lopsided smile. "Thank you for coming to see me," he said. "You are the only ones from Paulinum who have come."

Before we left his room, Lou said a prayer.

On the drive home we wondered if this stroke would force him to retire, and we imagined what a different place the seminary would be without him.

Chapter 18
Back to Work

*N*ews reports in the final months of 1999 were filled with predictions of the Y2K calamities that were poised to happen at the turn of the century. Especially troubling were the unsettling scenarios about how this centennial wedge would impact underdeveloped countries. The two that concerned us the most were the breakdown of air traffic control systems and the dysfunction of ATM machines. We changed our travel plans and flew back to Windhoek directly from our family gathering in Denver on December 28, a journey of forty-one hours.

The next day, I went to the bank and arranged for a hefty cash advance on my Visa debit card. We would carefully hide the currency in our flat. The local news media began to suggest that Namibians might experience disruptions in their telephone, electrical, and water service. I started filling up buckets and jugs of water.

At midnight on New Year's Eve, fireworks exploded throughout the neighborhood, which of course set all the guard dogs to barking. Since Namibia entered the new century seven hours before the big ball descended in Times Square, we woke up the next morning, switched on the television, and watched the new century arrive in the United States. Nothing awful happened in either country. Our electricity, telephone, water and computer still functioned. So did the ATM machines downtown.

Our Namibian colleagues brought us up to date on events that had occurred during our two-month absence, and I was reminded that I was reentering a system that continually struggled to order itself in the midst of chaos, no matter which century we were in. The seminary's chief maintenance worker was supposed to have returned on December 17, but no one had seen him, or knew where he was. A large international Lutheran conference was scheduled to take place here in two weeks, but no one had informed the bishop whose church was supposed to be making the arrangements. Dirk, our former colleague who had been ordered to leave, had never returned the keys to his campus house, for which I had a paying tenant waiting. A new faculty colleague announced that he had changed his mind and would be accepting employment in the private sector. Classes would start in four weeks—who would teach his courses? Lou and I reminded each other to corral the coping mechanisms we would need, chief of which was a sense of humor. We also decided to join a new health club that had opened downtown. For a mere thirty dollars a month for both of us, Lou and I had access to modern Nautilus equipment, squash courts, an Olympic-sized swimming pool, saunas, and whirlpools. The club's clientele included all races. Most seemed to be young professionals. Our friends in America would have been astonished to see such a facility in the heart of Africa.

Jonah arrived several weeks before the rest of the students for a follow-up ophthalmology procedure. He brought me a rust-colored clay pot with intricate patterns carved onto its surface, plus a large basket with handles and a lid.

"Meme Susan, my mother made these for you. She thanks you for helping me."

Most Ovambo women make baskets from reeds and grasses on their homesteads, but this basket, cream-colored with darker grasses tightly woven into the design, was one of the most elegant I had seen. Jonah had ridden nine hours with these precious gifts on his lap.

"My mother said since you are my parents in Windhoek, I must listen to you. She said she will always remember what you have done for her son."

I knew I had just been given a piece of her motherhood, as surely as she had woven dark grasses into the cream-colored ones.

In mid-January, I harvested my pineapple crop—one smallish pineapple. The previous January, I had planted a pineapple top in a pot on our deck. All I wanted was something cheap and green. To my surprise, it just kept on growing, and I kept transplanting it to larger and larger pots. When we were getting ready to leave for the United States, I noticed a new development in the center of the plant—tiny purple flowers. When those faded, a pineapple started growing. Franzina, whose family would be staying on campus for the holidays, had said she'd water my plants while we were gone. We savored every sweet, luscious bite, and shared a few pieces with Franzina's family, too. I wasn't at all discouraged by the fact that a large, juicy pineapple from South Africa could be purchased from the grocery store here for fifty cents.

When I went for a walk early the next morning, I passed by many black women walking from the bus stop to their jobs as domestic workers in this affluent neighborhood. Those women, who lacked the benefit of education, worked long arduous hours for white families, and returned home in the evening to care for their own families. I could probably have seen a similar scene in any good-sized American city. I tried to greet them, but the women averted their eyes as I passed them on the sidewalk, and I felt self-conscious of my skin color and embarrassed by my status. And then there were the throngs of unemployed young men. Each morning, they stood, hopeful and alert, alongside the main roads in Windhoek, hoping that someone would pick them up for a day's manual labor. By noon, those who remained were slumped against the trees or sleeping by the curb. I knew our seminary had, just that week, employed two of those fellows to dig up thorny weeds on our campus that grew in profusion during the rainy season. It was backbreaking work in the hot sun, but it gave those men a few dollars.

In Namibia, many husbands and wives had jobs in separate parts of the country. If a woman had a job as a teacher in the rural north and her husband located work in Windhoek, the wife would usually have to remain behind because highly prized teaching positions in the capitol city had long waiting lists. Since most families did not have cars, the husband or wife had to travel long hours on a bus or try to hitchhike to be reunited during the public-school holidays.

That afternoon, Lou and I attended what our embassy called a "town meeting" for American expatriates. The situation in the Kavango Region had turned ugly, and the thirty-three-year civil war in Angola had spilled over into Namibia. Angola's UNITA rebels, led by Jonas Savimbi, had been fighting the Angolan government army, also known as the Popular Movement for the Liberation of Angola (*Movimento Popular de Libertação de Angola*) or MPLA. Villagers in Namibia were in danger because the Namibian government had granted the MPLA permission to establish a base south of Rundu, and the MPLA was firing mortars from that base into the UNITA-held villages on the other side of the river. I worried about our former student, Paul Muha, whose house was on the bank of the Kavango River over which those death-givers were flying.

Although we had arrived fifteen minutes early, the embassy's small common room was already packed, and workers were bringing in more folding chairs. I looked around and recognized a few American expats as well as some Europeans and Namibians we knew. The embassy's Regional Security Officer told us the Peace Corps had removed all its volunteers from the Kavango Region, and the Namibian government was urging tourists to stay away. We learned that people in rural villages were afraid to sleep in their homes at night so they slept in the bush.

That evening I phoned Paul. I knew there was a public telephone near the village of Mupini, and I hoped someone would be close enough to answer it. I was in luck. Although the woman who answered the phone did not speak English, she fetched Paul when she heard me mention the name, "Pastor Muha."

"My family is still safe," he said. "No one in Mupini has been injured."

"How is the work going?"

"Oh, it's going very well. On the day after Christmas I baptized one hundred and twenty people in a five-hour service."

Meanwhile, Lou and I finished our course preparations and spent many long hours getting ready for the international conference that would take place on campus the following week. Lou repaired showers and toilets and broken cupboards in the students' dormitories. He and Michael painted rooms in the several vacant flats in our building. Conference guests from European, Asian and African countries began arriving the next day. One gentleman from the Congo told us that he had lost the key to his suitcase lock, so Lou located a hacksaw and cut off the lock. Despite all my preparations, each day brought surprises. One morning I had to go to town to buy eleven blankets and five towels; another time it was cases of mineral water. Every time I would return to our flat and start working on my lesson plans, there would be a knock on the door or a phone call from someone needing something.

While our campus guests were busy with their conference activities, we faculty members had our own tasks. We set the course curriculum, established the daily class timetable, and planned the program for the first-year students' orientation. Dr. van Wyk wasn't present, but he had sent word to Michael that his doctor had placed him on a one-month medical leave while he continued to recover from his stroke. The faculty worked out temporary arrangements to cover his teaching responsibilities. It no longer felt strange to me to be doing these things just a week before the students arrived on campus. Planning my own English classes was so much easier for me since now I could draw upon previous years' plans.

Meanwhile, the forty conference guests on campus were giving me fits. One of the German organizers told me that my responsibilities included providing medical care for the guests. (*What?*) My first two cases were easy—colds. I gave them free sample packets of Aleve that someone had left with us. I couldn't quite imagine how this would help, except for fevers and aches, but the two gentlemen assured me that they felt much better the next day.

That evening one of the organizers told me that the Indonesian lady staying in room E-11 was sick and needed some noodles. When I went to see her, she said that her neck glands were sore, she had a headache and fever, and that she had been vomiting. Definitely outside my range of medical expertise. She also said she was hungry and would like some ramen noodles. It was Sunday night and most shops were closed, but I managed to find a small convenience store next to a petrol station that was open and they had two flavors: cheese and curry. I bought one of each, and returned to her room to ask her which she preferred. She said she wanted the curry flavor. I hurried back to our flat to cook the noodles (our kitchen staff had already gone home for the evening.) When I returned with her bowl of hot noodles, I asked her if she had any medicine for her sickness, and she said that a doctor had given her some powder. I read the label—barium citrate, a medication I'd never heard of—and assumed that she had first become ill before leaving Indonesia and that this is what her doctor had given her.

The following morning, I was telling Hanns about her, and he said, "Oh, I took her to the doctor on Saturday. She has mumps, and there is no medication he could really give her, other than barium citrate."

Early Tuesday morning, about six-thirty, I was in my nightgown, sitting at the computer in our little office reading the news on the Internet, when the phone rang. It was Sophie, our kitchen supervisor.

"Didn't Matheus ask you to buy bread yesterday?"

"No."

"Our guests are coming at seven o'clock for breakfast and we have no bread."

I dressed quickly, and Lou and I ran down the steps to parking lot. We drove to one market after another. All were closed. At the third store, the guard posted outside the locked door told us the market would open at seven o'clock. We waited for ten minutes, bought the bread, and had it back to the kitchen by seven-fifteen.

Lou returned to the flat for a quick cup of coffee before taking Jonah to the doctor for his follow-up appointment. I remained in the dining hall talking with Sophie and was approached by the German conference leader, a severe, skinny young man, marching toward us. He was frowning and waving his arms around. "Madame, there are problems!"

He began ticking off his concerns on his fingers. Somehow, I knew he'd do that. "There is no hot water in my house. Everyone needs more bottled mineral water. The guests want clean towels and sheets."

"Dieter, we have solar-heated water and you must let the water in your house run a few minutes before you get hot water. I will get more mineral water for drinking. We don't have any extra towels or sheets. If your guests want clean towels, they will have to bring their towels to the dining hall at breakfast time and our staff will wash them. Then they can collect their towels from the staff in the afternoon." Sophie asked him if clean sheets were really necessary because our lady who does sheets wouldn't be here until tomorrow, and it is a big deal because she irons all the sheets. He wasn't very happy with our answers, and I reminded myself that this was his first African conference. Behind his back, Sophie and I rolled our eyes at each other.

Last Saturday, Lou, Sophie and I had purchased every case of bottled water available at the warehouse from which the seminary bought its food. This morning, I was back on the road, buying out the stock of two other shops, and placing an order for four more cases that I would pick up tomorrow morning. Windhoek tap water is perfectly safe to drink, but the Germans and the Asian guests wouldn't drink it. When some of the guests began asking for water "with gas" (carbonated), I made an executive decision that they would have to suffer with un-gassed water.

As tiring as my tasks were, I knew that Matheus's extra responsibilities were worse than mine. Each morning, our treasurer awakened at three o'clock and drove to the outlying neighborhoods to collect our workers so that they could be on campus in plenty of time to have breakfast ready for the guests. His trip took about an hour. Of course, he had to do this in reverse in the evening when the kitchen workers finished washing the dinner dishes, a task they did by hand because the seminary couldn't afford dishwashers. When the conference ended, the organizers told me they were going to pay each worker and each of our five student stewards (who had returned to school two weeks early to help) a bonus of what amounted to fifty American dollars, an enormous sum for those Namibians, but they deserved and had earned every penny.

The semester was becoming busier than I had anticipated. The thirty students in my first-year English class were a delight. Bright and eager. But the third-year students, who had to take English because their language skills were so weak, were a real challenge. They were already falling asleep in class. I would need to find ways to challenge them.

One morning Lou and I drove to the airport to pick up a new missionary colleague. Angie was a young African-American woman who would work as the administrative assistant to the bishop, a two-year contract position that had previously been filled by our dear friend Pamela. Angie was a spirited young woman of twenty-one, and we looked forward to having her nearby.

About two months into the semester, Lou took one of our favorite third-year students, Josephina, to an orthopaedic specialist. Phina, as she preferred to be called, had been experiencing severe back pain ever since she returned to campus for the start of the school year, and the doctors at Katutura Hospital could not help her. The doctor tentatively diagnosed a disc problem and scheduled a CAT scan. Perhaps the less qualified doctors at the State hospital had missed the diagnosis because they were looking at the wrong thing. They had told her that the problem was an old leg injury. Phina's leg had been mangled in a bomb blast in 1980 during Namibia's war for independence. The bomb had killed two of her sisters. The explosion left a nasty scar, a deep hole, in Phina's leg, but she told us she had not experienced pain from the wound for many years.

Meanwhile, we were beginning to wonder if the year's rainy season would ever end. Normally, the rains ceased by the end of February and the millet crops began to grow. Now it was the end of March, and the rain showed no sign of stopping. The tender shoots of grain were beginning to rot in the fields. Goats tumbled into the rivers and drowned. We heard stories of people in the squatter camps on the edge of the city. Their tin-roofed shacks had collapsed. We saw them on TV, knee deep in mud, carrying their few possessions to higher ground. Sewage overflowed the culverts.

On campus, rain flooded the classrooms and the first-floor dormitory rooms. Awakened by the sound of rushing water in the middle of the night, our students grabbed their clothes and their books and scrambled to join their friends on the second floor. Rain pummeled the block of flats where we lived. We turned on our TV at eight o'clock to watch the evening news. The road to the airport was flooded, said the reporter. The camera panned to film footage of a river in town, not far from our campus. It was the riverbed that was usually nothing more than a passive collector of plastic bags, soda cans and broken beer bottles. Sludgy water seethed and surged over the banks. Suddenly, we saw a woman's head bobbing up and down and a frantically waving arm. Farther and farther down the river she coursed, past shops and apartments, and under a bridge. Horrified, we watched as the angry river swallowed her. "Why was the cameraman filming her, and not saving her?" we asked each other.

The following week we sadly bade farewell to our gentle colleague, Tomas Shivute. In 1995, when we had made our first visit to Namibia, Tomas had been one of the first to welcome us to Paulinum. Several months ago, Dr. Shivute had been selected to be the bishop of the Northern Church, and was leaving Windhoek to take up his new duties.

Angie, our new missionary colleague, phoned us one evening to tell us that someone had broken into her guest flat on the grounds of the Southern Church complex in Windhoek—the same place Lou and I had stayed when we first came to Namibia—and had stolen her money and her Visa debit card. She was scared and angry. Fortunately, the next afternoon she moved into her own flat, which was in a slightly (but not much) safer part of town. Thefts and break-ins were ongoing problems in Windhoek, which is why those who could afford to do so lived in houses protected by six-foot high walls, guard dogs or security systems. It was the reason our seminary had installed an electrified fence around the perimeter of the campus last year.

The weekend after we returned to Windhoek from Bishop Shivute's consecration (Matheus kept calling it a "coronation"), fifty theologians from all over the country arrived on campus for their three-day CCN (Council of Churches in Namibia) Theologians' Symposium. Since I now seemed to be the seminary's conference manager, I was in charge of making sure that everything was set up properly. Normally, that wouldn't be a problem because I'd tell Sophie or the workers how to set up the rooms. But the previous day, which also happened to be Namibia's tenth Independence Day, I learned that all our male maintenance workers had taken the holiday off. Paulinum did not have very adequate conference facilities. There was no large meeting hall, so whenever we hosted conferences it was a big job to haul desks and tables out of storage, clean them off, and arrange them in our chapel which had free-standing seating. I asked Sophie if she could try to find some students to help.

By lunchtime, Sophie still hadn't found anyone to set up the conference room/chapel and I really began to fret. Suddenly, all my careful planning was unraveling. I was torn between a desire to allow everything to fall apart—to "teach them a lesson"—and the fear that if this became a total screw-up I would be blamed for mismanagement by both Paulinum and the theologians. I became angrier when I realized that while the task of managing conferences had more or less fallen in my lap, it was not my responsibility to supervise Paulinum's custodians and workers. I decided to wait until about 5:00 p.m. before asking Michael what he planned to do about setting up the chapel. As a follow up, I was mentally preparing an agenda item for the next faculty meeting about roles and responsibilities.

At two o'clock, Matias, one of our first-year students phoned our flat. "Mrs. Bauer, we are ready to move the desks into the chapel. Can you come over and show us how they should be arranged?" Matias had engaged the assistance of about eight other students, and an hour later they had arranged fifty desks and chairs in the chapel. I wondered if I would ever get used to the "African way"—that things somehow had a way of working out.

Meanwhile, the rain continued. I heard on the news that in some parts of Namibia, the rain was the heaviest it had been in twenty years. My students told me they were seeing varieties of insects and other creepy-crawly things they had never seen before. One morning, outside the dining hall, our workers were exclaiming about a seven-inch-long slug. It looked like a big cigar with antennae.

Shortly after the theologians' conference ended, a woman from the United Nations' AIDS Office phoned me looking for a three-week accommodation for a woman who was coming here from Ethiopia. We had a flat that had been formerly occupied by students, but which lacked the amenities of the other flats we rented to guests. Because the income from such a paying guest would be substantial, I hustled to get permission from our treasurer to buy a small refrigerator, hotplate, electric jug, utensils, and dishes to make this a self-catering flat. I rushed out to buy these things Thursday morning before my English class. The refrigerator was delivered Thursday afternoon. I expected the lady to arrive on Thursday afternoon, too. She never appeared. When I phoned UN-AIDS the next morning, the office manager was puzzled, but she assured me the Ethiopian woman was still coming, and they'd just learned that her husband would be with her. I asked our staff to make up another bed. The couple never arrived.

I was growing weary and was already looking forward to the upcoming term holiday. Our friends George and Nancy would be visiting us for the entire month of May, and would accompany us on a camping trip to a remote part of the country we hadn't yet seen.

With the return of cooler weather, I could turn on the oven without overheating our flat, so I decided to bake cookies. I was still wearing the apron I had sewn from colorful African fabric when I walked over to the office to collect our mail. Michael saw me and said, "Oh, I would like one of those aprons!" He did a lot of the cooking in his household since his wife was a nursing student at the University. I told him I would sew one for him, and ended up making aprons for all seven members of our kitchen staff, too.

During the semester I had acquired some more piano students. None of the five students could read music, so we began with the first John Thompson book. The only piano on campus was the one in the chapel, and I told the students they ought to try to practice several times between our weekly lessons. Only one of them ever did—Morekwa, our student from Botswana.

At our last faculty meeting of the semester, I was telling my colleagues about the various conferences we'd had here and how my little job of accommodations manager had turned into the much bigger job of conference manager. Before I realized what I was saying, I was telling the faculty that I wanted to resign this position by the end of the year. I had not planned to say so. Lou, sitting at the other end of the table, raised his eyebrows and grinned at me.

Chapter 19
Himbaland

George and Nancy arrived from the States just before Easter weekend. George was a large, happy bear of a fellow whose good-natured wonder at all things African—it could be a small herd of springboks leaping across a plain or the tarpaper squatter settlements on the edge of town—often burst forth in exclamations of "Amazing!" and "Would you look at that!" We'd had more than a few American visitors, but none matched George for enthusiasm. In the 1970s Lou and George had both trained in Washington, D.C. at St. Elizabeths Hospital which was home to the National Institute for Mental Health. In the 1940s, the St. Elizabeths complex occupied three hundred acres and provided care for seven thousand resident patients. The hospital offered the most extensive and acclaimed program in the country for training chaplains to work with psychiatric patients. Whereas my husband had returned to parish ministry after completing an internship and residency at St. Elizabeths, George had become a chaplain supervisor and now he directed a highly successful chaplaincy training program at a major American university's medical school. He was one of the most perceptive people I'd ever met. Nancy, a psychiatric nurse, was as petite and soft spoken as her husband was large and gregarious. We looked forward to a grand month with them.

On Easter morning, after attending church downtown, our friends happily joined us in our now customary Easter Bunny routine. George had brought with him T-shirts and caps from the university where he worked, and these were distributed to the students, along with the colored eggs and candy. The next day, Lou invited George to accompany him to the Katutura Hospital where Josephina was recovering from back surgery. They were surprised to find her sitting quietly on the side of her bed, suitcase packed, waiting for someone to take her to the seminary. Lou hadn't known she'd been discharged. They gingerly placed her in the back seat of the Venture and brought her back to the campus. She was reluctant to move from her bed, but Lou enlisted a few of Phina's girlfriends to help her to take a few steps each day.

Then it was time to turn our attention to our upcoming camping trip.

Our guide would again be our friend Lutz, the same man who, two years ago, had taken us and our children camping in the desert. We met Lutz at his home in Walvis Bay, where we loaded our gear into his dilapidated green Mazda 4X4. I heard George whisper to Lou, "Do you think this vehicle is going to hold up for the next two weeks?" Our drive through the veld again revealed to us how much rain had fallen during the past months. One could easily imagine lions stalking through the thick, lush grass. It was nearly sunset when we reached our destination, the Hobatere Lodge, located in a vast expanse of land kept as a game reserve by the owners. Lutz told us we should savor our last night in a real bed and our hot showers. The next morning he introduced us to his friend, Ulf, who would be driving the second vehicle, his Land Cruiser. Like Lutz, Ulf was also a third-generation Namibian. His family owned a farm in Otjiwarango, and Ulf also owned a clothing shop in Walvis Bay that was started by his father and still bore his name, Harry Schaefer's Clothing. Ulf was as quiet as Lutz was gregarious, but we soon came to appreciate his droll humor and the way he became the straight man for Lutz's jokes.

After we'd been on the road a few hours, Lou and I with Ulf in his Land Cruiser and George and Nancy ahead with Lutz in the Mazda, we saw Lutz stick his arm out the window and motion for us to pull over by the side of the road. A jet plane had just roared overhead and Lutz shouted, "It's Boeing Time!" He said the large, international jets that fly over Namibia from South Africa always seem to pass overhead at eleven o'clock in the morning. He and his cronies had dubbed this phenomenon *Boeing Time*—time for a beer.

Our first day's journey was eight hours, the last two through rocky mountainous terrain, the road little more than a corrugated wagon trail. Our destination was a campsite on the Kunene River, the northwest border between Namibia and Angola. We passed through Damaraland and into Kaokoland. The South African government had originally established these districts as tribal homelands and restricted travel from one district to another as a means of preventing an alignment among the tribes that could threaten South African governance. At the time of Independence in 1990, geographic regions replaced the districts. Although now, in a free Namibia, people are able to move about from one region to another, these areas still tend to designate territorial dwelling places of the various ethnic groups in the country. Kaokoland, a vast territory covering fifty thousand square kilometers, is home to the Ovahimba people. Although the majority of the Himba live in rural areas, their main town is Opuwa. In fact, Opuwa is the *only* town in the entire region. Here the traveler can stock up on fresh bread, cool drinks, and petrol.

Professor J. S. Malan, Chair of the Department of Anthropology in South Africa's University of the North, conducted his doctoral research among the Himba in northern Namibia. He writes:

The Himba are actually a dispersed remnant of the Herero tribe that first crossed into Namibia from Angola in the middle of the sixteenth century. The majority of the Herero proceeded farther south, where they settled as pastoralists and ranchers. They left behind a section of the tribe that later came to be known as the Himba. Cattle raids from other tribes forced the Himba people into a hunter-gatherer way of life. Today, the Himba still highly value their cattle, but also tend to roam from place to place in search of good grazing land. They are among the least developed of the Namibian tribal groups. Occupying such a geographically isolated region of the country, the Himba eschew modern practice—commerce, education, political systems. Their religion (ancestors are highly honored), social structure and clothing have not changed much in hundreds of years...The natural conservatism of the people, together with the geographic isolation and marginal ecology of their habitation, has contributed greatly towards restricting the diffusion of European culture to them. (Peoples of Namibia, Rhino Publishers, Pretoria, 1995, p. 85)

The Himba women are popularly featured on postcards of Namibia. Always bare-breasted, they cover their bodies with a mixture of red ochre and animal fat to protect their skin from the harsh climate. They are tall with finely chiseled features, and both men and women adorn themselves with distinctive jewelry made from leather, shells, and copper. A young Himba girl wears her hair in two thick braids. On approaching the age of puberty, these braids are loosened and made into thin braids that hang over her eyes. After the initiation rite, which follows puberty, the braids (Malan calls them "hair-strings") must hang at the back of the head. Young Himba men wear one long braid. When a young man is considered mature enough to marry, he is permitted to wear his hair in two long braids that hang down the back of his head.

Our two-vehicle convoy slowly entered Opuwa around noon. The place looked like most other small Namibian towns: a few petrol stations, some tiny markets, several churches, and a school. A group of traditionally dressed Himba women and children, the women's skin smeared with ochre, were sitting under a large, shady tree by the side of the road. We wanted to take their photos and Lutz suggested we negotiate a price with them. The women didn't smile, but were willing to pose for us and take our money. Perhaps posing for tourists was their livelihood, like Native Americans in parts of the Southwest.

We continued driving through town and after a quick roadside lunch, we journeyed through some of the most remote parts of Namibia we'd ever seen. Travel writers call this vast, bleak, mountainous region Namibia's last, true wilderness, and I was starting to wonder what we had gotten ourselves into. I tried not to think about how we would manage a medical emergency this far from civilization. It was late afternoon when we reached Epupa Falls, where we would be camping for three nights. The campsite was managed by the local Himba community, and at the entrance a group of Himba women and children had spread blankets on the ground from which they were selling their handicrafts to tourists: carved dolls, woven bracelets, and Himba "pillows." Because a Himba woman wears a thick wooden necklace that she never removes, she sleeps with her head on a wooden headrest. It resembles the letter "H" lying on its side.

The site Lutz and Ulf selected for us, on the bank of the fast-flowing Kunene River, was shaded by a grove of swaying makalani palm trees. Ulf told us that these trees could reach a height of sixty feet. Women use their leaves to weave baskets. The seed, a hard, small nut, is used to make jewelry. The fermented sap of the tree produces a strong, intoxicating beverage. Declining our assistance, the two gentlemen began hauling camping gear from the top and back of their vehicles. Now they were in their element! Within half an hour they had assembled our tents and even made up our cots with sheets and duvets. They set out six chairs and two long tables. They unpacked their cookware and built a fire. Not long after dusk, we were enjoying a delicious spaghetti supper, complete with garlic bread and salad. Nancy and I offered to help wash the dishes, but Lutz said this had already been taken care of. A few minutes later, we learned what he meant. Our guides had hired a young Himba woman to wash the dishes.

Adjacent to our campsite was a shower (cold water only). The circular privacy fence was fashioned from ten-foot-high palm branches. Also nearby was a little hut with a toilet (which sometimes flushed). That night we fell asleep in our tents under the stars of Southern Cross, so close you felt as if you could touch them. When I closed my eyes I heard the gentle gurgle of the river lapping the shore and the hushed whooshing and whispering of the breezes in the palm branches.

Shortly after we awakened the next morning, Lutz and Ulf had the water boiling for coffee. We were treated to a breakfast of muesli, bread, jam, cheese, salami, bacon, and eggs. "I thought I was going to lose weight when I came to Africa!" said George. The same young woman returned to wash the dishes. Ulf said that she would also stay to guard the campsite when the six of us went off to hike and explore the falls.

The unusually heavy rains of the summer had produced many wide, surging streams. Lutz and Ulf insisted that in order to get the best view of Epupa Falls we would need to forge these streams by stepping carefully on the slippery rocks in their beds. We managed to do this, arms flailing, and the six of us clustered together on a muddy little island in the middle of the Kunene River. From there we had a spectacular view of the gorge and the river tumbling one hundred feet over the falls. We crawled back across our slippery rocks, and hiked up an escarpment arising from the riverbank. We rested briefly on a narrow ledge, and climbed higher to get a better view of the mountains of Angola on the other side of the river. We saw a village over there—the houses were wooden dwellings, unlike the mud and thatch homes of the village near our campsite.

When we walked past the Himba vendors on our way back to our campsite, I decided to assist the local economy. The doll I bought was clothed in the full attire of a Himba woman, including a skirt made from animal skin and all the traditional jewelry. I also bought a Himba "pillow" and three necklaces made from leather strips, cowrie shells, and tiny metal beads that had been fashioned from pieces of fencing. Back at the campsite, I had to wash my hands because they were covered with the red ochre from the doll, the same ochre the Himba women rub on their skin.

The next morning we hired a guide. Jon, a young Himba man, told us he was taking a class right there on the campground sponsored by Namibia's Ministry of Tourism to train young men and women to be tourist guides. Jon wore sturdy sneakers, snug black shorts and a leather apron-like garment traditionally worn by Himba men. We noticed that his lower incisors were missing, and that his two upper incisors had been filed. Jon told us that removal of the teeth is part of a Himba teenager's initiation rite. Professor Malan describes the ritual:

The removal of these teeth, that takes place between the ages of ten and twelve, is an event of considerable religious and social significance in the life of a child, and is accompanied by a number of prescribed rituals.

The night before the event the boys and girls sleep in the main hut. This is done to ensure the protecting influence of the ancestors, thereby averting evil and dangerous influences. It is believed that serious complications will occur if this rule is not observed. Early the next morning the village-head goes to the ritual fire, followed by the children. He prays for the blessing of the spirits on the performing of the ritual so that the teeth may be removed easily and also that excessive bleeding and infection may not occur.

The actual knocking out of the teeth is accomplished by placing a specially sharpened sliver of mopane wood against one tooth at a time and tapping it with a heavy object until it has torn through the gums and may be removed with the fingers. When all four teeth have been extracted, they are given to the child who must wrap them in a mopane leaf and throw them in the direction of his birthplace, while expressing the words: "Mayo wanje, yaruka kotjirongo kumba kwatera." ("My teeth, go back to the place where I have been born.") At the end of the ritual the child's torn gums are attended to by heating a mopane leaf against a glowing coal and using it to press the wound shut. Should a serious infection occur, however, a red-hot arrow-head is placed in the wound. (pp. 94-95)

Our walk along a leafy trail adjacent to the river took us through a small village where there was a large brick oven. Something was baking, and it smelled wonderful! Lutz and Ulf bought loaves of warm bread from the people who operated this concession and we continued walking and munching. Unfortunately, our sightseeing revealed what we had been told about the alcohol problem here in Kaokoland. It was only mid-morning, but several village men were already staggering around, and one disheveled, wild-eyed old lady kept stumbling after our little group, pointing at us and shouting at Jon. We passed two men urinating on the path. Behind them was a small mountain of broken beer bottles. Lutz, sounding angry and embarrassed, reminded us that this was not a traditional Himba village, such as we would see later. Did the very tourism that provided people like Jon his livelihood, the tourist dollars that enabled schools to be built, also create that Carling Black Label Beer Mountain? Jon hurried us past the drunks and tried to divert our attention by telling us about the various trees and plants we were passing, explaining their uses and medicinal properties.

After lunch, George and Nancy accompanied Lutz and Ulf for a swim in one of the shallower sections of the river. Lou and I relaxed at our campsite. Later in the afternoon, Ulf told us that we were going for a sundowner. He set two frozen chickens on a rock to thaw, and we drove to the top of a mountain from which we had a panoramic view of northern Namibia and southern Angola. We sat on the chairs the gentlemen had thoughtfully brought along and enjoyed soft drinks, beer, chips, and pretzels.

When we returned to our campsite at dusk, the young woman who washed our dishes came running up to us and said that a wandering dog had stolen one of our chickens before she was able to chase it away. There was still enough spaghetti left over from last night to make an ample meal. As the sky darkened, Lutz and Ulf set out six luminaries, candles inserted in paper bags half-filled with sand, around our campsite. In this romantic atmosphere we savored our dinner of chicken and rice, spaghetti and more freshly baked bread. In the distance, we heard the sound of drumming and singing. We wished that we could investigate. There were several other villages in the area, in addition to the boozy one we had seen that morning, and the sound seemed to be coming from one of those other villages.

The next morning, Jon accompanied us on our drive to visit two traditional Himba homesteads. A tall stick fence encircled the compound. In the center of the homestead was a circular pen, the kraal, in which the cattle were kept. The chief's dwelling, a circular mud hut with a thatched roof, was opposite the entrance to the kraal. Jon said the space between the chief's home and the kraal is known as the Holy Fire, a sacred space where ceremonies occur. It is forbidden to walk between the kraal and the Holy Fire.

The chief in this homestead was a "lesser" chief, a middle-aged, bare-chested man with a generous belly who was sitting on a low stool in front of his hut holding on his lap a baby. Jon introduced us to him and he mumbled words of welcome, but did not offer to shake our hands. I bowed slightly, and then felt a little foolish. Why did I do that? He told Jon that the beautiful young woman standing beside him, who appeared to be about sixteen years old, was his second wife and the baby was their son. The chief's young wife invited us to come inside her home, a hut on the opposite side of the kraal. We followed her around the kraal, careful not to step into the holy space. Her dwelling was called a beehive hut because of its conical shape. We had to stoop to go through the doorway. A small fire was burning inside, near the entrance. On the floor was a cowhide—the bed. Hung from the mud-and-dung walls were small ivory-colored containers made from the tips of cattle horns. In these she stored the red ochre powder that she mixed with butterfat to rub on her body to protect herself from insect bites and the sun. Another horn container stored the black powder that was used by the men on their necks and chests. Jon showed us the aromatic leaves the Himba burn to perfume their garments and their home. These are burned in a small round metal pot covered by a conical, loosely woven basket—an incense burner. This home, no more than eight feet in diameter, also contained a variety of clay cooking pots of different sizes.

Outside, the young wife walked to a nearby square storage hut from which she withdrew some elaborate skin garments. She told us that these were her wedding clothes. She graciously modeled them for us: an elaborate cowhide headdress and a garment made from leather and goatskin that she tied around her shoulders like a cape. She was already wearing many ornate necklaces, bracelets, anklets and belts.

The second homestead we visited was about forty kilometers away. We drove past a cemetery, the final resting place of an important chief. The sign of his eminence was the display of about twenty cattle horns stuck into the earth surrounding the grave. When we drove our vehicles into the area outside the homestead, little children came running up to us, and we gave them handfuls of wrapped hard candies. This larger homestead was the home of the head chief of the whole area. When we parked outside the homestead, Jon went in first with the gifts we had brought: sugar, maize meal, tobacco and some wrapped candies. After a few minutes, he returned to us saying that the chief wanted tea and coffee. Unfortunately, those items were back at our campsite, but the chief allowed us to come inside anyway. He was a wizened old man—Jon said that he was his uncle—and he was sitting on the ground under a tree. With a sharp knife, he was carving a pair of sandals out of a piece of heavy leather. They were for a young woman who was standing patiently next to him. From time to time, he told her to put out her foot so he could measure the sandal against it.

We each shook hands with the chief, who didn't waste time looking at us, but through Jon he told us that we were welcome to his homestead. As we walked around, we visited one hut where a woman was churning milk by gently shaking a calabash back and forth. Jon said she would do this for about three hours until the butter formed. He said the Himba diet is primarily sour milk, meat and millet porridge. Another young woman walked into the kraal and demonstrated milking a cow for us. She tied the rear legs of the animal together and tucked the tail under her right arm before she started.

When we returned to the chief, he told us that a child here had injured her leg and asked us if we had any medicine. Nancy, a nurse, inspected the wound and saw it was very deep—a gash almost to the bone. We discovered that the first aid kit in our vehicle contained no antiseptic, only a cleansing solution. Nancy cleaned and bandaged the wound. Jon said the child lived in a homestead about thirty kilometers away and had been brought to the chief's homestead by his family members who were hoping to catch a lift to Opuwa where they could seek medical attention. We said we were sorry that we were not returning to Opuwa, and thus we could not take the child to the clinic. From what we had seen of Opuwa, we wondered what sort of medical care would realistically be available there.

On our drive back to the campsite, we encountered several police vehicles from Namibia and Angola. When we stopped to talk with them, a Namibian policeman said they were working together with the Angolan police to try to resolve a cattle-rustling problem. Lutz said that such cattle theft was not uncommon in the area.

After dinner, a delicious Namibian *braai* (barbecue), Lutz and Ulf told us they had a surprise for us and they said we must stay seated, near the fire. Since winter was approaching, it was soon very dark. The men again set the luminaries in a large circle. Suddenly, from the shadows and trees, we saw movement, and about thirty people rushed into our campsite, singing and dancing single-file in a sort of conga line. Soon the group swelled to over sixty. They were mostly young adults and teens, although there were a few middle-aged men and women, too. Except for three young women, all were wearing Western-style clothes. Lutz laughed when he saw our astonished faces, and said they were from the local Christian community. He and Ulf had invited the congregation to sing and dance for us. They had also brought their drummer. These were the people we had heard drumming and singing the previous night. For the next hour we were transfixed. Their dancing became a frenzied mass of twitching limbs, swaying hips, and swirling braids. Every so often they reformed their conga line and wove their way throughout the campsite. We were introduced to Amos, their leader, and we donated one hundred Namibian dollars (about fifteen U.S. dollars) to his church.

The next morning, while Lutz and Ulf broke camp and loaded up our vehicles, Jon took us four Americans to visit Amos. He told us that the Pentecostal Protestant Kirche had started this Christian community. Amos was so proud to show us his church. Inside the simple, square wooden structure, white plastic chairs rimmed the walls. The altar was a table covered with a white tablecloth. On the table were a Herero Bible and two jars filled with water and bouquets of colorful plastic flowers. Amos's home, next to the church, was a small square dwelling made of clay. Inside, a red and yellow curtain suspended from a clothesline separated it into two rooms: a sleeping room and a living room/kitchen. Amos called for his wife, a tiny woman in a blue cotton housedress, and she brought him four brass bracelets, which he gave to us. He said they had been made by poor people from Angola who had come to visit them, and he wanted to give us the bracelets so we would remember him.

When we returned to camp, Lutz and Ulf had secured all our supplies in their vehicles. Bertha Petrus, the young woman who had been washing our dishes every day, spoke a little English. She told me she was a member of Amos's Christian community, and she asked me if I could find her a Bible in her language. I wrote her address in my notebook and told her that I would buy her a Herero-language Bible at the Namibia Bible Society when I returned to Windhoek. I gave her a bottle of hand lotion. We bade farewell to Jon and climbed aboard for our seven-hour journey to Sesfontein. The landscape was ruggedly beautiful: grassy plains, rocky, purple mountains, and granite inselbergs, small rocky knobs that rose abruptly from the ground. Lutz called them by their more familiar Afrikaans name, *kopjes* (pronounced "copies").

Sesfontein, so named because of its six springs, used to be a German military fort in the early 1900s. Later it became a police station. Now the complex had been converted to an upscale lodge. There was also a camping area here (with *hot* showers), and that was the campsite where we would stay for the next two nights.

I awakened early the next morning before anyone else and sat quietly outside our tent as the canopy of stars overhead began to fade with the coming dawn. I listened to the village sounds: crowing roosters, braying donkeys, and loud singing and clapping from a nearby Damara village.

After breakfast, Lutz said, "Our mission today is to track and find the elusive Desert Elephants! They live in the Hoanib Riverbed." He rubbed his palms together and grinned like a little boy. "This is the most exciting part of our whole journey!"

We drove through narrow mountain passes, past abandoned villages with tumbledown huts, and across a grassy savannah where we saw herds of springbok, a few oryx, ostriches, and two giraffes. We reached the Hoanib around mid-morning. One of Namibia's major rivers, the chalky lines on the riverbank showed that during the rainy season the water had reached a depth of six to eight feet. Now it was mostly dry. Scattered throughout the twenty-foot-wide riverbed were large trees; there was lush growth along the banks. For the next two hours, we drove up and down the riverbed in our two vehicles, in search of the elephants. Occasionally we'd pass other 4X4 vehicles, their passengers also peering intently through the windows, seeking the beasts. Although we saw huge mounds of dung and plenty of tracks, the elephants eluded us, so we decided to search for a picnic site. Lou and I were riding with Ulf. Ahead of us, Lutz drove toward a shady spot beside a large cliff on the side of the riverbed. As he approached the base of the cliff, the rear tires of his Mazda 4X4 slowly began to sink into the soft sand. Ulf parked several yards back from the Mazda, and we three climbed out of the Land Cruiser. I approached on foot to investigate. Suddenly I found myself sinking into the sand. Oh my God, was I stuck in quicksand? My heart was pounding hard, but slowly and deliberately I picked my way back to more solid ground. Ulf tossed a strong rope to Lutz who tied it onto the rear of the Mazda. Ulf tied the other end to the front bumper of the Land Cruiser. He climbed in, put the Cruiser in reverse, and managed to tow poor Lutz out of the sand. We selected another spot, under a shady tree, and enjoyed a feast of bratwurst, which Lutz had grilled that morning in garlic butter. There were also roasted ears of corn, dill pickles, and bread from the Himba village. Lutz was calling this our "mature picnic." While we ate lunch, we all laughed at the image of the hapless Mazda sinking into the sand. Poor Lutz! Throughout the trip, his old Mazda had been falling apart. Somewhere, he had lost a mud flap. And another time, crossing a rough riverbed, his rear bumper came off. He always handled these small misadventures with good grace and humor.

After lunch, Lutz waved down three people in a Jeep to ask them if they'd seen any elephants. The passengers told us yes, they had spotted a bull elephant about twenty minutes ago. Hooray! We quickly packed up our picnic gear. Back in our own vehicles, we resumed our tracking, with George and Nancy riding atop the Mazda. Within an hour, Lou said, "What's that gray shape ahead of us?" Sure enough, moving slowly toward us was the elephant. We stopped and watched as he lumbered up the sandy bank, heaved himself up another ledge, and squashed a melon underfoot. We continued to watch as he slowly disappeared into the bush. It was nearly dark when we returned to our campsite, but our efforts had been rewarded and we continued to relive the day's adventures with each other. Trackers in the African wilderness.

We broke camp the next morning, and by nine o'clock were leaving Sesfontein. Several kilometers down the road, we stopped at a place where three springs had created permanent waterholes. Ulf said, "A few years ago, a fellow had begun to build a lodge here, but he went bankrupt and abandoned the project. The foundations remain. Let's take a look." As we tramped around the site, Lutz and Ulf excitedly discussed with each other how wonderful it would be for them to resurrect this project. I half believed they'd actually do it, these two joyful adventurers.

Our evening destination was Palmwag, where we stayed at the modern, comfortable Palmwag Lodge located amongst fan palms alongside a perennial spring in the Uniab River. Our rooms were spacious, with Italian tiled floors and large, soft beds. After five nights of camping, the bed and shower were glorious. Signs around the lodge warned guests to beware of elephants that wandered freely throughout the grounds, but we didn't see any.

When we boarded our vehicles the next morning, I was sad to think that by the end of the day our camping adventure with Lutz and Ulf would be over. We didn't realize that they had a few more adventures in mind. Our morning drive took us past the Burnt Mountain, formed millions of years ago by volcanic deposits that had baked the shale into what looked like huge, rusty slag heaps. By mid-morning we reached Twyfelfontein, an area of massive rock slabs with the largest known concentration of Stone Age petroglyphs in Namibia. Plentiful water and abundant game attracted Stone Age people to this area where they dwelt for several centuries. To date, more than 2,500 engravings have been recorded. Lutz hired a young girl, about fourteen years old, to serve as our guide to see these rock engravings and paintings. For the next hour, we clambered up and down the rocks, stopping whenever she pointed out carvings of lions, giraffe, antelope, rhino and ostrich. Some consider these engravings one of the richest collections of rock engravings in Africa, dating back to at least 3300 B.C. Ulf said, "I remember coming here as a young boy, before there were any guides. We had such fun seeing who could spot the next engraving or painting."

A short drive from Twyfelfontein we encountered another curious sight—an outcrop of vertical pillars or slabs of basalt, about fifteen feet tall, called the Organ Pipes. The Organ Pipes are exposed in a gorge roughly three hundred feet long and considered to be between 130 and 150 million years old. Lutz and Ulf knew a short cut that allowed us to climb to the base of this gorge and walk among the pipes.

After lunch, we started our hot and dusty drive back to Lutz's home in Walvis Bay, where we had left our vehicle. It was dark when we arrived, and surprisingly warm for this coastal town where the air had always felt so cool. Lutz's wife told us that the Berg Winds had passed through, those hot desert winds that sometimes send the temperatures up to one hundred degrees and fill all the buildings with drifts of fine-grained sand. We sadly bade farewell to our companions of the past week, those funny, competent, hard-working gentlemen who made this experience such a grand adventure for us.

Chapter 20
Campus Life

*T*he day before George and Nancy returned home to the United States, we had a visit from the Rev. Joseph Hupitho. We had met Joseph on Easter Sunday at a church in the part of Windhoek known as The Location, a township established by the South Africans during the apartheid era that was, today, rimmed with the tarpaper shacks of squatters. At that church service, he had learned that our American friend was in charge of the Clinical Pastoral Education (CPE) program at a major American university medical center. Now Joseph wanted to speak with George.

"Namibia needs more trained pastoral counselors," he said, "especially because of the AIDS pandemic in which we are living. Will your program consider me?"

The glint in George's eye and the eagerness with which he leaned forward and peered at Joseph told me this was probably as good as done. "Joseph, I think you have a strong chance of being accepted. Our medical center is interested in recruiting Africans. Because Lou has also been trained as a CPE supervisor, I'm going to have him formally interview you and mail me his evaluation."

Participants in American CPE programs are paid generous stipends—a fortune, by African standards—so Joseph could earn a comfortable income during his two years in the program. Members of local churches near the hospital would likely help him furnish a small apartment. If he managed his earnings wisely, he would even be able to send some money home to his wife, Rebekkah, and his two young children. What a win-win exchange! Namibia would acquire a well-trained pastoral counselor, and this eager young African would invigorate the American hospital's chaplaincy program. So enthusiastic were they, that neither George nor Lou did the kind of background check with Joseph's bishop or church board that they would have conducted with an American candidate. Such a screening would have prevented much anger, embarrassment, and heartache in the months to come.

Our friend, Veiko Munyika, the General Secretary of the Northern church, was in town to attend a meeting and had come to the campus to consult with Lou about the seminarians' summer internship program, the program that Lou had established two years ago. I invited him to stay for dinner.

"I love American food!" he said.

Veiko had earned his degrees in South Africa. I knew this bright young man represented his church well at international gatherings because I'd already had the privilege of editing some of the papers he presented at such colloquies. Despite his intellect and scholarship, he was a humble man. "I'm just a simple, rural person," he told us. When we sat down to dinner, he congratulated Lou for putting together an effective fieldwork program for the seminarians, and promised to continue working closely with him to strengthen the program.

Of all the Namibians we'd come to know, Veiko was the one we most admired. Educated and insightful, he helped us understand the culture and the church. We kept hoping that the Paulinum Governing Board would appoint him to our faculty, but his bishop preferred to retain him in his current position. Veiko helped himself to more meatloaf and mashed potatoes and turned to Lou. "You know, I have been wondering whether the Finnish piety of the missionaries in northern Namibia was really Lutheran."

Lou raised his eyebrows and Veiko continued. "No, really. I'm serious. It seems to me that this theological heritage, combined with the traditionally quiet and compliant disposition of the Ovambo people, is responsible for the state of the Northern Church today. You have seen what our church is like, highly structured and traditional. Our congregational pastors are not free to make any changes to the liturgy. They have no stewardship theology because the Finnish missionaries had taught Namibians that the material things of the world were to be shunned. When clergy get together, unlike in Europe or in the States, there is no animated theological discussion or debate. Our pastors would consider this rude. That's why I'm so glad that people like you and Susan are teaching here. You bring us a breath of fresh air." It was after eleven o'clock when Veiko left. He told us he hoped we would come north again soon, and we promised we'd do so.

When we returned from the gym the next morning, a Friday, two of the seminary's maintenance men were standing outside our flat with a broken switch in their hand. They didn't speak any English, but Lou was able to determine that the switch was from the meat-slicing machine, used almost every day in the seminary kitchen. He accompanied the men to the seminary's dining hall. Within an hour Lou had found a replacement switch at a hardware store and had repaired the machine. After lunch, Michael Shangala phoned to tell Lou about a broken toilet in one of the men's dormitories. That afternoon Lou repaired both the toilet and a leaking shower in the women's dormitory.

On Saturday afternoon, Lou and I met Ndiku at Friendly Haven, the small, two-bedroom house that served as the shelter for abused women and children. Ndiku introduced us to the five women who made up the board of directors. She told us the board gathered there every Saturday afternoon. Although the Namibian government's Woman and Child Protective Unit, headquartered at the State Hospital, made referrals to the home, Friendly Haven received no government assistance. Abuse of women and children was a horrible problem in Namibia. Nearly every week an article would appear in the newspaper about one distressing case after another, and most of the cases were incredibly gruesome. A few months earlier, a man had blinded a woman who had tried to break up with him by throwing acid in her face. Not long after that, we read about a man in Otjimbingwe who had burned his ex-girlfriend to death.

The women on the board said that they would like to expand the house. A local architect and a contractor were offering their services gratis. I told these women I'd contact our sponsoring congregations back home to see if we could garner some support, and Lou suggested that some of our seminarians might do some counseling with the residents.

By the middle of June, all the students had returned to campus and the second semester classes were well under way. Michael welcomed everyone to the first meeting of the term and said, "We particularly want to welcome back Dr. van Wyk. We hope and pray you are recovering well from your stroke."

"I did not have a stroke," grumbled van Wyk. He pasted a smile on his face and glanced around the table. "My doctor said it was a diabetic coma. I'm fine now."

Our agenda that afternoon was lengthy. Just before the food break, Lou was invited to update the faculty on the student internship program. He reminded everyone that the third-year students, during their three-month summer holiday, November through January, would be placed in congregations with veteran pastors who would supervise them. Incorporating fieldwork, such an integral aspect of seminary education in America, was a new concept here. Establishing such a program was one of the primary reasons the Namibian bishops had been eager for Lou to come here. The previous year's student interns had returned to campus praising this addition to their training. Since many of our students' families depended upon their sons' and daughters' assistance during the summer holiday time, the students were particularly pleased that Lou was able to secure funding from our Division for Global Mission that provided them with small stipends for their work. The Namibian churches had already begun seeking ways to make those stipends a permanent item in their budgets.

Dr. van Wyk was probably still fuming because Lou, and not he, had been chosen dean of students six months earlier. Forgotten was his gratitude for our hospital visit. The man was sly. He knew how to cloak his attacks in rhetoric that would sound reasonable to an outsider. He would say something like, "I understand our churches, and this is not part of their tradition." Or, simply, "This is not the African way," accompanied by a withering look at the foreigner he was skewering. The point on which he chose to attack the internship program was on its financial sustainability after Lou left Namibia. Lou said that DGM would happily entertain the request for a long-term grant until the churches were able to bear the full financial obligation. Van Wyk retorted that it was unwise to make the seminary donor-dependent, but we had already seen his own willingness to avail himself of handouts from abroad in the form of sabbaticals and expense-paid guest lectureships. Michael wisely tabled future discussions about funding to another time.

A month into the new semester, thirty of our students were preparing for a class trip to Swakopmund, the seaside town on the coast. Many students who had grown up in villages or on homesteads in the interior part of Namibia had never seen the ocean, even though it was only a three-hour drive from Windhoek. The air crackled with their excitement. They reminded me of youngsters getting ready for a class trip to Disney World. In the chapel one Wednesday evening, at the conclusion of the vespers service, Immanuel, a first-year student, announced that someone had donated T-shirts and caps with the Paulinum logo for all trip participants. The students also received some sweater vests from Caltex, one of the local petrol stations. In appreciation for my husband's helping them organize their trip, the students called Lou forward and presented him with one of the vests. Everyone applauded.

The students were probably eager to get away from the unpleasantness that was again engulfing the campus. I'm sure our faculty colleagues were wishing they could get away, too. Because of Johan van Wyk's obstructionist behavior, it had taken us twelve hours, spread over three days, to get through the agenda of our last faculty meeting. Van Wyk vigorously opposed every innovative faculty suggestion and all of the requests from the students. He sought to cancel the students' trip, to refuse permission to Jermaine, who wanted to commute to classes from his home in Windhoek so he could care for his ailing mother, and to deny permission to Phillip, who'd had his driver's license for eight years, to become a student driver.

The most troublesome issue was dealing with Thomas, a third-year student who had apparently fathered a child before coming to the seminary. Van Wyk wanted to expel or suspend him immediately. The faculty delayed taking any action, concluding that this was a matter that should be handled by the Southern Church, and decided to meet with Bishop Diergardt and two other Southern Church pastors. We were all astonished when the bishop pointed out that another of our first-year students, Henrico, had fathered *four* children before coming to the seminary. He was unmarried, and the Church Board had accepted him, apparently without reservation. When Michael and Lou had initially spoken with Thomas, he denied that he'd fathered a child. He later recanted, and admitted he had lied to them. The Paulinum faculty dealt with the lying by requiring Thomas to make a public apology to the student body. In the midst of all this, tempers flared. Lou stormed out of one faculty meeting and van Wyk out of another.

Two days after our meeting with Bishop Diergardt, the bishop phoned us to say that the Southern Church Board had voted to reassign Johan van Wyk to another post, probably as pastor of a congregation, effective at the start of the next academic year. Unfortunately, the goodwill on campus over the news of van Wyk's departure didn't last very long. Five days later, at the conclusion of a chapel service, Thomas made his half-hearted apology to the student body. He surrounded his declaration with defensive statements about why he had lied to Lou and Michael. At the end of his statement, Lou stood up and confronted him.

"Are you saying that the principal and I are to blame for your lying?"

"N-no."

Then another student, Johannes, jumped up from his seat, went to the lectern, and berated the faculty for forcing Thomas to make such a confession before the student body. There were only three of us faculty members present at that evening's vespers service, and Lou, as dean of students, bore the brunt of the students' anger. It had only been one week since they had publicly applauded him for supporting their beach trip.

Two days later, the seminary grapevine buzzed with the news that van Wyk, the only faculty member who had wanted Thomas suspended, now had Thomas running errands for him and was inviting Thomas to his home for tea. The grapevine also informed us that the students' trip to the coast the previous weekend had not been as positive as they had initially told us. Several unhappy students told us there had been excessive drinking and that one intoxicated student had driven the seminary's minivan into a ditch.

In the midst of this unpleasantness, we received a phone call from Rev. Hasheela, the general secretary of the Northern Church. He told us that an American pastor who had been visiting northern Namibia had died suddenly that afternoon from an apparent heart attack. The pastor's wife and the two American traveling companions would be returning to Windhoek the following night. We told Rev. Hasheela to send them to us, and we offered them accommodation in seminary flats for as long as necessary.

The American pastor, Michael Wuchter, his wife, Shirley, and another couple, Dick and Beatrice, had been in Namibia to attend the dedication of a new church building for a congregation that their Minnesota congregation had supported for ten years. Within hours of Rev. Wuchter's death, thirty members of the Namibian congregation had gathered at the church guesthouse to comfort Shirley, Dick, and Beatrice.

For the next five days, Lou and I offered what assistance we could. There were so many details, including transporting the body from the rural area in the north to a mortuary in Windhoek for an autopsy, and to a funeral home for embalming and preparation for transport back to the USA. Shirley and her friends had to reschedule their own flights back home. We gave them meals, access to our e-mail and phone, and transportation to the embassy, travel agents, and the coroner's office. Lou helped Shirley begin planning for the funeral back in Duluth. He accompanied her to the funeral home to view the body of her husband before the casket was sealed for shipment. I took the three to the Namibia Craft Center so Shirley could buy three hand-carved picture frames for herself and her two children, frames that would contain photos of her husband. Her eyes filled with tears when she whispered to me, "I never thought I'd be doing this sort of souvenir shopping."

As the semester progressed, life on our campus calmed down. One

Sunday morning we took about twenty of our students to an ecumenical service at Christuskirche, the Lutheran church in town whose members were mostly German expatriates. With its gleaming stained-glass windows, modern chancel furnishings and fine pipe organ, it was unlike any church most of our students had ever seen before. The fifteen students who comprised the seminary choir sang two anthems at the beginning of the service. Our German faculty colleague, Hanns, leaned over and whispered, "It is always a strange sensation to come here. It makes me feel as if I am at home in Dortmund."

What was difficult was explaining to the students the reason for the five huge brass commemorative plaques that completely covered one full wall of the nave. Engraved on those plaques were the names and death dates, going back to 1893, of at least one thousand German soldiers who had died while fighting in Namibia. This church was honoring those Germans who had killed their ancestors.

One afternoon, I received a telephone call from a Namibian pastor I had never met.

"My name is Rev. Ileka, and I have just returned to Namibia from South Africa. I have been studying for my master's degree in theology. One of my Namibian colleagues told me that you are the seminary's English teacher."

I knew what was coming, and I knew I wouldn't be able to deny his request. I was right.

"Mrs. Bauer, I'm hoping you will be able to help me. I need someone to proofread my master's thesis. It is about the eschatology of liberation theology."

I told Rev. Ileka I would meet him in the seminary's library the following afternoon. I probably would not have agreed to take on the task if I had known that his paper was 130 pages long, and that it was all handwritten. I did draw the line when he suggested that maybe I could type it, too. Oh, and had he mentioned that he needed it in a week? Lou and I had already booked a flat at the coast for the upcoming weekend. We'd be gone for three nights. I knew how I'd be spending my time at the beach.

When he learned that we would be driving to the coast, Jomo asked us if he could ride with us. His parents lived in Swakopmund, and he wanted to go home for the weekend. I told Jomo he was welcome to accompany us, but on our way out of town we would need to stop briefly at the doctor's office so I could have a few stitches removed from my leg. The previous week, Dr. Rohn had excised a mole from my right shin.

In the past, Lou and I had always stayed at the church guesthouse, which was a lot like staying in a dormitory room. It had the advantage of being cheap. This time, we chose a more elegant alternative, telling ourselves we had earned a bit of luxury, given everything we'd been through this semester. Our weekend flat contained a television with satellite connection, CD player, VCR, microwave, and even a dishwasher, the first one I had seen in Namibia. Despite the fifteen hours I spent correcting the English grammar on Rev. Ileka's master's thesis, Lou and I had a good time. The weather was temperate, and there wasn't as much fog as there usually was at the coast. On Saturday we bought most of our Christmas gifts, carvings and batiks, at the outdoor vendors' market. I found a cozy knitting supply shop in Swakopmund's trendy shopping district where I purchased yarn for an afghan I planned to crochet for Jason. During our three-and-a-half-hour-drive back to Windhoek, I gave Jomo the task of rolling skeins of yarn into balls.

Shortly after our return from Swakopmund, Dirk was back on campus to remove the rest of his belongings from the house he used to occupy. He kept telling everyone how hard it was to find room for these things in the tiny house in town, the church's parsonage, where he and his family were living. He was particularly unkind to Mia, our next-door neighbor from Finland who, with her husband, would be moving into his former campus house. "If you had moved all your things out of this house ten months ago," she said, "we could have moved in and the seminary would now have earned thirty thousand Namibian dollars (about four thousand U.S. dollars) in income from our rental."

Dirk exploded. "All you white people ever think about is money! You don't understand Africans. You don't know the pressures I have been under since the Church kicked me out of the seminary."

By the end of the week, he had relinquished his key. Just in time. The Southern Church was hosting an international conference of German and Cameroonian guests, and I had booked accommodations for fourteen people in that house. The day after Dirk handed me the key, our workers were busy setting up extra beds in the living room and study.

At six o'clock on the morning the Cameroonians were scheduled to return home, I heard a loud banging on our door. It was one of the German women. "Madam Bauer, one of the Cameroonian ladies, Giselle, is in labor!"

"How long has she been in labor?"

"It has been some hours now. I think the baby is coming soon!"

"Okay. Go back to Giselle and tell her that we will get her some help." I had no idea what I meant by that. My first thought was to phone Ute, our German colleague who had given birth to her second child here in Windhoek. Ute suggested that we could either take her to Central Hospital or that perhaps the midwife she had used would be willing to come. I shook Lou awake and told him to get ready to drive Giselle to the hospital. Soon the German woman was back at the door saying that the contractions were five minutes apart. I told her I would bring some extra sheets and towels and a large basin from the dining hall. I found my robe, shoved my feet into slippers, and grabbed the large key ring that opened all the storage cupboards in the kitchen complex. It was still dark when I shuffled across the road to the kitchen building. While I was pulling sheets and towels off the shelves, another German woman came running into the storage room to tell me that the baby had just been born. Ute's midwife arrived ten minutes later and was able to cut the cord, deliver the placenta and determine that the baby and mother were healthy and safe.

The students were excited about the news of the seminary's first-born. Luckily, that house was not booked for anyone else, and our Finnish neighbors weren't moving in until the end of the month, so Giselle was able to remain there for another week. Securing a passport and appropriate travel documents for the baby required time-consuming negotiations with the Ministry of Home Affairs because Cameroon did not have an embassy in Namibia. Hans and Ute took care of that.

One morning Lou and I were sitting on our balcony having breakfast. Neither of us had any classes that day, and we were enjoying the warm spring morning and the symphony of birdsong when we heard a knock on the door. It was Jomo. Like many of our students, Jomo came from a complicated family. His father, who had left his mother when Jomo was a young lad, lived with his second wife and their children in Otjiwarango, a town in Windhoek's interior, about a three-hour drive north of Windhoek. Jomo, his mother, and his stepfather lived on the coast, the place we had recently taken him for the weekend. These were the parents we'd met at the beginning of the school year. Jomo was engaged to a young woman who had a five-year-old daughter from a previous relationship. Jomo, himself, was father to another five-year-old daughter who lived with the girl's mother. When we had taken him with us to Swakopmund, Jomo had told us that he, along with his fiancée and the two little girls, were planning to live in a flat on campus next year after the wedding.

Jomo's usually cheerful demeanor was gone, and worry lines creased his forehead. He told us his sad tale. His stepfather had been having an extra-marital relationship. The woman with whom he was having the affair had recently given birth to a baby who had tested positive for HIV. Jomo's mother and stepfather had just received their test results, and they, too, were HIV positive. Few in Namibia had access to antiretroviral medications, so positive diagnoses were almost certain death sentences. Jomo's sisters had consulted a witch doctor who told them that the spirit of their deceased brother, who had drowned as a child, was now living inside their mother and had returned to punish her for allowing him to drown.

As if this weren't trouble enough, Jomo said he just learned that his brothers were telling everyone that since his fiancée had been previously married they would not attend his upcoming wedding. Apparently their parents' second marriages didn't bother the brothers. Although more complicated than most, Jomo's tale was so similar to others I'd heard. Lou was a well-trained family counselor, but sometimes the troubles of our students defied even his skills. We just listened to Jomo that morning and assured him that we cared. What we didn't know was that our own personal lives were about to be turned upside down.

Chapter 21
Monster Leg

*T*he first Thursday in September had been an unusually busy one. After a morning filled with classes, I drove into town for some errands: getting applications for a renewal of our visas and work permits at the Ministry of Home Affairs and buying a few more Christmas presents. Normally Lou would have accompanied me, but he was busy teaching a seminar that afternoon. About four o'clock I sat down with a stack of students' homework papers when the jangling ring of the telephone troubled the air in our tiny flat. I wiped the sweat from my neck and put down the grammar assignments.

"Susan, I've just received the pathology report on the lesion I removed from your leg. I am so sorry to have to tell you this. It's malignant melanoma. But you mustn't worry. It's very treatable."

I felt as if I had fallen from a swing at the height of its arc. When I opened my mouth, my words came out in little puffs. "Dr. Rohn. That pathology report. Last week. It said the mole was benign."

"Yes. Well, apparently our local pathologists weren't entirely certain of their diagnosis, so they sent the specimen to Cape Town. This new report is, uh, more extensive. And it definitely shows Stage One Melanoma."

"I'll be there in twenty minutes."

This was the third mole I'd had removed in Namibia, and I had come to regard the procedure as routine. Nothing more than a mild inconvenience. I wasn't about to let these small, dark skin-invaders, these freckles with attitudes, rule my life. Even as my doctor's words began to register, another self insisted, "He's made a mistake. It really isn't *me* he's talking about."

I desperately needed my husband, but Lou was still across campus teaching his seminar. I forced myself to take deep breaths as I drove through the gates of the campus and headed north, toward town. I barely noticed Windhoek's earnest street vendors peddling their batiks and carvings, the women in gaily colored head wraps selling their roasted ears of corn by the side of the road, the children in their uniforms laughing their way home from school, images that always made me feel happy I lived here. I couldn't even hear the grumble of the passing cars because the word *cancer* had begun screaming in my brain. Was I going to die? How soon could I return to the States? Would I ever see Africa again? Who would teach my classes?

Half an hour later, I sat in the car outside Dr. Rohn's office reading the report. At that time, I had no idea what was meant by terms such as Clark Level or Breslow thickness. It was the word "malignant" that made the papers tremble in my hands. As I drove back to the campus, I tried to talk myself down from the mountain of fear. It's Stage One. There are treatments.

When I returned home, Lou was sitting in his favorite chair in our living room, working a crossword puzzle. "Where have you been?" Hearing my silence, he looked up. My face must have told the end of the story while my voice still struggled to tell the beginning. "Susan! My God, what's happened?"

I described the past two hours. Finally, "Dr. Rohn says this can be treated easily. He said I could have the surgery right here in Windhoek. He gave me the surgeon's name and said I should phone him in the morning."

"And are you comfortable with that?" Lou asked.

"I think I'll send an e-mail to John." Our longtime friend was an oncologist in Chapel Hill, North Carolina. I already knew he would tell me to return home for treatment, but, more importantly, he could also tell me what I was dealing with.

Fortunately, our temperamental Internet connection was working that night. After I sent my e-mail, I did an exhaustive search for anything related to melanoma. My search gave me new things to worry about, things like lymph node involvement and metastases to other body organs.

As expected, John's prompt response urged me to return home. When I wrote back that I wanted to consider all options, he gave me the name of a reputable Cape Town surgeon. I felt better knowing I had choices. I decided to explore the Namibia Option first and made an appointment with Dr. Lauschke, the local surgeon. I was surprised when he said he could see me the next day.

We drove to Klein Windhoek, the affluent "white" section of town, and found the house number neatly painted on the curb. Blood-red bougainvilleas smothered the whitewashed wall, and a tasteful, bronze plaque on the gate assured us we'd come to the right place. The doctor's office appeared to be an extension of his elegant, adobe-style home. We walked into a deserted office dominated by a shiny executive desk, as empty as the waiting room. To the right, a doorway opened into an examining room. Lou and I stood by the desk, wondering if we should sit down in the chairs in front of it or call out that we were there, when a tall, middle-aged man in a white coat strode though the examining room door. He looked like Freud. The same intense eyes and neatly trimmed beard. When Dr. Lauschke introduced himself to us and invited us to sit down, his accent identified him as an Afrikaner, a descendent of the Dutch settlers of southern Africa. I handed him the pathology report.

"Hmm. Stage One Melanoma. Well, that doesn't sound too bad. Let's see what the literature says."

He stood up, reached for a book from the shelf behind his desk, and started reading. The punched-in-the-stomach feeling returned, and I started twisting a piece of my skirt. Why did he need to read a book to know what to do?

He ushered us into the examining room, told me to climb onto the examining table, and peered at the little spot on my leg that was still healing from the biopsy. Removing a ballpoint pen from his pocket, he drew a large rectangle around the spot, about three inches wide and four inches long.

"We have to make sure we have good margins, so we must remove an area this size. We will close the wound with a skin graft taken from your thigh. I will phone you and let you know how soon we can schedule the surgery theater."

I nodded, mute with fear, and paid the doctor his fee, the equivalent of forty U.S. dollars.

"Well?" asked Lou as we drove back to the campus. That's always my husband's shorthand for: "I have an opinion, but you tell me your thoughts first."

"Lou, this is a doctor who had to *read a book* to know what to do. Did you see the size of the circle he drew on my leg? I'm scratching the Namibia Option."

"Absolutely!"

Then came the guilt. Would I be a bad expatriate if I refused treatment in my adopted country? I often felt uncomfortable living among people who would never have the wealth and the choices available to us. But this was cancer. And this was my life.

"I'm going to phone the Cape Town doctor," I told Lou.

My guilt faded the next day when Dr. Duminy's office manager made all the arrangements, including the recommendation of a comfortable guesthouse where I could stay during the post-op period. When I inquired about the doctor's credentials, she told me the doctor had a web site. I found his photo online and learned that he'd studied in Europe.

Next I phoned Dr. Lauschke and told him that I had decided to have the surgery in Cape Town. He protested. "That really isn't necessary. Besides, I have scheduled your surgery for seven o'clock tomorrow morning."

"I am sorry to inconvenience you," I replied. "I must ask you to cancel it."

Silence. Then, "As you wish," and I was listening to a dial tone.

I kept reassuring myself that I would get state-of-the-art medical treatment in Cape Town. After all, that's where Dr. Christiaan Bernard performed the world's first heart transplant. How could that be selfish?

Three weeks later, we rented a compact car at the Cape Town airport and drove to Claremont, an upscale suburb twenty minutes away. There was something comforting about returning to Cape Town—this was our third visit—but it wasn't the stunning scenery that appealed this time. It was the reassurance of stepping back into civilization as I remembered it.

Dr. Duminy's office looked like a small, stone house set in an English garden. Above the door was the sign "Rose Cottage." Nurse Morrisey explained that after this visit I would be going to Kingsbury, the small, private hospital across the road for blood samples, a chest x-ray, and an ultrasound of my liver. "That's to make certain there isn't any organ involvement," she said. "They will also measure your leg for the special surgical stocking you will wear when the bandage comes off."

I already felt more comfortable.

Dr. Duminy, a genial, middle-aged man with a British accent, carefully explained his approach to my treatment. After examining my leg, he took out his ballpoint pen and drew a rectangle on my shin. It was the same size as the one Dr. Lauschke had drawn.

I felt alarmed. And embarrassed. Was I naïve in my hope for a less invasive procedure?

"Does it have to be that big?" I whispered.

The answer was the same one I had received in Namibia. He told me that melanoma cells had long tendrils. A wide surgical excision was essential to insure there would be no recurrence in the skin surrounding the lesion. He explained that my melanoma could be the result of sun exposure many years, even decades, earlier. It may not even have been a sunburn at the site of the lesion.

I swallowed hard, thinking less about the inevitable disfigurement and more about the cancer. I remembered the lazy summer days of my childhood, most of them at the community pool. Our annual Outer Banks vacations when our own children were small. I remembered telling my friend Angie, "I want to come back with tanned legs." And there was that week in Miami, the one where I'd fallen asleep and the silver cross around my neck had burned its imprint into my chest.

Back in our elegant room in the guesthouse, I read the lab results. Some were written in Afrikaans, and I learned that the Afrikaans word for laboratory specimen is "monster."

I returned to the hospital the next morning. As soon as I filled out all the paperwork, a friendly young man escorted us to the surgery floor. The nurses all wore military-looking shoulder boards on their starched white uniforms. I stowed my clothes in a tiny locker and gave Lou my handbag.

Lou gave me a tight hug, and the nurse wheeled my gurney into the surgical theater. I recognized Dr. Duminy's eyes above the surgical mask, and he introduced me to the anesthesiologist who began inserting the IV line.

Even though I knew what was going to happen, I was shocked when I awakened in the recovery area to see my right leg swathed in a bulky white bandage, from my knee to my ankle. I felt a wide steel brace at the back of my leg. Another thick bandage covered my thigh, from which the skin for the graft had been removed. Monsters. Give them a few inches, and the next thing you know, they want your whole leg. After an hour, Dr. Duminy came into the room and said I could return to the guesthouse. He gave me an appointment card for my return visit the following week.

For the next five days, I lay in bed with two fluffy pillows supporting my back and another three under my leg, a vial of pain pills on the nightstand. From the window I could see the early spring-blooming trees. Bored, I flipped through the TV channels, usually settling on the Sydney Olympics. The guesthouse staff brought gourmet dinners to our room.

One afternoon, our American colleague, Phillip, visited me. He pulled his Queen Anne chair closer to my bed, and I told him about my experience with the Windhoek doctor, and how difficult it was choosing where to have the procedure done. "You know, Susan, *choice* is one of the fundamental differences between people who live in the Western world and those who live in Africa." Of course, he was right. I felt the expat guilt creeping back.

When Nurse Morrissey removed bandages four days later, I had to look away from the hideous-looking cavity of raw meat. My mouth began to water, and I hoped I wouldn't shame myself by vomiting. The nurse touched my hand. "The first glimpse is always a bit shocking," she said.

"But will it always be that deep?"

"Well, yes. This is what we call a partial thickness skin graft. All the fatty tissue on your shin has been removed. Maybe, in time, you could consider reconstructive surgery but we don't recommend that for at least two years. It makes it more difficult to determine if there is any recurrence."

She rewrapped my leg, told me how to change the dressings, and handed me a brown paper bag full of bandages and ointments. "In about ten days you should have the surgical staples taken out. I suggest you visit the casualty section of your Windhoek hospital. Please phone me if you have any questions. Here's a card with my e-mail address."

On our way to the Cape Town airport, I looked out the car window and saw a grim urban ghetto of shanties extending toward the horizon: the renowned Cape Flats. I peered intently at a woman hanging her washing on the clothesline and a man repairing the corrugated tin roof of his tiny shack, and I thought again about choices: the medical choices available to me, and the gut-wrenching poverty that obliterated any choice.

Low-flying aircraft signaled our approach to the airport, but I couldn't stop thinking about those Cape Flat dwellers. And I thought about all the students we had taken to clinics in Namibia. Sometimes they waited the entire day to see a doctor, only to be told to return the next day. It seemed the only ailment those physicians could treat with any measure of competence was malaria. How many of our students had returned to campus telling us they'd been given aspirin and vitamins for their sprained ankles, rashes, and stomachaches? When a complaint seemed serious enough to require further follow-up, we'd take them to a specialist and pay the doctor ourselves.

While I recuperated on campus, the students welcomed me with flowers and bedside visits. They came in groups of three or four, and I felt as if I were holding court, my braced and bandaged leg propped up on three pillows. These young men and women had grown up in traditional homesteads without electricity or running water. During school holidays they would return home to help harvest the family's millet crop, pound the grain for the day's porridge, or collect water from communal wells.

I thought about my visits to those homesteads, where Lou and I had been welcomed so graciously. I thought about people who lived in the elegant mansions of that Cape Town neighborhood and the others who lived a few miles away in the corrugated tin shacks. I thought about an elderly Namibian couple I knew who had given up two months of their meager pensions so their granddaughter could attend the university for one semester. I thought about those young men who stood on the street corners of Windhoek, waiting for someone to offer them a day-job doing "casual labour" such as gardening or construction work. They had thought, after their country gained its independence in 1990, that life would be better. They had thought that they'd have choices. Like those who lived in the mansions. Like me.

Two weeks later, I made an appointment to have the surgical staples removed at MediClinic, Windhoek's private, state-of-the-art hospital. The same hospital where our young colleague, Heather, had been treated after her automobile accident. A nurse phoned me back.

"The surgeon said the removal of staples is so painful that many patients prefer to have this done under general anesthesia." Dr. Duminy hadn't said anything about this. I wondered what would happen if I just left them in. After all, they were high quality staples. They probably wouldn't rust.

I found Nurse Morrisey's phone number in the brown paper bag with the ointments and bandages, and quickly placed a call to Cape Town. She assured me that she had never had to anesthetize a patient for this procedure.

The doctor met me at "casualties" and efficiently removed all twenty-nine staples. Without anesthesia. It didn't hurt any more than having stitches taken out.

I spent most of the next month lying on our living room sofa, which was about as comfortable as the nubby back seat of my dad's 1957 Chevy, pillows under my leg to reduce the edema. The heat made my leg swell, and the tight, surgical stocking didn't seem to help. I felt a twanging sensation in my shin, as if currents of electricity were coursing up and down my lower leg. I sent Nurse Morrisey an e-mail. She wrote back the same day and said that the nerves have all been disturbed. She said that nerves are supposed to work in shifts, but mine are now always working together, "firing" all the time. She suggested that lightly stroking my shin with a piece of cotton or a soft brush several times a day would help the nerves get back on their proper schedule. I was glad when Lou gave my English students their final exams. Grading them gave me something to do.

Four weeks later, I was able to accompany Lou for short trips into town, and one of these was a visit to the US Embassy to mail our absentee ballots. A few days later, I was able to remove the bandages for good, and Lou took me shopping for some lightweight slacks, better than my usual skirts for concealing the disgusting surgical wound. I still had trouble looking at this angry, puckered red dent in my leg,

I had been planning to relinquish my job as accommodations manager at the end of the year anyway, and my surgery provided the opportunity for me to do so a few months earlier. Matheus, the seminary's treasurer, agreed to take over these duties. What a relief!

Our students continued to visit us. One afternoon, two of our Ovambo students, Phina and Nambili (he had once told us his name meant "a man of peace") sipped glasses of chilled orange juice in our living room and told us about the latest incident with Dr. van Wyk.

"We were in our New Testament class," said Nambili, "and he said, 'I hate Germans, Americans, and Ovambos.' He was acting like a crazy man!"

Phina nodded vigorously. "Yes! He said, 'I could kill all you Ovambos—just like we did in the South African army camps.'"

"I think you ought to tell the members of the Governing Board," I said.

"No," said Lou. "Don't you remember what happened when the students tried to do that two years ago? Van Wyk made life hell for the students." He turned to Nambili. "I think you should tell the principal. Dr. Shangala will know the best way to handle this."

Sadly, Michael never did anything about out students' complaint, confirming our hunch that he was afraid of van Wyk, too. Michael was also an Ovambo.

When the last of the students had left the campus and we had finished grading all the final exams, Lou and I went to the Etosha Game Park for three days. We brought out short-wave radio so we could tune in to Voice of America and learn the election results. On Election Day, as Lou and I sat in our vehicle watching the zebras at a dusty water hole, I whispered, "I guess if an elephant comes to the water hole, that will be a sign!"

Weeks later, our Namibian friends were still teasing us. "What? Your country hasn't got a new president yet? Maybe you should have had Africans there to monitor your elections."

Dorothy, the seminary's American librarian, and I decided to host a small Thanksgiving dinner. We invited Angela, our missionary colleague working in Windhoek, Sophie, the seminary's kitchen supervisor, and Matheus, our treasurer. Since turkey wasn't available in Namibia, we bought two chickens to roast. I made a sweet potato casserole and Dorothy made stuffing and baked a pumpkin pie. We were pleased to find cranberry sauce in the large downtown grocery store. Angela was happy to be with other Americans on Thanksgiving, a day that would otherwise have been another hot, summer workday in Namibia. We sent leftovers home with Sophie and Matheus, and Dorothy and I still had enough food remaining for several more dinners.

When I returned to Dr. Rohn's office for a final check-up, he was pleased with the healing, but concerned about the risks of edema from the two long airline flights. He gave me a good quality elastic bandage and showed me how to wrap it properly. I mentioned that, even with the letter he had given me, I had been having trouble getting South African Airlines to guarantee me a bulkhead seat in economy class where I could at least elevate my leg a bit. Half in jest, I said, "Maybe I should wrap it in gauze and limp a lot." He thought that was a good idea, and even suggested that I buy some cotton wool to make it look bigger.

When we returned home from seeing Dr. Rohn, we learned that Dr. van Wyk had been readmitted to the hospital because he'd had another stroke. That evening, Michael accompanied Lou and me to the Roman Catholic Hospital. We were shocked to see our irascible colleague lying in his hospital bed looking so feeble. His face was ashen, and when he tried to speak, his words were barely audible. He told us he had pneumonia, as well as the stroke. Before we left his bedside, Lou took hold of his hand and said a prayer. A tear trickled down the older man's cheek. In the hallway, just outside his room, his daughter told us that he was also in renal failure.

Dr. van Wyk died two days later, at about four o'clock on Sunday afternoon. At seven-thirty that evening, there was a memorial service for him at our chapel attended mostly by members of the coloured community and representatives of the Southern Church. It felt very strange to be attending a memorial service for a person who had been so openly hostile to so many people, particularly the whites and the blacks, and who had been such a stumbling block to unity and progress at the seminary.

The formal funeral service, which would also be held at the seminary, was scheduled for the following week. We would be in North Carolina by then. The family had asked the seminary staff to provide a meal afterwards. Michael and Matheus decided that the seminary would give the family about one hundred dollars to help with funeral expenses. Before they even had a chance to prepare the check, representatives of the van Wyk family told Michael they expected the seminary to bear the entire cost of the post-funeral meal.

"We bought enough food for three hundred people," Matheus reported to us later. It had cost nearly $1,000. "Only seventy or eighty people showed up. Rather than leaving the leftovers behind, which could have been frozen and used for our students, the people grabbed everything. I saw some people walking away with four or five cans of soda."

We had all expected that Dr. van Wyk would be buried at Rehoboth, the coloured community south of Windhoek that was the family's hometown. Instead, the burial occurred in Windhoek at what is known locally as The White Cemetery. During the apartheid years, there existed two cemeteries on the south end of town, a beautifully maintained and landscaped one for whites only, and one for blacks that was not much more than a scruffy field. Today, the black cemetery has been tidied up and is primarily used for war heroes and government officials.

As I limped around our bedroom, taking winter clothes from the cupboards and placing them into the open suitcase on our bed, I thought again about choices and my own privileged ability to choose where I would have the melanoma surgery. As Phillip had reminded me, most Africans have few choices. Dr. van Wyk, a colored man, had had many more choices than black Namibians during the country's decades of apartheid captivity, but what had he chosen? As a person of mixed race, he lacked the heritage, traditions, and cohesion that bound together members of Namibia's black tribes so, when he was offered the opportunity to acquire rank and status, he had turned his back on his countrymen and joined the occupying government of the white South Africans. Later, when the spotlight of international attention illuminated the plight of Namibia, Johan van Wyk did an about-face and publicly excoriated the oppressors. The Southern Church rescinded its excommunication of van Wyk, but no congregation would accept him as its pastor. This bitter, unhappy man continued persecuting blacks—now they were his students—until the day he died. Perhaps his final choice of burial in the cemetery that had been reserved for whites allowed him peace in death, a peace he'd never enjoyed in life.

Chapter 22
Cultural Collisions

*M*y home country had never felt so welcoming. In previous years, I couldn't wait to visit my children, to see what was new on supermarket shelves, to drive on the right side of the road again. This time, all I could think about was my visit to the melanoma specialist in Chapel Hill.

I hoisted myself onto the examining table and tucked the paper sheet snugly around my legs. Was it my imagination, or did the cupboards, the sink, the few instruments on the shelves gleam a little more brightly than those in Africa?

A knock on the door, and in walked a smiling, middle-aged woman who extended her hand and introduced herself as Dr. Thomas. She carefully read all the medical notes I had brought with me. "Your treatment was appropriate," she said. She examined the surgical site. "Oh! The excision is awfully large, isn't it?"

"Do you mean it didn't have to be that big?"

"I haven't removed this much tissue for years. Recent studies have shown it to be unnecessary." She suggested I try Dermablend, a thick concealing makeup used by lupus patients, to soften the appearance of the wound. Like Nurse Morrisey, she advised against plastic surgery. "We need to watch this site for recurrence. And be sure to get quarterly melanoma checkups from a qualified dermatologist when you return to Africa."

Forty-eight hours after we arrived back in Namibia, our suitcases caught up with us. It wasn't unusual for luggage to linger a while—or forever—at the Johannesburg airport where we had changed planes. We never checked through any baggage that contained medicines or anything else that would be a horrible hassle to replace. After unpacking, I drove to Baines, the small neighborhood shopping center, for a quick take-away pizza and a few grocery items. My hairstylist, Nikki, waved hello as I walked past her little shop, and I was surprised how happy I was to be back at my tiny, local grocery store with its limited selection. I didn't miss the overwhelming aisles of an American Super Giant. The shop assistant carried my bags out to the little parking lot and loaded them into the car. I gave him the usual tip. As I drove back to our flat on campus, I wondered about how it was possible to feel so completely at home in two very different continents.

We settled back into life in our campus home. Feeling sluggish from two months of relative inactivity, we decided it was time to resume our daily visits to the health club. When I donned my workout shorts, I also carefully wrapped my right shin in an ace bandage, to avoid attracting attention. Some Africans have a disconcerting trait. They don't consider it rude to stare at someone with a disability or deformity. A few days later, I forgot to wear the ace bandage. I noticed a young fellow on the stationary bike next to mine peering intently at the angry red crater on my shin. When he glanced up, I just shook my head ruefully. "Lion," I whispered.

Our classes and our daily chapel services resumed. Three years earlier, on our visit to the San (Bushman) community, I had bought a small purse made by the Bushmen: white ostrich leather decorated with leather fringe and tiny shells. Its long, thinly braided leather strap made it a convenient shoulder bag to take Sunday worship services, and it had just enough room for my keys, some money for the offering, and a couple of tissues. When I was not using this bag, I hung it on the living room wall as a decoration. From time to time, students or faculty members commented about it when I took it to chapel services, but I never thought much about their comments until one Sunday when Michael said to me, "Do you know what that is?"

"Yes," I replied, "it's a handbag that I bought from the Bushman community."

"Oh, no it isn't," he laughed. "It is a witch doctor's medicine bag."

My mouth dropped open. The very next day, another Namibian pastor stopped by our flat and commented upon the bag when he saw it hanging on the wall. This pastor had just returned to Namibia after completing the course work for his Ph.D. in the United States. When I told him about Michael's comment, he shook his head, smiled, and said, "You're lucky you weren't thrown out! Until recently, people were forbidden to bring items of witchcraft into a church."

I wondered why—in the three years I had been carrying this "purse" to church—no one had told me. I wondered what other embarrassing behavior I had inadvertently engaged in. Then I had another thought. Perhaps Michael Shangala finally felt comfortable enough to say such a thing to me.

At the end of the month, we took an extended weekend trip to Swartfontein, a guest farm located about two hundred kilometers south of Windhoek. Swartfontein ("Black Spring") was owned by a young Italian couple, Roberto and Silvia, who had lived in Namibia only a year longer than we had. Silvia was the daughter of the Italian ambassador to Ethiopia. Until his move to Namibia, Roberto had been a highly paid lawyer who specialized in international corporate trade. When I asked him why he had chosen to alter his lifestyle so radically, he said, "I found that I had everything I wanted and needed in Italy—everything money could buy. But I was not deriving any pleasure from these things anymore. My Alfa Romero was parked in the garage all week. I remembered the carefree days of my youth when I would ride my motorcycle all over the country, and I decided that I did not want to spend the next twenty or thirty years in corporate law." They had a four-month-old son, Lorenzo, and Silvia told us that she had just discovered that she was five weeks pregnant.

This farm boasted a variety of wild game, and Roberto said the real profit from his farm was not from the guest accommodations, but, rather, the sale of the game to hunting lodges. We learned that hunters would pay seven thousand U.S. dollars to shoot a black wildebeest, which is considered "trophy game." I had always hated the idea of hunting. Something inside me shuddered at the thought of raising these magnificent animals to be hairy, tusked wall ornaments for wealthy Europeans, but I held my tongue. The couple had plans to make their farm self-supporting. They already grew all their own vegetables.

During dinner, Roberto talked to us about how long it took to build the trust of neighboring farmers. Their biggest problem, he said, was keeping dependable workers. They had tried hiring black workers from a Windhoek trade school, but found them to be unreliable. One young woman left after one month, saying she had to return to school. She didn't comprehend that she had been hired on a one-year contract. The workers they hired who were supposed to be trained gardeners seemed unable to understand the concept of staggered vegetable planting to provide a continuous variety of crops.

"One month," Silvia said, "we had nothing but radishes. The next month, spinach. The month after that, Chinese cabbage."

"And it is so difficult," added Roberto, "to try to make them understand the need to keep the place looking nice. I keep telling them this is what encourages guests to return and will help them earn more money for themselves. We used to have such a big problem with littering. When this continued to happen, I took a dustbin full of rubbish and dumped it inside their house. Even today, when you arrived, I noticed a pile of shit-of-the-dog on the grass, and I told the yard worker that there would be five Namibian dollars (about seventy-five cents in US currency) deducted from his pay that week. 'Did you not see that our guests were arriving?' I asked him. The worker said, 'Yes.' 'But still you did not remove it!'"

During our game drive the next morning, I asked Roberto if he knew why Namibians seemed to export so few artifacts to other countries. "I recently visited the woodcarvers market in Okahandja," I said. "I asked one of the craftsmen whether anyone had ever discussed with him the export of his beautiful teak tables and chairs to Europe or the United States, and he said, 'No.'"

"Don't believe it!" exclaimed Roberto. "Some time ago, I made an arrangement with one of those vendors to purchase a large quantity of his wares: chairs, tables, large carved hippos. I sent a big crate of these items to a furniture dealer in Milano. I told the woodcarver that we could make a profitable arrangement with him, and that the dealers in Italy were pleased to receive nice African artifacts. But when I returned the following month, the woodcarver was uninterested in continuing the arrangement. It seems so difficult for Africans to understand long-term planning."

I nodded, recalling my own experiences at the seminary. I had heard about so many schemes for developing our seminary into a first-rate conference center to provide valuable income, but I had seen so little effort toward actualizing those plans. Lou and I had thought—and had been taught, by our national church in America—that all these Africans needed was a small boost, a helping hand, but we were running out of ways to explain or excuse behavior that seemed to suggest something else.

Roberto continued. "To live day-to-day is deep within the culture of these people. And maybe that is the right way for them. When they see some of the nice things I have, such as a good car or a television, and I tell them the path they must follow to have those things, they do not find it acceptable to work so hard for so many hours a week."

I thought about what everyone laughingly called *African Time*. Even our Namibian friends used the term to explain away their tardiness. But I had also noticed that Namibians valued time spent visiting and socializing with friends and family, and maybe that wasn't such an undesirable value. Our young African-American colleague, Angie, secretary to the bishop of the Southern Church, had told us a typical workday at the church office in Windhoek was punctuated with two long tea breaks, mid-morning and afternoon, plus a ninety-minute lunch "hour." Our seminary grounds keepers appeared to spend as much time lying under a tree as they did trimming, weeding and sweeping. These workers had no job description, no training, and no supervision. And yet, so many young people, including Priscilla who was a maid at this guest farm, told us of their desire to "go for further studies" so they could advance themselves. Priscilla said, "Even if you go abroad for a single course of study, not even a diploma or degree, you are much more likely to find a good job in Namibia when you return. Often, it does not even matter what you have studied."

With a countrywide unemployment rate of around forty per cent, we kept hearing about a rising level of frustration and despair among young Namibians. And also a rising number of robberies, pickpockets and break-ins. Every month, six hundred impoverished, unemployed Namibians from small villages and rural homesteads migrated to Windhoek, seeking work. The majority were unskilled and ended up living in squatter camps which the city officials euphemistically called "informal settlements." The new arrivals placed a burdensome strain on the city's resources and also upon their extended families, with whom they often moved in. Their Windhoek relatives were barely making it themselves.

Unlike our usual restorative getaways to the Namibian countryside or the coast, our weekend conversations with Roberto and Sylvia left me feeling frustrated and confused. As we drove back to the campus, Lou and I told each other that we had thought, after four years of living among Africans, we would have acquired a better understanding of the people with whom we lived and worked. I wonder if our discontent ignited the spark of the Ash Wednesday fiasco.

We entered the chapel for our usual Wednesday evening vespers service. Ash Wednesday and the penitential season of Lent, such a major part of our own liturgical tradition, were unknown to our students. Apparently, the nineteenth-century Protestant missionaries had found these observances too Catholic. As Lou and I approached the chapel, we heard loud music blaring from the synthesizer and speakers. Second-year student Henrico, a talented musician, was playing what sounded to us like rock music. Students from the Southern Church, Damaras, Hereros, and coloureds, were in charge of leading that evening's service. When students from one tribe or another led worship, they frequently used some of their indigenous-language hymns. Rather than enhancing the multi-cultural dimensions of life on the campus, our often-xenophobic seminary community tended to resent this practice.

Fourth-year student Jermaine greeted the congregation at the beginning of the service and declared that he was "the M.C. for the evening." I sensed Lou stiffen in the seat next to me. Lutheran worship services are led by clergy or trained lay people, not masters of ceremonies. All the hymns were unknown by the non-Damara members of the community, and some were not even known by them. There was a lot of faltering and stumbling through the service, with Jermaine alternately preening or admonishing.

At the conclusion of the service, during the usual time for announcements, Lou stood up, walked to the front of the sanctuary, and turned to face the congregation. "When Moses encountered God, he was told to take off his shoes because he was standing on holy ground," Lou said. "When we come to chapel services we are entering holy ground. The task of worship is to lead people to God. Tonight's service was not a service of worship. It was a production. It is the task of the worship leader to bring the congregation into closer contact with the Holy, not to entertain them. I have no quarrel with using elements from our traditions—it is what makes us a stronger community—but I do have a quarrel with worship that is sloppy and unprepared, as it was tonight. I am not speaking to you now as the Dean of Students, but as an ordained pastor of the Lutheran Church. If I see this kind of careless worship leadership again, I will personally ask the student worship leader to sit down and I will replace you." Unfortunately for us, none of the Namibian faculty members had attended that Ash Wednesday worship service.

The next day, several Ovambo students came to our flat and said that a group of Damara students left campus as soon as the chapel service ended and did not return until after midnight. We were told that they had gone to visit local pastors to complain about Lou. One of the pastors they visited was Dirk, our former principal. The Ovambo students said that the Damara students wanted to bring Lou before the Southern Church board to accuse him of favoring Ovambos. Just as we had witnessed during the student strike of 1997, large groups of Damara students began congregating with one another under the trees and in the roads. From our balcony we again heard loud, heated conversations. For the next week, these students from the Southern Church boycotted all the daily worship services. One of them, the Damara student librarian who had the library keys, was off campus all day, so students couldn't use the library.

The tension between Damaras and Ovambos was escalating. Nambili said, "They are calling us baboons. In our Namibian society, Damaras always treat Ovambos as their slaves. They ridicule us because we come from poorer backgrounds. When some of us Ovambos arrived at Paulinum last year, we were shocked and confused. We had thought that this place—a school of theology—would be different." He sighed. "Now we are used to it. That is just the ways things are."

During the apartheid years, the Ovambos suffered from Bantu education, an inferior type of schooling designed to keep blacks uneducated. They were given courses about agriculture, but no science or mathematics. Historically, the Damaras had always had better schools, more textbooks and class materials, and better-trained teachers. When Namibia threw off the shackles of South African rule ten years earlier, the Ovambos became the predominant cultural and political group in Namibia, a new reality that antagonized the Damaras. Nonetheless, although we preferred the companionship of our Ovambo students, we tried not to play favorites. I remembered, unhappily, that two weeks earlier Lou and I had hosted a dinner in our flat for three Damara couples and their wives. They seemed to have conveniently forgotten.

The next week, we all had a shock that took everyone's mind off our tribal conflicts. Lou and I had just finished supper and were washing and drying our dishes when we received a breathless phone call from our second-year student, Hainane. "Morekwa has been stabbed!"

Lou hurried over to the dormitory. Morekwa, our student from Botswana, had been walking back to the campus from soccer practice in an adjacent neighborhood when a young man accosted him with a knife. In an attempt to defend himself, he put his hand up in front of his face and his assailant slashed his hand with the knife. His turquoise-blue Charlotte Hornets T-shirt, given to him three years ago by some of our North Carolina friends, was speckled with blood. He had wrapped his hand in a towel, and the red stain was spreading. He was barefooted; his assailant had taken his soccer shoes and socks. We put him into the back seat of the Venture and rushed to the emergency room at Medi-Clinic.

What we had thought would be a fairly simple matter of a few stitches turned out to be significantly more serious. Dr. Rohn, who happened to be on call that night at the hospital, told us that the flexor tendon on his fourth finger had been severed, and that Morekwa needed a very complicated surgical procedure. We left our student in Dr. Rohn's competent hands and returned home around ten o'clock to find the campus and the surrounding neighborhood plunged into darkness. Another power outage. They were becoming more frequent.

The following week, I took Morekwa to an orthopaedic specialist who constructed a dynamic splint for him. The splint allowed him to exercise and flex the finger so it would not lock into place. A week later, I took Morekwa back to the surgeon's office to have the stitches removed. He was wearing the Cornell University T-shirt we'd given him. When we had told him our son, Jason, was in graduate school at Cornell Morekwa had worn the T-shirt for the whole week. (I wondered if I could—tactfully, of course—tell him it was okay to wash the shirt.) As I was backing the car out of the parking place, I complained of having a stiff neck. I said to Morekwa that I must have slept on it wrong. He replied, "In my village people would say that the witch doctor visited you during the night and walked on your neck!"

When I asked him to tell me more about that, he reminded me that witchcraft in Botswana is very common. While we were driving back to campus, Morekwa began to tell me about his family. "This past summer, when I was doing my internship in a congregation in Gaboronne, I never once returned to my village. Because my mother is unmarried, my uncle has legal responsibility for my sister and me. But those people—my extended family—all believe in witchcraft. They are not happy that I am studying to become a pastor, and I am uncomfortable being around them."

"Have they said this to you?"

He was silent for a few seconds, as if he were considering how much he could tell me. Finally, he said, "Let me tell you what happened last year. In my Setswana culture, the father role is important and people say a home without a man is not a real home. Since my mother is not married, I am considered the man of the house because I am the first-born son.

"After my second year here at the seminary, my mother got some land in Gaboronne. She wanted to build a house. When starting a new home you need to perform some rituals before building anything on the land. I was in Windhoek when my mother wanted to begin building. The land was still traditionally untouched—it wasn't made clean—but my mother couldn't wait for me because I wouldn't be coming home until the end of the year, so she hired a builder.

"During the process, the chief builder started to feel pains in his fingers after work. The surprising thing was that this took place only when he went to work at *our* home. At some other places where they had contracts there were no problems.

"When I went back home I met the builder and he told me the same story. I was not convinced. I asked whether he had consulted a doctor, but he said that was unnecessary. He said it was most definitely a traditional problem."

"What do you mean, Morekwa? What is a traditional problem?"

"The house—or the land—was bewitched."

"So, what did you do?"

"By then, the term holiday was over and I had to return to Windhoek, so my mother consulted the *Ngaka*." He glanced at me quickly, and then stared straight ahead, out the window. "That's the witch doctor. He said our homesite was endangered by witchcraft, and this was disturbing any progress of building. He said this was because the land had never been healed traditionally. My mother asked the *Ngaka* to perform the healing. He agreed but only if I, the first son of my mother, was present. Without my presence the *Ngaka* said he could not enter that home.

"The extended family—my uncles, grandmother, aunts, and my mother—phoned me. They were aware that I didn't like traditional healing and such stuff, but I had no alternative. I went back to Botswana. Maybe you remember that week I had to leave Namibia to go home."

I nodded. "You must have felt uncomfortable doing that."

"Not just uncomfortable. I was scared! I was afraid of being cut by sharp things by the *Ngaka*. That is what these witch doctors do. It was midnight when we went to the land. We were each carrying torches. On the way I asked the *Ngaka* if he would cut me. He promised that he wouldn't do it, provided I use his medicines. I was carrying the container, a calabash. I looked inside and sniffed. There were lots of herbs mixed with a liquored thing and some medicines that I can't describe. We had to walk in a straight line behind the *Ngaka*. I was behind him and my mother was behind me. The *Ngaka* started right at the gate, putting some medicine on it and covering it with dirt. He did the same in all four corners of the yard and in the center. Then he took the tail of a horse that was tied to a stick and dipped it into the calabash and sprinkled water all over the yard. Later we came to the middle of the yard.

"He lit some candles and handed one to me, and then he called the ancestors. He told us to kneel down. After a long exorcism with ancestors he came back to life. I was still holding the candle. He poured healing water on us from the calabash he had been carrying. There were some slight changes in my body, but I cannot exactly describe them. Maybe I was afraid. He took a pouch from his clothing and gave us little packets of some medicine to wash with whenever we took a bath. He said we must use the medicine until it was finished. He looked right at me. The *Ngaka* told me that if I didn't do this I would have problems. I did precisely as I was told.

"A week later I came back to the seminary to continue with my studies. I told my Namibian lecturers what had happened and they were very interested to hear how I felt after this rite."

"How *did* you feel?"

"Sometimes when I was relaxing I felt, or maybe I imagined, that something sharp like a razor or needle was cutting me inside my body. I stayed with this feeling for two to three weeks in Windhoek. If I saw something that was sharp, the imagination of a demon of some sort just came immediately. I was really scared about that. As a Tswana I knew something was wrong, but I continued to put my trust in God. It was not long after that when I was attacked by those gangsters with knives."

Morekwa looked off into the distance. We were approaching the campus, and I turned onto the same road on which he'd been attacked. He continued with his story. "The evening I was attacked, I took my usual way to the soccer training. One guy grabbed me from behind and demanded money. Another one wanted to stab me with a knife. He cut my hand, but I managed to kick his hand and the knife. I still do not know how I escaped. I just ran away. I still haven't been able to sleep well. I'm worried God may be punishing me for the traditional rites I performed in Botswana. But maybe not. Perhaps the feelings I had before the accident were foretelling what would happen to me. Maybe I did not perform the whole rites of healing wholeheartedly because I was influenced by Christian faith. All these thoughts are still bothering me." He shrugged and forced a weak smile. "I try to ignore them."

From time to time, our students would mention witchcraft to us, but rarely did they speak with us as openly as Morekwa had. I knew that, as a Botswanan, he felt he was an outsider in Namibia. Like we did. Maybe that bond, along with my taking him to his many doctors' appointments, had allowed him to feel close enough to share his thoughts and fears with me. I was grateful. I hoped his telling me had, somehow, made him feel better.

At the end of March, another American missionary arrived in Namibia. Our national church in America had sent us an e-mail saying that Adam, a recent college graduate, would be teaching math for two years at Oshigambo High School, where our friends Ray, Lois, and Heather had previously taught. Lou and I had e-mailed our supervisors in Chicago to assure them we would meet his flight.

We waited for Adam in the arrivals lobby until long after all the passengers had cleared customs and immigration. This was not a good sign. Lou approached one of the airport officials and explained that we were awaiting the arrival of our colleague. Could the gentleman kindly allow us into the immigration clearance area, because there seemed to be a delay of some sort? The man nodded, and we walked past the baggage carousel into the immigration area. A tall, handsome young man with tousled blond hair and a very red face appeared to be pleading with the immigration official, a portly woman in a navy blue uniform. "It is no good," she was saying. "This letter," she waved a document in the young man's face, "is *not* a visa! You are trying to enter Namibia illegally."

"Excuse me." My husband stepped forward. I was glad he was wearing his clerical collar, something he rarely did here in Namibia. I wondered if he'd had a premonition. "Is there a problem?"

"Yes, Reverend. This man says he has a Namibian work permit, but all he can show me is this letter from the principal of a school in Oshigambo."

Lou quickly introduced himself to Adam, and asked him if he had any other documentation. "No, they told me this letter was all I'd need." Poor Adam. Namibia's immigration officials required delicate handling. I knew he'd probably been traveling for at least thirty-six hours, and was in no condition to negotiate his way thought the situation. I wondered why and how our national church had allowed him to leave the States without a visa.

The official was beckoning Lou and Adam into a small, glass-walled office. She ordered me to return to the lobby. About fifteen minutes later, the two men emerged, Adam dragging two heavy suitcases.

"Let's get out of here before she changes her mind," whispered Lou.

"What happened in there?"

"Well, let's just say it's a good thing I've learned how to grovel and cajole. For some reason, Chicago allowed Adam to come before anyone there in our church office checked to make sure he had his visa in hand. I had to assure the woman everything was in order, except for the stamp in his passport. She agreed to give him a two-day visa, and said he'd have to go to the Ministry of Home Affairs tomorrow. She said if he stayed in the country longer than forty-eight hours without a visa, she'd have him arrested and deported. Oh! And did you notice what was right next to her office?"

I hadn't.

"A jail cell! If we hadn't met Adam's flight, that's where he'd be spending the night."

Poor Adam looked sheepish and exhausted. "It's okay, Adam," Lou said. "We'll get it all sorted out tomorrow. One of our American colleagues who works in the bishop's office knows someone who works at Home Affairs. Come on, let's get you to the guest house. You must be dead on your feet."

Adam nodded. Fifteen minutes later, as the sun was setting behind the mountains, we were speeding along the highway on our way back to town. Adam was already able to laugh at his Namibian welcome.

The next evening I hosted a warmer welcome in our flat: a buffet dinner for Adam and five other American missionaries who happened to be in town. After everyone left, I went out onto our balcony. On that quiet evening, the sky was filled with stars close enough to touch. I located the Southern Cross. The troubles on this campus felt as inconsequential as the little insects swimming lazily through the night sky. From the flat below us, I heard several students talking quietly in Damara-Nama (the "click" language). Across the way, our Finnish neighbors were dining with friends on their patio, and I smelled roasting sausages and heard snatches of conversations in Finnish. Despite the turmoil of recent weeks, I already knew would miss our international life when we left this place. I felt the clock ticking.

Chapter 23
Attacked

*A*t the end of the term holiday, we went out to dinner at a new Cameroonian restaurant with our American colleagues who were living on campus this semester. These were our friends, Peter and Solveig, whom we had first met in 1995 during our three-month teaching sabbatical in Otjimbingwe. Peter was teaching two courses, New Testament and Greek. Solveig was working on an oral history project with her longtime Namibian friend. Dorothy also joined us. She was a widow from Kansas in her mid-seventies who had been Paulinum's librarian for the past two years. Sometimes, it just felt good to be around other Americans with whom we could laugh and share outrageous experiences we'd all had. We all defined *normal* the same way.

This year, Lou was teaching a course on spirituality to our first-year students, the same course Dr. van Wyk had taught last year. Whereas van Wyk had assigned his students books to read and long papers to write, Lou believed that one couldn't really teach spirituality without a significant experiential component. Twice a week, since the beginning of the year, we had been hosting in our flat small groups of students from his class. These groups of students would come for an hour of conversation, Bible study, and cookies and juice. Since a few of the American congregations that sponsored us had made available some funding, Lou and I decided to take these students on a weekend retreat at a nearby church retreat center.

We knew that music would be a primary component of the retreats. Lutheran missionaries of the previous century had convinced the Namibians to give up their traditional music. Those Germans and Finns had believed that pagan music profaned sacred space, so now almost all worship services used European hymnody. But when we had attended masses at the Roman Catholic seminary, we had seen how successfully the Roman Catholics had incorporated lively, indigenous music into worship settings, and we wondered if we might attempt something similar. We shared our thoughts with Sakari, an ethnomusicologist who had grown up in Namibia as the son of Finnish missionaries.

"I'd like to buy some African drums in the marketplace," I said. "Do you think you could help us select some?"

Not only did Sakari advise us, he also took us to a music shop where we bought maracas, tambourines, and percussion sticks. Sakari volunteered to conduct a quick training session with our students. Afterwards, he led a special worship service in the chapel using these instruments as accompaniments for a liturgy he had composed. He told us he had spent the past year visiting villages throughout Namibia, asking people to sing traditional songs for him. He recorded the villagers' singing and incorporated those melodies into his liturgy.

Meanwhile, I began collecting art materials for another retreat project. Since one of the retreat themes would be reconciliation, we planned a project for the students in which they would create greeting cards to send to a person with whom they wished to reconcile, or to reestablish a relationship that may have diminished. I had decided to offer the students a variety of objects—fabric, paint, beads, and colored markers—to use for their cards.

We left the seminary after lunch on Friday. Lou drove the seminary's minivan, and I followed with our Venture. The retreat center, constructed of cement block buildings, was clean and well maintained. There were even small plots of brightly colored flowers throughout the grounds. We all stayed in double-occupancy bedrooms. The communal bathrooms, one for men and one for women, had plenty of shower stalls and tub cubicles. In addition to the three daily meals, the kitchen staff also provided mid-morning and mid-afternoon tea breaks.

One of the retreat activities that Lou and I had used many times in the United States was to have participants create lifelines. I distributed pages of newsprint and several colored markers to each student, and Lou gave instructions: "For the next hour, you are going to be drawing a picture of your life. I want you to indicate significant events. Your lifeline can look like a road, with special road markers along the way: births, deaths, spiritual and educational milestones, whatever you think are important. If you prefer, you can draw pictures instead of using words. Be sure to include your birth date. And I also want you to name your death date." When the students finished making their lifelines, we divided them into small groups of six or seven students per group. Lou and I each took two small groups. We told the students that each of them would have twenty minutes to share his or her lifeline with the others in the group, and that the other participants would be encouraged to respond to what they had heard and to ask questions. We deliberately created tribal diversity within each group.

Several students in my groups had grown up during the apartheid years on farms owned by white South Africans. These students' families were farm hands, but their lives resembled those of the black slaves in nineteenth century America. Phillip, a thirty-one-year-old married Damara student, told us that his family couldn't ever attend church when he was growing up. Instead, he said, "The Boer farmer would gather his workers together about once a month and read Scripture passages to us."

Kai, another Damara student, said, "I used to be paid five dollars a week, a cup of sugar, and a cup of sweets every Friday for my weekly work. I really looked forward to Fridays." The situation is not much better today, even after independence. The white Namibians still own the better farms, and the farm workers are still the Damaras and the Namas.

Hainane, an Ovambo student, told of being sent to the cattle post as a young boy. (The cattle post is where young boys and men take their herds to graze. They live in makeshift dwellings, like tents, for several months at a time.) He said that his father was an uneducated man who did not believe in sending his children to school. "When I was eighteen years old, and was hospitalized for a serious medical condition, a kind nurse began to teach me to read and write. I was very determined. I remained hospitalized for about a year, and when I was finally discharged, I chose not to return home. I went to live with some friends who helped me get into school. I was embarrassed to be a twenty-one-year-old student in the fifth grade, but I just kept up my studies. When I finally graduated from high school, I had different jobs before I made my application to the seminary. Even now, on holidays, I work as a translator for a Windhoek construction company."

Saara, an Ovambo woman with sad eyes, said she was twenty years old when she became pregnant. She married the father of her child, but her husband died two years ago. Her twelve-year-old child was living with Saara's sister while Saara attended the seminary. In addition to her diploma studies at Paulinum, Saara was also studying for a bachelor of theology degree by correspondence through the University of South Africa.

At the conclusion of our Saturday evening vespers, one of the Ovambo women sang a short, lively hymn in her language. The Nama student seated next to her, a bright, talented musician, translated it into Damara-

Nama, and Afrikaans. We all practiced singing the song in those three languages, and concluded by singing it in English. At the end of the retreat, after our Eucharist on Sunday morning, Lou invited everyone to remain seated in a circle and to share their impressions of the weekend. Kai said, "I learned things I never knew about some of my Ovambo classmates." Others nodded. Kleopas said, "On campus, we are always with our own tribal groups. We don't know the stories and the backgrounds of those outside our own tribe. After this weekend, I have some new friends." Thomas, the student who had given us so much trouble the previous year, jumped to his feet and said, "I give thanks to God for creating white people like Pastor Lou and Mrs. Susan!" Tears filled my eyes when everyone applauded.

Not long after we returned to the campus, our African-American missionary colleague, Angie, came to visit us. Angie worked as the administrative assistant to Bishop Diergardt. She had recently become engaged to Benhi, a Namibian musician. Angie told us the other young women with whom she worked in the church office liked to bait her. "Last week they said they wanted to take me out to lunch at a traditional Namibian restaurant, to celebrate my engagement. One of the secretaries ordered lunch for everyone. You I know I always try to be a good sport, but I almost gagged when the waiter brought lunch to the table. It was a big bowl of maize meal porridge...and a goat's head, with the eyes still in the head! Everyone was supposed to pick meat off the head and dip it into the bowl of sauce. It was all I could do to remain at the table, staring into the eyes of that goat!"

Angie said that she and Benhi had been planning to get married quietly and inexpensively by the city magistrate, but the Bishop and his wife had other ideas. They told Angie they thought of her as a daughter, and they wanted the Bishop to preside at a traditional church ceremony. Since her parents couldn't afford the trip to Namibia, Angie asked Lou if he would walk her down the aisle, and Lou agreed. Her wedding was scheduled for January—midsummer—in Rehoboth, a small town south of Windhoek.

A week later, the third week in July, a mass of cold, Arctic air swept across Namibia causing the nighttime temperatures to plummet. Early one morning, our outdoor thermometer registered twenty-three degrees Fahrenheit. We turned our little space heaters to their highest setting and still shivered. That morning, the water froze in the pipes from the solar water heaters, located on the roof of each building, and no hot water flowed from our bathroom or kitchen tap until the sun had been shining on the pipes for several hours. We were glad the pipes did not burst because the seminary could not have afforded to repair them.

The following week, Lou celebrated his sixtieth birthday. I ordered a large sheet cake from the bakery department of Pick 'n' Pay and bought four dozen cans of soda. After lunch we had a little celebration with the students in the seminary's dining hall, and invited the kitchen staff to join us, too. Later that afternoon, we received an e-mail from Chicago informing us that our teaching contracts had been extended for one more year.

We were surprised, a few days later, when Joseph Hupitho stopped by our flat. He was taking a brief leave from his chaplaincy-training program in the United States and had returned to Namibia for a short visit. He brought us greetings from our friend, George, and he told us he had also brought with him ten suitcases of health care supplies, donated by the medical center where he was studying and working. The American congregation that was supporting him and had furnished his apartment had given him a $900 check for a program that supported AIDS patients in Namibia. Joseph told us his training was going well, and that when he returned to the States his wife, Rebekkah, and his little son, Uno, would be able to accompany him.

One day, I noticed bright yellow posters tacked up on telephone poles around town. The posters shouted: "Screw the War!" The National Theatre of Namibia was performing *Lysistrata*, and the advertisements said this production mingled African themes with Aristophanes' ancient Greek comedy about women who withhold sex from their men as a way of protesting war. An article in the newspaper extolled the creativity of the costume makers in designing costumes that combined elements of both cultures. It seemed to be a play that we would enjoy, especially since Angie's fiancé, Benhi, was a percussionist in the orchestra.

When I told Angie that Lou and I had tickets, she rolled her eyes and started describing how the producers had been treating the actors, dancers, and musicians. "At first, none of the Namibians were going to be paid anything more than taxi fare. When the performers protested, they were told that they would be paid seven hundred Namibian dollars for each of the three performances (about US$90 per performance). A few days after that, the producers said to the performers, 'No, we can't pay you that much after all. You'll be paid N$210 (about US$26) for the entire run of the show.'"

"The production company has brought in a black choreographer from England," said Angie. "They're paying him over five thousand U.S. dollars!"

"Can't Benhi and the others take their complaints to the union?" I asked.

"Fat chance! Benhi did two months of work for the union last year, and has still not been paid anything for it."

The following night, Benhi and about fifteen other performers again protested to the production company. They were told, "You are actors and musicians. The privilege of performing ought to be payment enough." Benhi and his friends walked out.

We threw our tickets in the trash, and I wrote an angry letter to *The Namibian* newspaper and to the various embassy and corporate sponsors who had supported the show. When I saw Benhi a few days later, I said I hoped that he and his fellow performers would never again allow themselves to enter into an agreement such as this without a signed contract.

We seemed to have reached another one of those times when it felt as if we were pushing a heavy boulder uphill. This was not the first time we had contemplated the Sisyphean nature of our missionary endeavor. "It's time to get away for a few days," said Lou. Since neither of us taught on Fridays or Mondays this semester, we would leave classes after lunch the following Thursday. I phoned a local real estate company that leased holiday flats on the coast, and arranged to stop by on Tuesday afternoon to pay for our four nights in the same condo where we had previously stayed.

The estate agent's office was in the Ausspannplatz section of Windhoek, an attractive part of town just a block from the United States embassy. I handed the clerk my Visa card, and while I waited for her to complete the transaction, I glanced at the television set behind the counter. A news program—it appeared to be CNN—was showing film footage of what looked like a bad fire somewhere. Smoke was pouring from a skyscraper. Was this New York City? I couldn't tell, and the sound was turned down so I couldn't hear what the announcer was saying. When I returned to our flat, I said to Lou, "Honey, why don't you connect to the Internet and see if there's some news about a bad fire in New York?" We did not have cable television in our flat, and there was no continuous news on the one channel we received, so I didn't expect to learn anything that way.

"I can't seem to connect to the CNN or the Washington Post web sites," said Lou.

"Try the BBC."

That is how we learned what had happened on Tuesday, September 11, 2001, in the United States.

I switched on our television, and was surprised to see that NBC, Namibian Broadcasting Company, had pre-empted its afternoon programming and was broadcasting, without any commercial interruptions, the live feed from CNN International. This looked bad. I hurried downstairs to tell Peter and Solveig what seemed to be happening, and invited them to come and watch with us since they did not have a television. Next I phoned Dorothy and invited her to join us, but she said she'd prefer to return to her house, just off campus, and watch on her own television. I learned later that the students were all gathered around the TV in the recreation room on campus.

As afternoon faded to evening—we were seven hours ahead of Eastern Standard Time in the United States—we four Americans sat transfixed in our small living room as CNN played and replayed the horrifying footage of the airplanes smashing into the tower, of bodies plummeting from the two buildings, of terrified people running from the smoke, of planes that had smashed into the Pentagon and crashed somewhere in Pennsylvania, of reports that the President was in an airplane and the Vice President was in an undisclosed location.

Never had Lou and I felt lonelier than during the next few days. I was surprised how few of our Namibian faculty colleagues and students seemed to be able to say, "We're sorry for what has happened in your country." One who did was our elderly friend and former colleague, Rev. Amaambo, who phoned us from his home in Oniipa. He and Meme Esther had just gotten a phone installed in their home. "This is terrible, just terrible," said our friend. "We remember the people of your country in our prayers." Our principal, Michael Shangala, said nothing to us. Our German colleague, Hanns, said, "I hope Washington doesn't do anything foolish, such as going after Afghanistan." But what really hurt was that at our usual vespers service on Wednesday night, not one person uttered a single word or even offered a prayer for what had happened. I was glad to be leaving campus the next morning.

As soon as our classes ended, we loaded our car with suitcases, food and books. On the three-and-a-half-hour drive to the coast, Lou and I kept talking about our deep sadness over the terrorist attacks on our country and our resentment about the insensitivity of our colleagues. Why were they so silent? I told Lou I wished that we would be returning home permanently in a few weeks, rather than just for our home leave.

The condominium in Swakopmund had DSTV, and we looked forward to being able to see CNN coverage of the ongoing events in the States, but we had some difficulty figuring out how to get the television to work. We returned to the rental office. Tina, the young woman who was filling in for the manager, wasn't able to help us very much, so we went back to the condo and tried again. About fifteen minutes later, Tina came by with a white South African man. She told us he was a guest staying in another condo nearby. He soon identified what we had been doing wrong and fixed it.

I thanked him and said, "We're Americans and we really want to be able to watch CNN and see what's happening at home."

"Well," he replied, the smile on his face becoming a sneer, "now you Americans have a taste of what those of us in the rest of the world have experienced for years. What are you going to do now? Go to war against all your enemies—Iraq, Libya, and all the others?"

Tina, obviously embarrassed by the man's remark, tried to offer an expression of sympathy to us, but the man continued his harangue. Having no desire to engage in a debate with this stranger, I raised my voice to cut him off. "Thank you for helping us with the television," I said. "I hope you enjoy your holiday here."

Not all our encounters were so painful. Friday morning, Lou and I walked around town. Not far from the ocean was an open-air market where Namibian craftsmen and vendors sold their wares: wood and stone carvings, batiks and jewelry. At the far end of the market was a small amphitheatre. It was empty that morning, and we sat down on the steps for a few minutes. A young Namibian man in tattered clothes was sitting several feet away from us. He stood up, and we knew, as he approached, that he was going to ask us for money. "I'm so sorry to disturb you," he said, "but could you perhaps give me two dollars (the equivalent of about twenty-five cents) so I can buy some bread?"

"Yes, I can do that," I said. As I reached for my wallet he asked where we were from. I told him we were teachers in Windhoek, but that our home country was America.

"You have heard what happened there?" he asked. We nodded. He continued, "Those people who did this are lions who lie in the grass waiting to attack. You Americans must now be like lions, too." Before he walked away, he told us, "Have faith in God and in His son Jesus Christ, who died for our sins."

It was 6:00 p.m. in Namibia when we watched the Service of Prayer and Remembrance broadcast live by CNN from the Washington National Cathedral. As painful as it had been to watch the continuous news coverage all weekend, there was a feeling of healing when we heard the familiar hymns and listened to the words of comfort from the clergy and the sermon delivered by the Rev. Billy Graham. When I saw the red, white and blue ribbons worn by the former presidents and others, I said to Lou, "I'm going to buy some ribbons tomorrow and wear them for the next month." I was grateful we had those few days to ourselves. When we returned home to the campus, the students told us that the morning chapel service had been a prayer service to remember those who had died in America.

Every Friday—and only on Fridays—*The Namibian* newspaper published letters to the editor. I had forgotten about the letter I had written protesting the treatment of the actors in the "Lysistrata" performance, but there it was, on September 21, along with two full pages of letters addressing the attacks in the United States. Nearly all of them condemned the United States, suggesting our country had brought these events upon itself because of its arrogance and its isolationist stance toward developing countries. I stopped buying the newspaper.

My dad sent me an e-mail telling me that Mom had stopped watching all news broadcasts because she found them too upsetting. This was the woman who had been president of my town's League of Women Voters when I was growing up in Ohio.

Four weeks later, at the end of another academic year at the seminary, we packed our suitcases and gratefully prepared for our two months of home leave and vacation back in the States. When our flight from Windhoek landed in Johannesburg, before we could check in for our flight to Washington, we had to carry our suitcases to tables that had been set up in a special roped-off area of the terminal. South African Airways agents rifled through our underwear, sweaters, Christmas presents, books, shoes, and toothbrushes. They told us that all passengers on flights bound for the United States had to join long queues. We lined up behind the other passengers in a long, windowless corridor. After thirty minutes, most of us were sitting on the floor, our backs against the rough concrete wall. Two hours passed. The idle chatter ceased. By now we all knew we would miss our connecting flights when the airliner arrived in the States the following morning. Eventually six agents arrived, three men and three women. They told us to form two queues: men on the right, women on the left. When I reached the front of my female queue, an agent told me to open my tote bag and purse and she rummaged through them. Another security guard patted me down. She seemed to be as embarrassed as I felt when she ran her hand up and down my thighs.

We stayed two nights with our daughter, Megan, in Chapel Hill. Our first full day in North Carolina, we bought a Nissan Pathfinder. We needed a four-wheel-drive vehicle to navigate the mountain road in Fancy Gap, Virginia, that led to our cottage. Since we would be concluding our missionary service the following year, buying a car now seemed preferable to spending two thousand dollars, as we had the previous year, to rent a vehicle for two months. Megan said we could keep the car in the parking lot of her apartment complex when we returned to Namibia for our final ten months.

Our cottage, a simple, two-story house we had built ten years earlier as a place for weekend getaways, looked forlorn and abandoned. The gravel path from the dirt road to our front door was hidden underneath the tall grass and thick blanket of pine needles. Lou and I were glad for the physical exercise of late autumn yard work: mowing, raking and pulling weeds. While Lou repaired leaks in the roof, I bleached mildew stains from the interior walls and repainted the small downstairs bedroom. We drove into town to buy groceries and to take our clothes to the laundromat and were surprised to see so many American flags on cars, homes, and shops. Signs along the roads and in restaurant windows proclaimed: "God Bless America!" and, "United We Stand!"

I would have been so happy to stay on the mountain those entire two months, but we had many trips to make. The first was a visit to my elderly parents in northern Ohio, and another flight to Denver to see our son, Jason, and my sister's family. Following the family visits, we traveled to some of our sponsoring Lutheran congregations in North Carolina, Ohio, and Virginia. The national church office would have preferred for us to visit all twenty-four congregations that sponsored us, but they settled for six. I wondered, given the terrorist attacks and the anthrax scares, if people in those congregations would even be interested in hearing us talk about global mission. Lou and I also struggled with all the things we felt we couldn't say: the episodes of racism, Nandi's alleged abortion and suspension, the cold response we had received after September 11th. But we could talk about the students' retreats, and our hope to conduct two more the coming year. When we did that, we were overwhelmed with contributions that would make those retreats a reality.

On one of our many trips down the mountain to Chapel Hill—this time for dentist appointments—we heard on the radio that American Airlines flight 587 had crashed in Queens, New York. Almost everyone, of course, assumed this was another terrorist attack. The nation was jittery. When we left the dentist's office, we paid a visit to our dear friends, John and Mary. John was a retired professor of medicine who had been my first supervisor at the medical school where I'd worked for eleven years. He offered us tickets to a Carolina basketball game. Lou gratefully accepted. Then he asked me if I would be interested in returning to my former job when we concluded our missionary work the following year. I couldn't quite say why, but I had the strong feeling that returning to my previous life and vocational identity would somehow obliterate the five years of living in Africa. It would make that experience irrelevant. Maybe that would happen anyway. Would anyone remember us, say, five years after we'd left Namibia? Would our work have mattered? I told John I would have to let him know closer to the time of our return to the States. Despite all the frustrations, contemplating leaving Africa was starting to feel painful.

Finally, all our visits and medical appointments were behind us, and we had three weeks left to enjoy mountain life. We replaced the glass door that opened onto our deck and Lou rebuilt the frame and attached new molding. We put new glass in the skylights and had caps installed on the chimney.

Jason and Megan arrived the day before Christmas. Fluffy flakes of snow had begun falling. Just after the sun set, the power went off, so we scrambled to light all the candles and oil lamps. Lou had built a fire in our wood stove so at least we would be warm. With Megan holding the flashlight, Lou grilled steaks on a small grill on the front porch. Jason and I made a salad and sliced bread by the glow of candlelight. It felt like an African moment.

Chapter 24
Storytelling

*D*on, a friend from North Carolina, arrived for a visit shortly after we returned to Namibia. He had business in neighboring South Africa and wanted to see us and a bit of the Namibian countryside. Although our schedules wouldn't allow an extensive journey, we suggested a weekend at the Schonfeld Guest Farm, about a four-and-a-half hour drive from Windhoek. Namibia's rainy season had arrived. The grass along the road had become noticeably greener and the mountains wore a green tint. This would be our fifth, and probably final, visit with Schonfeld's owners, Hartwig and Elke von Seydlitz, a couple we had come to call our friends. On Saturday afternoon, Hartwig took us on an extended game drive, and we saw parts of this vast farm we'd never seen before. It rained heavily that night, assuring the von Seydlitz family that their many animals would feed well during the coming dry months. On Sunday morning, when we stepped into the courtyard and looked up, we saw the Stars and Stripes flying from the flagpole atop the roof of one of the towers. Hartwig and Elke had done this in our honor, and they told us our flag would remain there throughout the day.

When I took Elke aside and told her that I wanted to settle the bill, she said, "No, there is no charge." I was astonished, because I knew from our previous visits that their rates were not low. But she insisted. "We have enjoyed getting to know you during the past several years," she said. "Please consider this visit a small blessing from the Lord."

Don had said he'd like to meet some of our students, so we invited several students to join us for dinner. Our students always returned to campus so very thin after the summer holidays. During the months of their summer vacation, just before the rainy season, there isn't much food available in the rural north. Saara and Hainane came, along with Hafeni, Hilja, David, and Esron. The evening's menu included a couple of new food items for these students—broccoli and blueberries—but there was enough other food I knew they liked: pork chops, rice, bread, and salad. Saara said that some people from her village thought eating salads was very strange. "The villagers wonder why someone would want to eat uncooked vegetables." Don invited the students to tell him about their families. David said, "At home there are five of us, plus my mother and my grandmother. My father has fifty-two children from other wives. He was a pastor." To his credit, Don's fork barely hesitated on its way to his mouth. As I was clearing away the dishes, three strangers came to the flat, two men, and a woman who were looking for Saara. I invited them to join us for dessert, a medley of fresh fruit with whipped cream and a platter of cookies. As they were leaving, one of the men laughed. "Now that I know what time you have dinner, I'll be back."

The next afternoon, after Don had flown back to the United States, Hafeni returned to our home carrying a copy of *The Namibian*. Printed on the front page was a story about an elderly woman in the north whose twenty-one-year-old grandson had killed her with an ax for her pension check, worth about sixty American dollars. Accompanying the article was a color photo of the mutilated, naked woman with the ax protruding from her head. (Even after five years, it was hard to look at the newspaper photography here.) Hafeni said, "I was so shocked and upset when I saw this photo because this woman was from my village—she lived next door to my family. I was her grandson's Sunday School teacher." He got up and paced up and down our little living room. "He was a good boy. I can't understand how this could have happened. In this newspaper he said that it was Satan who made him do it." He shook his head. "I just don't know."

Hafeni sat down and began to tell us about his own family. "My father is a man rich in animals. We have many cattle and goats, and the kids are too many to count. There are seven of us children in my family and whenever school fees or clothes are needed, my father will simply sell some animals. He is very proud that he has never had to ask for help from anyone. I remember the time in 1996 when there was a terrible drought. All of our animals died. My father said that we must not lose hope, and that God would provide for us. He bought one cow and a few goats. Now his animals are many, and he boasts about what he has done. I reminded him that it was God who provided all this and he said, 'My son, I can see that you really are a pastor already.' That made me glad, but I know that being a pastor isn't so easy," he looked down at the newspaper he was still clutching in his hand. "Especially when things like this happen."

One evening I returned to our flat after doing some research in the library to find Jomo sitting in our living room. He had come to talk with Lou. I greeted him and went back to our little home office to grade papers. When Jomo left, Lou said to me, "We have the Niamey toilet problem." I immediately knew what he was talking about. When we were visiting Niamey, Niger, in 1992, our American guide had told us that during his first year in Niger, he used to wonder why all the toilet seats were broken. Finally, he realized that the people from the rural areas had never seen toilets before and didn't know how to use them. They assumed that the correct procedure was to stand on the toilet seat and squat down. This is what Jomo, with great embarrassment, had been explaining to Lou when I arrived. Some of our first-year male students from rural villages didn't know how to use toilets.

The next morning after the morning chapel service, Jomo announced that there would be a short meeting for all the first-year male students. It seemed the training session wasn't explicit enough. After chapel service the following morning, another student, Thomas, addressed the student body. "We are having another problem in the men's bathroom," he said. "*Please*, gentlemen, when you are finished using the toilet, push down the little handle at the back. The rest of us are *suffering*!" All the women laughed out loud.

When we went to lunch in the dining hall the first day of classes, Sophie, our kitchen supervisor, handed Lou a list of repairs needed in the kitchen and the classrooms. She knew he had a well-stocked toolbox. After lunch, a new student came to our flat with another list of dormitory repairs that were needed: cupboards without hinges or knobs, leaking showers, broken windows.

At our first evening vespers service of this new academic year, we noticed the new Southern Church bishop seated in the front row. Bishop Zephaniah Kameeta was hard to miss. He was an albino. But what was he doing here? We had heard that the seminary's governing board would soon be announcing its selection of new seminary officers, and Bishop Kameeta stood up in front of the student body and made that announcement at the conclusion of the service. The choice of Rev. Hasheela to be vice-principal and dean of students was no surprise. He was a good, gentle man, the former General Secretary of the Northern Church. Lou felt relieved to be stepping down after serving in this capacity for the past four years. But our hearts sank when we learned that our new principal would be Rev. Dirk Cloete, the lecturer whom the governing board had dismissed from the seminary four years ago because of his role in the student strike. When I looked around at the faces of our colleagues and students, it was clear that no one was happy.

Outside the chapel, after the service had ended, I quietly asked our current principal, Dr. Michael Shangala, when the appointments would be effective. He replied, "I will have the principal's office cleaned out by Monday morning." Since I had served as faculty secretary for the past four years, I asked him if he thought it would be all right for me to also step down from this position. "I think that would be a good idea, Susan. You have always taken accurate minutes of the meetings, but we know that Dirk would probably find fault with what you write. He might even ask you to change the minutes to reflect what he wants them to say." I hadn't even considered that possibility, but hearing Michael's observation confirmed my decision. I would tender my resignation as secretary at the next faculty meeting.

The upcoming wedding of our friends Angie and Benhi took our minds off seminary politics for a while. Although the couple had been married last year by the public magistrate, this was the formal wedding ceremony Angie's former boss, the recently retired bishop, had insisted upon. Bishop Diergardt would conduct the service, Lou would give the bride away and deliver the homily, and I had been asked to read a lesson. Our other American missionary colleagues from around the country would be coming for the event, which would take place in the town of Rehoboth, just south of Windhoek.

The morning of the wedding I collected from the local bridal shop the candelabra and the bridal arch, a plywood structure in four pieces, painted white. It would be decorated with ribbons and paper flowers and placed in the center aisle of the church. We had also agreed to transport the champagne and whiskey, the table favors and the cake. Instead of a purse, I brought a large, deep Ovambo basket with handles and a lid. It was the basket Jonah's mother had made for me. I packed it with a bottle of water, sunscreen, our cameras, and the dark blue cotton bandana I always brought to hot events. The day was already sizzling at ten o'clock. In the parched brown fields beside the road, the cows and the baboons were seeking shelter under the few trees tall enough to provide a bit of shade. Beyond the dusty fields, purple granite mountains thrust into the clear blue sky.

We arrived at the church a little past eleven o'clock. One of Benhi's brothers told us to park at the edge of the packed-earth parking lot, and when Benhi greeted us, I handed him the cake to put in a cool place. Earlier, Bishop Diergardt had told us that we could meet him there for an eleven o'clock rehearsal, but when we saw that he had not yet arrived, we went searching for Angie. We found her in a small flat behind the church. She was sitting on a narrow iron bed, the only item of furniture in the small bedroom. Scattered around her on the bed and floor were gold and purple decorations for the reception. Mascara, lipstick, tubes of makeup, a stick of deodorant, a vial of perfume, a curling iron, and brushes and ribbons were spilling from the bed. Angie, wearing pearls and a frilly petticoat, looked as if she were about to burst into tears. "I've been in this room since Tuesday!" She said that in the Damara culture, it is the custom for the bride to be "locked up" for the week before the wedding. During that time, she is supposed to be visited and cared for by the family.

"But no one has come! They didn't even bring me food. Yesterday, I walked across the street to the little take-away place to get a sandwich to eat because I was hungry. One of Benhi's sisters saw me there and scolded me, telling me that I shouldn't leave my room. 'Fine!' I said to her. 'And you are supposed to make sure that I have something to eat!' Now all the sisters are at the beauty shop getting their hair done. Do you think anyone asked me if I wanted to get *my* hair done?"

Angie had told me that she and Benhi had recently been having some disagreements with Benhi's family because the family had provided so little assistance with the wedding. My young colleague was nervous, and was probably missing her parents who were in Iowa because they could not afford to travel to Africa. I assured her the wedding would be lovely, and that I would send digital photos of the event to her parents as soon as we returned to Windhoek that evening. "Now," I said, "what can I do to make sure the church and reception hall are properly set up?"

Angie handed me two large swatches of burgundy tulle, a spool of white and gold ribbon and ten gold candles for the candelabra and bridal arch in the church. Was the church open? One of Benhi's younger brothers hurried over to the pastor's house. About fifteen minutes later he returned, breathless. The pastor could not find her keys to the church, but she thought that perhaps her son had them. He'd gone shopping, but was expected to return shortly. In the meantime, Angie and Benhi were summoned to the florist's shop just down the road to inspect the flowers. No one seemed worried that she was leaving her cell.

While we waited, Lou and I found some shade under an acacia tree in a corner of the church compound where there was a pile of building rubble. We took out our liter bottle of water and gingerly sat down on some stacks of ceramic tiles next to a broken toilet. I was already sweating profusely, and the water in the bottle was hot. An old white car pulled up next to us, and several happy fellows with dreadlocks, ragged clothes and knitted woolen caps climbed out. One of them had a guitar. They sat down on the ground in the corner of the lot, beside a small shed. Next to the shed some young people were cooking sausages on a charcoal grill. I heard voices in the road, and when I looked up I saw Angie and Benhi returning from the florist. Angie saw the group by the shed and exclaimed, "Oh, good! Our reggae band is here!" By now, it was nearly noon. A little boy walked up to us and told us that the church was open. There was still no sign of the bishop, but at least we could begin setting up the candelabra and bridal arch.

The solid-looking church building had apparently been constructed during the time of the German missionaries, and the beautiful wood carving adorning the sanctuary was in sharp contrast to the other Namibian Lutheran churches we had seen, with their functional concrete walls and tin roofs. The massive, mahogany pulpit overwhelmed the chancel. I took a photograph of a plaque on an interior wall. I could not read the Afrikaans, but noted the word, *bastardvolke* at the top of a list of names. I recognized the surnames Beukes, Cloete, Van Wyk, and Diergaardt. They were the same as those of some of our lighter-skinned seminary students. Rehoboth was home to the Baster community, those people of mixed descent whose status was higher than the people of various black tribes during the years of apartheid rule in Namibia. Rehoboth had been the hometown of Johan van Wyk.

Benhi helped us carry the candelabra and the four pieces of the bridal arch into the church. He switched on the ceiling fans, and I walked up and down the rows of pews, opening windows. The church felt like a sauna, and I could feel myself becoming light-headed as I wiped the sweat from my forehead, eyes and neck with my bandana. Lou realized that he would need tools to assemble the arch, so he went back to our car for his small tool chest. He and Benhi completed the construction of the arch while I finished swathing the candelabra in tulle and ribbon. More of Benhi's brothers appeared, along with the bishop who was wearing his distinctive violet clerical shirt. He was only an hour and a half late. We greeted him and his wife, Lissie, and he began talking quickly to Benhi in Afrikaans. Switching to English, he rapidly told me the order in which everyone should march in, and who should sit where. The congregational pastor, Rev. Kristina Beukes, entered wearing her long black robes and the bishop immediately began telling her about how the chancel should be set up, and where various chairs and tables should be placed. Then the bishop left.

I stood in the center aisle with my mouth open. When I had discussed the rehearsal with the bishop several days before, he had appeared unfamiliar with the concept and said that he assumed this simply meant telling people how to enter the church. I had tried to explain that it might be helpful to rehearse the service so that everything would proceed smoothly. Oh, well. It wasn't my place to tell a bishop how to conduct a wedding.

My scalp tingled with perspiration. Lou looked alarmed and told me that my face was very red. He ordered me to sit down while he went to refill our water bottle. As I rested, I wondered how the family members and the wedding party would know what to do. At two o'clock, the scheduled time for the wedding to begin, there were no more than ten people in the congregation, most of them our American colleagues and their friends who had traveled here from various parts of Namibia. At ten past two, the bishop returned, looking distracted. He had not yet vested. "Where is the program leader?" he demanded.

"Do you mean the master of ceremonies?" I asked, remembering that every ecclesiastical event I'd ever attended in Namibia was led by an M.C., and not by the officiating clergyperson. "I don't think one was chosen," I replied, suddenly realizing the large planning gaffe.

The oversight was resolved when the bishop spotted Dr. Paul Isaak, the Chairman of the Department of Religion and Theology at the University of Namibia. Dr. Paul was recruited and agreed to serve as master of ceremonies. By two-forty, everyone was in place and the wedding could begin. Benhi's Damara family and friends began singing hymns in their "click" language. The groom, his parents, and the groomsmen were all standing in a row in the first pew on the right, but they didn't turn around as the four bridesmaids, wearing short purple dresses trimmed in gold, began their procession. Each was carrying a lighted gold candle. Angie, smiling and serene in a gold satin gown trimmed with purple, walked slowly down the aisle on Lou's arm.

The service proceeded joyously without any major stumbles (perhaps wedding rehearsals were overrated?), and the reception was a festive United Nations general assembly of so many hues and languages, food, drink, and customs. By eight o'clock that evening, I was back in our flat on campus, editing digital photos of the wedding and sending them as e-mail attachments to Angie's parents in Iowa as fast as our Internet connection would transmit them. A big jug of cold water was sweating on the desk next to me.

The academic year was well underway when we received a phone call from Rebekkah Hupitho, the wife of Joseph, the Namibian pastor who had recently completed his year of clinical pastoral education (CPE) at the American university hospital under the direction of our close friend, George. George had sent us an e-mail saying that Joseph and Rebekkah, along with their young son Uno, were returning to Namibia because Joseph had been unsuccessful in his attempt to extend his US visa for another year of study. George told us he was angry and embarrassed. He wrote that Joseph had fallen out of favor with the American congregation that had been supporting him when he'd returned to the States the previous July with a new gold watch and an expensive leather coat. The congregation suspected he'd purchased these in Namibia with the money the congregation had given him for ministry with AIDS patients.

Lou and I had never met Rebekkah, but we knew that George thought highly of her, and that she had been enrolled in a master's degree program at the American university. I wondered why his wife was calling us. She had a soft, sweet telephone voice.

"George took us all to the airport in September," said Rebekkah. "We were ready to board the flight to Namibia, but after George left, Joseph said that he needed to make a short trip to Pennsylvania first. I did not know what was going on, but he told me that he would be joining us in Namibia in a few days. But he never did—he just disappeared! I sent George an e-mail after we had been back here in Windhoek for two weeks. George told me that Joseph had gone to New York."

"Why did he go there, Rebekkah?"

"It seems that he was accepted into an unaccredited CPE program. I had no idea he was going to do such a thing!"

Then Rebekkah said something that left me speechless.

"Joseph has also been having an affair with a Namibian woman living in New York." She sighed and was silent for a few moments. "I know that George thinks very highly of your husband. Do you think I could come to your flat to talk with both of you?"

We suggested she come the following afternoon.

Rebekkah Hupitho kept her Sunday afternoon appointment with us, and brought along her friend, Dorothy. Rebekkah was a slender, attractive woman with short hair. She wore a modest, navy dress with a high white collar and white sandals. She sat on the edge of our sofa, her hands on her knees. She leaned forward, an earnest, pleading look on her face, and told us Joseph had been a pastor in a Namibian congregation for several years at the beginning of their ten-year marriage. "My family and I thought he was a good man. He was so handsome and so kind to my family." But there were problems, she said, in the marriage and the congregation. She did not elaborate. Rebekkah went to Bishop Diergardt about the situation. Joseph chose to leave the congregation and had a series of part-time, non-church jobs. "He had one full-time job, for only a year, but he quarreled with his boss and was dismissed. It was only recently, the year before he went to America, that he seemed to regain his interest in the church." That, of course, would have been the year he met our friend, George.

"When he learned he had been accepted by the chaplaincy training program in the United States, Joseph met several times with the administrator of Central Hospital here in Windhoek to discuss starting a chaplaincy program there. That is what he said he would be trained to do while he was in America." Joseph also told Rebekkah that he was being considered for a position at the University of Namibia in the Department of Theology and Religious Studies, but that statement appeared to be pure fantasy. We knew Joseph was not qualified for that position.

When she returned to Namibia this year, Rebekkah had been allowed to resume her teaching position. She and her three sons were now living in the government house the family had lived in prior to their year in the United States. As we had learned from our student Paul, the provision of such housing was often a benefit of public school teaching. Rebekkah told us she was hoping one day to purchase the house from the government. Eight-year-old Uno, their oldest son who had accompanied his parents to the United States, did not yet know that his father was not coming back. Rebekkah told us that he had been having some emotional problems.

"The woman Joseph was living with in New York was a very old friend of Joseph's family. She had been living in the United States for twenty years, working for an accounting firm in New York City. When we were in America last year, this woman phoned Joseph every day." She looked up, paused, and gazed out the window, as if she couldn't quite believe all this had happened to her. "I am attending church regularly and I'm getting a lot of support from my friends." Dorothy patted her hand. "And I am working to remove my name from all the debts Joseph incurred."

Lou asked, "Rebekkah, if Joseph apologizes, would you take him back?" I knew he was asking because Namibian women are very dependent, compliant and submissive. I was glad to hear her say, "No, I am ready to move on with my life." Before she left, we told Rebekkah we would do what we could to help her.

She phoned again the next morning. "I have just received a notarized letter from Joseph. Let me read it to you: 'To whom it may concern: I give permission to Rebekkah to proceed with the divorce she has requested....' This is untrue! It is Joseph's way of avoiding child support. I will divorce him on *my* terms."

I advised her again to get a lawyer to protect herself, her children, and her assets. We said we would help her find money to proceed.

"Thank you. I think I might contact the American embassy here in Windhoek and give them the address, phone and fax numbers contained in the letter," she said. "Joseph is in the United States illegally. I think the U.S. authorities would be interested to know that. Especially these days."

At the end of the week, I gave the first-year students an English quiz. As usual, I told them they were free to leave when they finished. When all the other students had left the classroom, Alfeus Hausiku, a quiet, serious young man, approached my desk and said softly, "I'm sorry, Mrs. Bauer, I was not able to give you the vocabulary assignment that is due today." He told me that he didn't have a composition book. "I asked my parents to send me money to buy one but it has not arrived." He continued, "I have never used a computer before, but one of the students has told me that she would help me, so maybe I could do my assignment on the computer and hand it in later." Paulinum had about half a dozen computers in the library for the students' use. I realized that he was thinking of this as an alternative because students don't have to pay for the computer paper they use to print out their assignments.

I explained to Alfeus that it takes some time to learn how to use a computer, especially if one doesn't know how to type. "Alfeus, you are telling me you cannot do class assignments because you have no paper and pens, and no money to buy any." His eyes filled with tears and he just nodded. I told him to stop by our flat a little later in the afternoon.

After classes ended for the day, Lou and I went out to lunch with our English friends, Robin and Penny. On the way home, I asked Lou to stop at a small supermarket where I bought Alfeus two small composition books, a packet of ballpoint pens, and a package of lined notebook paper.

I was still a member of the worship committee. We had finished all our agenda items and were gathering our belongings together when the third-year student, Hainane, said, "I wasn't going to mention this, but perhaps I could add one more item to the agenda?" Rev. Hasheela, the chair of the committee, agreed. Hainane said, "Can the committee tell us student sextons what to do if a faculty worship leader fails to show up for a service?"

"Hainane, are you referring to a Sunday service?" I asked.

"Yes, two Sundays ago, Rev. Cloete was supposed to lead the Sunday service, but he never showed up. I think he had left town for the weekend. The other sexton and I didn't know what to do, so we had to send everyone home, including some members of the outside community. People who live in the neighborhood. We were embarrassed."

Rev. Hasheela frowned and clenched his fists. "That is irresponsible of a faculty member!" he said. Addressing the students, he continued in a softer voice, "If that should ever happen again, *please* do not send the people away. You can always sing some hymns, read the lessons for the day, and offer some prayers. It's all right if there isn't a sermon."

Our newly appointed principal was not starting his term on a very positive note. Our friend Matheus, the seminary's treasurer, had told Lou the previous evening that he had yet to see Dirk occupying the principal's office.

One March morning, I stood in front of my class of third-year English students. "I wish you could stand here and see the bored looks on all your faces." They smiled, self-consciously, and nodded. I suggested that we think about doing English differently. "I know you all enjoyed the African novel that we read together last year. Would you like to write your own stories?" Their response was an enthusiastic, "Yes!" These students had all written fables for me the previous year, the five best of which I had published in a little pamphlet that was distributed to all the faculty and students. When I asked them if they'd like to have their short stories published, there was some silence. Finally, Otto spoke up.

"Madam," he said, "We *did* like writing the fables, but we were unhappy that you only chose five to be published."

I told them I would do my best to find some funding to make it possible to publish a book that contained everyone's story. "But you're going to have to work really hard and study all aspects of story writing. And you're going to have to revise your story several times so it is as good as it can be." Kleopas Nghikefelwa, a first-year student with artistic talent, had shown me his portfolio of sketches, and when I asked, he agreed to illustrate the book cover for us. The next day, I combed the bookstores and found two collections of short stories written by southern African writers. I knew that reading short stories within their own context would be an essential element in teaching these students how to write stories of their own, especially since so few of them had ever read any fiction besides last year's novel.

The next evening I was grading homework from this same English class. This was a reading comprehension assignment, and one of the questions was to define five words from what they had read. One of the words was "sporadically." One student defined it as "a receptacle in which spores are kept."

Robert Mugabe had just been re-elected to his fifth term as President of Zimbabwe, and many Namibians were nervously watching the events in the tumultuous country to the northeast. Hundreds of white Zimbabweans whose families had lived in the country since it had been Southern Rhodesia were fleeing the country. Those who remained feared the takeover of their commercial farms by marauding groups of disenfranchised blacks. On the front page of *The Namibian* was a photo of the body of a man identified as Mr. Ford, a white farmer who had been slain by thugs in Zimbabwe. The body was covered by a bloodstained light blue blanket, and curled up on the blanket next to the body, staring into the camera's lens, was the dead man's little white dog. Some Namibians were beginning to wonder, "Could this happen here?"

Meanwhile, my students were enthusiastic about their short story projects. To help them understand characterization, I asked them to write a description of a childhood friend. For the lesson on setting, their assignment was to write a letter to one of my children in the United States, giving a detailed description of either their campus dormitory room or their family home. I told my students I would mail these letters to Jason and Megan. Before the students departed for their winter holiday at the end of April, I told them that while they were at home, their assignment would be to interview some elders in their village and to take notes about the stories they heard. After they had heard several stories, they were to choose their favorite story and write it down.

Although the faculty had decided that the last day of classes for the semester would be on a Thursday, no one told the students. Most found out via the sturdy African grapevine that wound its way around the seminary. The Damara, Nama, and coloured students planned to leave campus on Thursday, right after lunch. When Matheus, our treasurer, learned that some of the Ovambo students also wanted to leave early, he told them, "No, you must stay for the closing worship service on Friday morning." Matheus was an Ovambo and a former freedom fighter with a strong sense of duty.

On Thursday night Matheus stopped by our flat to ask Lou to cosign some checks. Although two months had passed since Lou had relinquished his position as dean of students, the current dean and principal hadn't yet gone to the bank to sign the signature cards for the transfer. Matheus was frowning. "When I returned from town about four o'clock, I saw that all the curtains in the dining hall were closed, and that the kitchen staff was preparing to go home. I asked Sophie, 'What about the students' supper?' Sophie told me that Principal Dirk had said the students weren't getting any supper—the dining hall was officially closed now for the term holiday. When Sophie asked him what she should do with the food that had been bought for the students, Dirk had said, 'Give it to the kitchen workers.'

"I feel very bad," said Matheus, "because I was the one who told the Ovambo students to stay, and now they have no food. I tried to tell the principal this isn't right, but he didn't want to listen to me. We've always made provision for those few who must stay a little longer. Why didn't he ask me?"

I said, "Matheus, what about the dean? Can't Rev. Hasheela do something?"

Matheus shook his head sadly. "The dean isn't on campus," he said. "And even if he were, he is afraid of the principal. They do not communicate well with each other."

When our dinner was ready, Lou and I each had a small piece of our lasagna. I wrapped up the rest in foil and carried it to the four students who were staying in the flat below ours. Later, about eight o'clock, Lou went over to the women's dormitory. A few minutes later, he returned. "There are four young ladies there who haven't eaten since lunch," he said. "Can you give them some food?" Luckily, I'd gone shopping that morning, so I stuffed two grocery bags with bread, butter, cheese, peanut butter, honey, coke, bananas and cookies. When he returned from the dormitory, Lou told me the women students had said: "We will deal with the principal when we come back from holiday." But they wouldn't. Ovambos go to great lengths to avoid confrontation.

I wondered if the old apartheid fears were still at work. The dean of students, Rev. Hasheela, was an older, black, Ovambo gentleman and a genuinely nice fellow. Dirk, about twenty years younger, was coloured. Even though Rev. Hasheela had been general secretary of the large Lutheran Church in the north, he appeared to be afraid to challenge Dirk.

I felt sorry for the students who would have to suffer with Dirk as principal for the next two years. I wondered if his behavior would incite another student strike like the one we'd endured five years earlier. As much as I knew I would miss Namibia, our departure at the end of this academic year was starting to feel well timed.

Chapter 25
The Value of One Ox

*D*uring our month-long term holiday, we decided to visit Jonah and his congregation at Oshali. Johnny Haufiku, another former student, accompanied us. Once we left the highway, we became hopelessly disoriented. The roads were little more than tire tracks on the grass. Namibian men have no hang-ups about asking for directions, and Johnny told us to stop at three homesteads along the way. At each, we parked the Venture close to the five-foot-high stick fence surrounding the dwellings inside. We knew the fences were designed to keep the animals away from the living spaces, but we'd been inside enough homesteads to know that as many chickens and sleepy-eyed donkeys wandered about inside the fences as outside them. While Lou and I waited in air-conditioned comfort, Johnny hurried through the fence for a quick exchange with whomever he encountered. I watched the women, their heads wrapped in colorful scarves, hanging the family laundry on the fence. A little boy cast glances at us over his shoulder as he pushed his toy car made of wire through the dust. Two other boys were kicking a soccer ball back and forth. Their ball was a lopsided sphere of plastic bags bound together with rubber bands.

At the last homestead, Johnny emerged with a smile on his face. "We're almost there!"

Oshali wasn't much more than a smattering of homesteads in the bush, scarcely large enough to be called a village. Parched, stunted stalks of millet bore witness to another year of drought. The midday sun penetrated my wide-brimmed hat, and I had to peel my damp skirt away from my legs as I climbed out of our Venture.

An old man napped in the shade of a tree and two little girls in threadbare dresses peeped at us from behind the neglected church building. Several villagers, skinny and dressed in tattered clothes, had heard our vehicle and appeared from somewhere. Jonah came running, clad in his formal, black clerical shirt and trousers. He hugged us tightly. His effusive greeting surprised me. I wondered if he had felt like a castaway when his bishop assigned him to this forlorn outpost. He must have read my thoughts.

"When I first came to this place and saw the church building, I cried," he said. "It was in such bad condition. But I was able to help the congregation put glass in the windows, and we're doing what we can."

He took us to his home, a simple concrete-block building a few yards from the church. In the Ovambo culture, it is considered rude not to serve visitors some sort of a meal when they arrive at your home. Jonah invited us inside, and I saw four women working in the kitchen. They smiled and nodded when Jonah introduced us. On the kitchen door Jonah had taped a sign: "Wanted: A Wife." I pointed to the sign and raised my eyebrows. Jonah just grinned and shrugged.

A long, dark wood table consumed most of the space in his small dining room. Against one wall was a tall, matching sideboard cluttered with Bibles, books and papers. Jonah hurried back to the kitchen. A few minutes later, two ladies brought us the customary plastic bowl filled with hot soapy water and a towel. We washed our hands, and they served us lunch: fried liver and cans of Sprite.

All I really wanted was another cold drink and a nap, but Jonah insisted on showing us the border town of Oshikongo, so we climbed into the blessed air conditioning of the Venture. Until recently, Oshikongo had been off-limits to foreigners because it had been overrun with freedom fighters and refugees from Angola. I felt apprehensive about this trip, remembering that Angola was the country in which an entire generation had grown up knowing nothing but guerilla fighting, wrenching hunger, and fields strewn with land mines. Almost all vestiges of civilization in Angola, their schools, municipal government, and hospitals, had disappeared. A Namibian colleague had told us that many of these young Angolans, uneducated and unsocialized, were little more than savages.

The border crossing was teeming with activity: not gun-toting freedom fighters, but a steady stream of commerce. Over-sized trucks were lumbering back to Angola laden with furniture, cartons of food, and a few protesting goats tied to the top of the heap. I hadn't expected to see all the foot traffic. Women with impossibly huge burdens on their heads, babies swaddled on their backs, trudged through the checkpoint. I heard the soft slap-slap of their shoes, and I noticed that the Namibian guards rarely stopped them. I wondered what they had come to sell, or buy, in Namibia.

Jonah introduced us to his friend Petrus, a young man who worked in a furniture shop. Dressed in a crisp white shirt and tie, Petrus was surprisingly fluent in English which, he told us, he had taught himself. He described what it was like working in a retail shop in this border town. "You would be amazed to see how much money these Angolans have, probably from diamonds. Every week, big trucks come across the border, and these guys buy sofas—maybe six at a time. They always pay in cash, American dollars, and when they return to Angola they'll sell these sofas for five times what they paid for them." Black market "blood diamonds," converted to U.S. dollars, bought the sofas that were furnishing Angolan homes.

We returned to Oshali in mid-afternoon to meet the congregation. Jonah seated us on white plastic chairs at the front of the church; the parish hadn't yet come up with enough money to buy pews, or even plain wooden benches. In his pocket, Lou had a $200 check to present to the congregation. An industrious row of ants scurried in and out of the large crack in the wall next to my chair.

About forty congregants filed in, most of them wizened elders. Jonah invited Lou and me to step forward while he explained to his parishioners who we were and why we were there. When Lou handed Jonah the check, everyone applauded and a few women stood up and ululated. Several members of the congregation came forward with gifts for us: two clay pots and a basket.

Jonah asked one of the parishioners to join us. "Meme Susan, I would like you to meet Mrs. Shikomba. She is one of our deacons."

I recognized her as the elderly lady who had been supervising the kitchen workers at Jonah's house. She placed a necklace of white and pink beads around my neck.

"This part of the necklace is very valuable," she said, pointing to a thin strand of delicate, lavender-colored beads. "The beads come from Angola, and it is the kind of necklace that is worn by the wife of the king. Its value is one ox."

I was speechless. Although I had been the recipient of numerous gifts from generous Africans, none had the intrinsic value of this necklace. How do you thank someone for a gift that could have been exchanged for enough meat to feed dozens of people in this drought-plagued village?

The next day, when Jonah took us to the Shikomba homestead, we learned that in addition to her full-time job as Jonah's housekeeper, Mrs. Shikomba was also the primary caregiver for her blind, diabetic husband.

The twilight was casting deep purple shadows on the sand when we all walked over to the parsonage for the feast. Some of the white plastic chairs from the church now rimmed the walls of Jonah's dining room, and we squeezed in with the elders and their families. Other guests spread blankets in the sandy yard. One of the elders had donated a goat for the meal, and there were also chicken, rice, pumpkin, cabbage and the traditional millet porridge, *oshifima*. Jonah lit candles and oil lamps. After dinner, the women silently cleared the dishes and began washing them in huge galvanized tubs.

"How far must the women walk to get water, Jonah?" I asked.

"The well is about one kilometer from here."

The men left for home while the ladies continued washing dishes. Jonah sat and talked with us in the flickering light of the oil lamp. He told us about his experiences during the past two years. "It was hard to know where to begin this ministry. There is so much to do, and we have so little money. The name of this village, 'Oshali,' means 'a gift.' I hope that I can be a gift to these people."

He was particularly proud of his youth group, and he told us he was constantly encouraging them to stay in school and improve their education. "And I myself am taking correspondence courses to improve my academic standing. Can you send me an English grammar book, Meme Susan?" When we returned to Windhoek, I sent him several. I kept thinking about Oshali, the village that means "gift."

The new term began the first week in June, and Lou and I fell headlong into our classes with renewed energy. Perhaps it was because we knew this would be our last semester in Namibia. We were already feeling nostalgic—and worried, wondering what we would do when we left Namibia. The recent downturn of the economy had damaged our earlier plans for Lou to take early retirement, buy a low-maintenance townhouse, and make ourselves available for short-term, unpaid, missionary work. We had lost a lot of equity from the sale of our home, and both our pensions had been hit hard. But after five years of working and living in Africa, neither of us could easily imagine ourselves back into the careers we had left behind. As if he could read our thoughts, Harold, the Director for International Personnel in the Division for Global Mission in Chicago, sent us an e-mail asking us if we would consider going to Ghana in January to teach in a seminary there. His offer tempted us, but we knew our young adult children and my elderly parents would be disappointed—even angry—if we were to do that. We asked Harold to give us more time to consider his offer, and he agreed.

I scarcely had time to wash our clothes before we were repacking our suitcases for our two back-to-back weekend spirituality retreats, this time with the first-year students. They were splendid, and the students were so touchingly grateful. During the second retreat, Lou and I celebrated our thirty-fourth wedding anniversary. In one of our sharing groups, Kleopas said that this past December he was out tending his family's cattle when he encountered a lion! Against the advice of his friends, he chased it away. From that point, I began calling him The Lion King, and when he came by the flat a few nights later for his spirituality group meeting, we played the CD, "The Lion Sleeps Tonight" for him. Kleopas beamed.

The next morning I drove Angie and Benhi to the airport. Angie was returning to the United States having completed her two years working in the bishop's office in Windhoek. She said she would be finishing her college degree work and was thinking about enrolling in a Lutheran seminary. Benhi would also try to go to school to study music. I wondered how they would survive. Perhaps the church was providing them with generous scholarships.

Winter arrived; the nighttime temperatures were close to freezing, and we were glad to have small space heaters in our flat. We were the fortunate ones. There was no heat in the student dormitories or classrooms, and the students sat in class bundled up in their padded winter jackets and warm hats. Many of them took their lecture notes wearing woolen gloves. Even when it warmed up to what I considered a comfortable temperature in the afternoon—upper 60s to lower 70s—they were still shivering.

My third-year students were making progress with their short stories. Most had already submitted their first drafts to me. As I was leaving class one morning, Esron told me how much he had enjoyed the African novel we all read together in English-2. He said, "I would really like to read it again."

"Walk with me to the English office, Esron. I have extra copies of *Nervous Conditions* there."

"You know, it's really good that we are writing our own short stories this year. It puts us back in touch with our culture."

"What do you mean?"

"Oral tradition and telling stories used to be important in our culture, especially in the north. It was how parents taught their children. Every evening, after supper, we would all gather around the fire pit. All the families used to do this. The father gives everyone a chance to tell a story, even the small children.

"Many storytellers favor animals, especially the rabbit, jackal, and the tortoise. These are clever and brave animals, even though they are small. People even name their children after these animals: *kavandje* (jackal), *kalimba* (rabbit) and *kashima* (tortoise). But animals like the hyena and the monkey are thought to be bad and greedy, so they are never the heroes in Oshiwambo stories. You would never find someone naming their child *shimbungu* (hyena) or *lunghindji* (monkey)."

"So the parents used these stories the same way people have used proverbs or parables?"

"Exactly. And the elders told stories to teach children about the history of our culture."

"Is that still being done on the homesteads?"

Esron shook his head sadly. "Not so much these days. Our families are adopting Western culture and ways of living. Many children now go away to boarding schools, and there is no time for them to talk with their parents. Those who remain at home must do their homework in the evening. Some are working in shops, and some are not interested anymore. They would rather go to visit with their friends. There is no time for them to sit around the fire."

I unlocked the door to the English office and found a copy of the novel for Esron. "There are lots of copies of these here. Why don't you just keep this?" His eyes widened and he gripped my hand. "Thank you, Meme!"

As the days passed, Lou and I found ourselves spending more and more time thinking and talking about our return to the States. Our Division for Global Mission would be providing us with five months of resettlement salary to allow us time to find jobs and a place to live. Sitting at the computer in our small flat in Windhoek, I examined web sites of North Carolina real estate agencies. I told Lou I was going to make a file of townhouses and condominiums available in our price range. Lou said he would be looking for positions where he could serve as an interim congregational pastor within the synod. I found a surprisingly large number of positions in clinical research administration at Duke University Medical Center. One such position, nearly identical to the job I had left in Chapel Hill over five years ago, posted a salary that was $10,000 more than Lou's and my combined missionary salaries. We wondered why we weren't feeling very eager to return home.

I thought, too, about our Namibian faculty colleagues, who were considered well paid among their clergy peers. Although their housing was provided as a benefit, Namibian faculty members earned less than five thousand dollars per year. On this salary, most of them were still able to send their children to good schools and, with the assistance of their working spouses, provide for the needs of their families. The cost of goods and services in Namibia wasn't substantially different from what it was in the United States.

At the end of June, we traveled north again to attend the Northern Church's ordination service in Eenhana, a village in the far northern part of the country, not far from the Angola border. In our five years here, this was the one class of students that we had accompanied throughout their entire seminary career, and we had become close to many of these students. It was a joy to see them through to this moment.

On our way to Ovamboland, we enjoyed a quick visit to Etosha Game Park. We knew it would be one of our last trips to this special place. As we drove down a narrow gravel path leading to a small water hole, we met a herd of about twenty elephants leaving the hole, with several young ones in the group. We were busy taking photos when Lou looked up, sensing some movement on the right side of our vehicle. A large bull elephant was slowly heading our way. Apparently Papa Elephant was the rear guard for this family outing, and he didn't seem pleased at our intrusion. Lou respectfully put our car in reverse, and I was able to snap a photo as we backed away.

We crossed into Ovamboland mid-morning on Saturday. Oshivelo was a governmental veterinary checkpoint to screen the transport of meat and livestock for the control of hoof-and-mouth disease. During the war for independence, it had been a patrol point used by the South African army to monitor the movement of the Namibians, and many tales are still told of Namibians who had been retained for questioning—and worse—in the small stone buildings adjacent to the checkpoint. Two hours after we passed through the checkpoint, we arrived in Oniipa, where we would be staying at the home of our elderly friends, Pastor Eino and Meme Esther Amaambo. As had become our custom, we stopped to buy groceries at the local supermarket so that our two-night visit would not financially burden our hosts.

When we drove past the head offices of the Northern Church, we noticed a familiar white minivan parked in front. It was full of students who had left the seminary at four o'clock that morning. "Let's stop and see what their plans are," said Lou.

We all got out of our vehicles and greeted one another with hugs—as if we hadn't seen each other for months. They told us they were staying at the church guesthouse. Lou asked them what they were going to do for supper that evening and they told us the seminary kitchen staff had given them each two slices of bread and an apple. Lou and I quickly conferred, and decided that we had enough money in our discretionary fund to treat the group to supper at the local hotel, along with Rev. Amaambo and Meme Esther. We drove to the Punyu Hotel and arranged a menu with the restaurant. The bill that evening for sixteen of us was under $100.

We awakened with the crowing roosters on Sunday morning. Meme had been up since five o'clock, boiling water for us, and she called to me, "Meme Susan! There is warm water for washing." Although the Amaambo's home now had indoor plumbing and electricity, there was no hot water, so this was still a daily morning task for Meme Esther. She had filled a large tub with hot water, and had carried it into the bathroom, placing it next to another tub full of cold water. It was still dark at this hour on a cool winter morning. A small candle in a dish flickered on the stone shelf above the sink.

We left the Amaambo's home at seven o'clock, stopping along the way to pick up two elderly women who would be accompanying us: a neighbor, Meme Anna, and Meme Esther's sister, Meme Aina. We passed by the villages of Oshigambo and Ondobe, driving on a good gravel road. We were surprised to see all the trees in this part of Ovamboland, and Rev. Amaambo said that the Kwanyama people who lived in this part of northern Namibia had been better conservators of the land by not chopping down all the trees for their dwellings and for firewood. As we approached Eenhana, we began to see many people walking to church carrying their black Bibles and white plastic chairs. Unsure about where the church was located, we stopped to pick up a young man, and he directed us.

To accommodate the crowd, the service had been set up outside. Large sheets of webbed canvas lashed to wooden poles created an awning to protect people from the sun. An usher directed us to some chairs near the front, close to the altar. The service began with the clergy procession, Presiding Bishop Kaulinga resplendent in his mitre and cope. The ordinands were standing for a long time in front of the altar rail, and two of them, Paulus and Nandi, appeared to be unwell. Someone brought them chairs, and Meme Esther asked me if I could let them have the liter of water that I was carrying in my tote bag. Later, I asked Nandi if they had malaria, which was common among Namibians this time of year. "No," she said, "I think we may have eaten some bad meat last night."

I was remembering that the ordination service we attended two years ago had lasted five hours, and I wondered whether this one would be the same. The actual ordination was about an hour, and was followed by a full worship service, with two of the ordinands, Josephina and Nambili, leading the liturgy and a third, Selma, preaching the sermon. Seven separate choirs sang selections during the service. Following that, there were speeches and greetings by special guests, including the regional governor.

I glanced at the ordinands listening to the speakers. Their faces were somber. Were they contemplating the life of service—and penury—to which they had been called? Some of them would be placed in congregations that could barely support a pastor, and they would experience times when their salaries would not be paid for several consecutive months. Like Jonah. Others might have been thinking about the remote villages to which their church was sending them, forcing the separation of husbands and wives. Spouses who were fortunate enough to have jobs would have to remain behind to earn the money for their children's school fees, uniforms and other basic family needs.

Following the service (only four and a half hours this year), I greeted Josephina Mulongeni. When we hugged each other, our eyes filled with tears remembering all that we had experienced together at the seminary. This was our student who, in January 2000, had returned to the campus for her third year, barely able to walk. We had helped to nurse Josephina back to health when she returned from the hospital, providing meals, ice packs and encouragement, and today she was pain-free. Her mother, aunts and sisters embraced us, and although we couldn't understand their words, we knew they were expressing their gratitude. We walked across the dusty road to the diocesan centre where women of the congregation had been busily preparing a meal to feed the several hundred guests. Josephina told Lou that she hoped we could stop at her family's homestead later for a family party.

The sun was low in the winter sky when we reached the town of Ongwediva. Our elderly friends, Rev. Amaambo and Meme Esther, assured us that we would find the Mulongeni homestead by asking people along the way. We stopped at a service station, and Meme jumped out of the car. She approached the young man who was pumping petrol, and after a few minutes of his pointing and gesturing, Meme returned to the car. We drove through the town, and Meme said we should stop and ask more detailed directions at the next homestead, so Lou drive the car up to the compound. An elderly gentleman explained the way to Meme, and we set out across the sandy field. We hadn't gone more than a few meters when our wheels became hopelessly stuck in the deep, soft sand. We all climbed out and began to push: the three old ladies, Rev. Amaambo, and me. The old gentleman from the last homestead was hurrying toward us. He told us his name was Tate Simon, and he said that he would take us to the Mulongeni homestead. He squeezed next to us on the back seat, and called out directions to Rev. Amaambo who translated them to Lou. We zig-zagged along small paths through the millet fields and within a few minutes we arrived.

The Mulongeni compound was a large, well-established traditional homestead, consisting of about twenty small, round, thatched-roof huts. It resembled a maze. Several generations of the Mulongeni family lived here. An eight-foot tall wall constructed from branches and limbs surrounded every three or four huts, marking out family spaces. As we approached, we heard a family choir singing a hymn. We stood quietly at the back, leaning against the outer wall. Josephina was proudly wearing her black clergy robe and clerical collar, as well as her Paulinum graduation hood and cap. The choir sang another hymn while the guests came forward and placed their small cash offerings in the basket. The older women in their gaily-colored Oshiwambo muumuus could not restrain their exuberance any longer, and they burst forward into the center of the crowd, ululating, dancing, and waving horses' tails attached to stick handles. After a few moments, an older gentleman in a brown suit stepped forward and waved his hands at the memes, signaling that they should stop their dancing. He offered a prayer, and then Josephina invited Rev. Amaambo, Lou, and me to step forward. "These were my lecturers at the seminary," she said. For a moment she was halted by emotion as she explained her relationship to us. "These two white people from America were my Mommy and Daddy when I was suffering because of my back."

After the speeches, a young woman took my hand and led our group through the maze to a section of the homestead where we would be served a meal. A full moon was rising over the fields, but there was sufficient light for us to see the clay pots, gourds, and baskets hanging on the stick fences. Shirts, trousers, and dresses hung from the branches of a large, leafy tree, and the fork of the tree provided storage for more pots and baskets. Someone hurried to bring us some plastic chairs, but most of the guests just sat on the sandy ground. A pink plastic tub of soapy water was provided for hand-washing, and several teenagers served us our meal: pieces of roasted chicken in a clay pot and a mound of *oshifima* heaped high in a round, flat, tightly woven basket. Beverages included soft drinks and a large calabash filled with *oshikundu*, the traditional Ovambo millet beer. There were no dishes or utensils. We joined the other guests in selecting a piece of chicken from the pot. Each guest pulled off a portion of porridge from the mound, rolled it into a ball in the right hand, and dipped it into the cooking juices at the bottom of the chicken pot. An elderly gentleman brought a candle and thrust it into the sand in front of us.

As soon as we finished eating, Rev. Amaambo said we should leave. (We had learned that Ovambo people never linger after a meal.) Josephina gave us a final hug, and urged us to come back in two months for her wedding to Otto Akwaake. Otto worked in a mine in the far southern part of Namibia; Josephina had been sent by the Northern Church to serve a congregation in the far northwest. They would begin their marriage living about seven hundred miles apart.

Lou and I were having trouble thinking about our departure from Africa, only four short months away. When Lou said, "I'm not at all sure I want to give up my missionary identity," I knew what he meant. As a clergyman, Lou was accustomed to living and working within his "call," but this was the first time I had ever had a religious vocation, the first time I had felt total harmony between what I thought of as my spiritual self and my paid employment. As a commissioned missionary, I could say, "This is what I do. This is who I am. They are one and the same." I knew it would be different when we returned to the States. I would have to set aside *vocation*, and in its place simply look for *employment*.

The next week we received an e-mail from the Division for Global Mission, their standard form letter about reintegration: "Adjustment to life in the U.S. after a long period of time overseas is as difficult, or even more difficult, as the adjustment to living overseas." We learned that we would be required to attend a re-entry conference in Chicago.

Our first-year students continued to come to our flat twice a week for their Spirituality Group meetings. I served them all hot chocolate, and they shared with us some of their concerns. Fillemon, a quiet, gentle young man, said he was worried because he thought he wasn't being a good enough Christian. He had recently taken a part-time job working as a gardener for a man who lived near the campus so that he could earn enough money to pay his seminary school fees, but he was afraid that this was somehow causing him to be less of a Christian. We reminded him that Jesus' followers had to support themselves.

Toward the end of our gathering, Lusati Shimbike said, "We students are worried about what is going to happen to us next year when you are no longer here. You are the only faculty members who seem to care about us. The only ones who ask us how we are doing and really mean it."

One day I went to the small neighborhood grocery store for a few items. When the cashier learned I would soon be returning to America, she wanted to know if I had anything to sell. She wrote down her name and cell phone number for me. The young man who carried my groceries to the car said, "You are American."

"Yes,"

"But you speak English!" He was accustomed to most white people speaking Afrikaans.

"That's right," I said. "English is my first language."

From the surprised look on his face, I'm not sure he really believed me.

Chapter 26
Can Anyone Really Leave Africa?

*W*hen the large photo of rebel leader Jonas Savimbi's blood-splattered body sprawled across the front page of *The Namibian*, we knew that Angola's long, vicious civil war was over. The Kavango Region had reopened its roads to tourists so, one month before finishing our missionary service in Namibia, we decided to make a final visit to Mupini. Paul Muha had invited Lou to preach to his congregation for a special family service.

The sun was well up, and families were gathering outside the church when we arrived at eight-thirty. I noticed there were few cars in the wide sandy lot surrounding the church; almost everyone had walked. After prayers with the elders in Paul's small office, Lou and Paul donned their vestments and stepped outside to join the procession. More than one hundred children had lined up, most of them wearing white shirts and dark skirts or trousers.

October was springtime in Namibia, but the temperature was at least ninety-five degrees, probably higher inside the church. I struggled to stay alert, grateful whenever Paul told the congregation to rise so I could peel my damp skirt from my legs. Knowing that I was one of the guests of honor helped me keep my eyes open. When the congregation knelt for prayers on the hard mud-brick floor, I hoped they hadn't noticed I merely perched on the edge of the wooden bench. My American knees had already tested their limits of endurance through many similar services.

Four hours later we were getting ready to sing the final hymn when Paul stepped forward and pointed to the back of the church. Everyone turned around. Five more children's choirs had just arrived. Two-by-two, the children solemnly marched up the aisle, their skin glistening with perspiration and their eyes shining. Their parents squeezed into the few open spaces along the walls. These were families who lived deep in the bush and usually attended worship at one of the small synagogues. They had heard this was a special service and had walked many kilometers to worship at their mother church. The children formed neat rows, the teenagers in the back and the little ones grinning proudly in the front.

Their merriment banished my drowsiness, and we all settled back down for another hour of songs.

Paul told us the elders would be joining us for dinner at the parsonage. Twenty-two of us crowded into the dining room of the old Finnish mission home which, with its thick cement walls and high ceiling, felt twenty degrees cooler than outdoors. As was customary, we first washed our hands in bowls of soapy water. The meal included the traditional stiff gray millet porridge, pieces of fried chicken, smoked fish heads, liver, and a bowl of something that seemed to be goat intestines. We politely helped ourselves to a little of everything, but when no one was looking I slipped the intestine back into the serving bowl. It seemed a shame to let this delicacy go to waste, and the gentleman seated across from me was already enjoying his second helping.

After dinner, the elders invited us to see their new gardening project next to the Kavango River. To keep the animals away, the villagers had fashioned a fence from broken, tangled branches of thorn trees. They had planted new crops in neat, hoed rows, ready for the coming rainy season.

Paul said, "I am praying this congregation can raise enough money to buy a pump, so we can pump water from the river. Then we could really expand our garden. We could even set up a little shop on that new, tarred road to Nkurenkuru and sell our vegetables there. If we did that, the people in the village would have money for shoes and clothes and their children's school fees."

As we walked half a kilometer to the congregation's newly expanded cemetery, Paul told us that the previous week he had conducted seven funerals, most of them for victims of AIDS. He said this was not an unusual week. Dozens of mounds of fresh dirt—new graves—spoke louder than all the statistics we had read.

"I'm becoming exhausted." He sighed. "I enjoy doing pastoral counseling, and many are coming to me. Even people from other parishes. But there isn't enough time. I cannot visit the bereaved families the way I want to, and some weeks I hardly have enough time to prepare my sermon."

The next morning, Paul and a few men from the village took us fishing on the banks of the Kavango River. They had no rods, just a hook attached to a length of fishing line they baited, twirled around in the air, and tossed into the river. One young man came by in a dugout canoe and held up his catch for us to admire. Sitting there under a tree, listening to the mourning doves and gazing into the clear blue water, I began to understand why Paul loved this place so much.

As noon approached, Lou and I realized we would need to leave soon in order to reach our hotel in Tsumeb before dark.

"Wait!" said Paul. "The villagers have some gifts for you!"

One of the men from the fishing expedition gave Lou the fish he had caught, and a young woman hurried to where we were standing behind the parsonage. She handed me a chicken, its leathery little feet tied together with a piece of twine so it wouldn't run away. I knew she would have been shocked to learn that I had never held a live chicken before. Lou and I looked at each other, and the silent expression we exchanged said, "Here is another of those awkward expatriate moments."

"Paul," I said, "Lou and I will be staying in a hotel tonight. I don't think we can take these gifts with us. Maybe there is a widow in the village who can use them?"

"Oh, I know there is."

Embarrassed, we returned our gifts to him. I hoped the donors would understand. I felt tears welling up in my eyes, wondering if I would ever see Paul again. I wanted to hug him, but you don't do that with these formal Namibians, so I shook his hand and let my fingers linger on his.

"*Karenipo nawa*, Paul." Stay well.

Only a few more weeks remained before we would leave Namibia. What mixed feelings we had. On the one hand, the time felt right for us to be concluding our work here. On the other, we continued to grieve for what Lou kept calling our missionary identity. "It isn't just what we *do*, Susan. It's who we *are*. I have trouble even thinking about resuming our previous lives in the States." Exactly.

Just as always happened whenever we had left one congregation to move to another, these final weeks were filled with farewell parties and dinners. My dear friend, Penny, the seminary's Greek lecturer from England, was also leaving the country. She invited us to a dinner at her flat, the one just below ours. She introduced us to the other dinner guests, two white Namibian lecturers at the University of Namibia. Christo had taught theology for many years in the Department of Religion and Jean, his wife, taught Afrikaans literature. Christo said he would be retiring in February. He and Jean would be going to Princeton for two years. He said he had become disillusioned with the political, intellectual, and religious situation in Namibia.

"Just this week, I attended a meeting of department chairs at the University and I became so frustrated by this intentional drifting we always see."

"What do you mean?" asked Lou.

"Most of the Namibians are afraid to rock the boat. They're afraid, in this conservative political climate, to embrace any sort of vision that would stimulate these institutions to greater heights and depths of learning."

"You're right," said Lou. "It's what we've seen here, too."

"Yes," added Penny. "Even though I have only been here one year, I can tell that change only seems to happen when it is proposed by a foreigner. And unless the foreigner doing the suggesting is also the one to implement the change, nothing happens."

"Exactly!" said Lou. "And even when a change is implemented, it seems to wither and expire once the foreigner leaves."

"This behavior is similar to what I observed when I was faculty secretary," I said. "It's a form of magical thinking, isn't it? The notion that lengthy discussion of an agenda item is tantamount to taking action. Everyone leaves the meetings exhausted and mysteriously thinking that exhaustion means that work has been accomplished."

Christo and Jean nodded, knowingly.

And yet...Namibia was changing and would continue to change. In its own way. In African Time.

While the students wrote their final examinations, Lou and I continued our packing and sorting tasks. We sold our TV, copier, and evaporative cooler. We donated our printer to the seminary and our computer to our friend in the north, Dr. Munyika, who said he'd pick it up the next time he drove to Windhoek. A young woman at the head office of the Southern Church bought my sewing machine. We had to limit the size of our shipment to the States to avoid paying excess shipping costs. To make room for the clay pots and baskets we had been given by our Namibian friends, as well as the artifacts we had purchased, Lou and I created our own free rummage sale. We took armloads of clothing, books, house wares, and toiletries to the dining hall, and spread them out upon the tables. We told the students to help themselves to whatever they wanted.

One afternoon, Lou went to the post office to collect the mail for the seminary. We found our usual quarterly packet of material from our Division for Global Mission in Chicago, including the monthly church bulletin inserts called *Prayer Ventures*. These leaflets, sent to Lutheran congregations throughout the United States, contained daily prayers for particular missionaries in dozens of countries, many of whom we knew personally. I always read these carefully because it was a good way to learn what was happening with our missionary colleagues around the world, and I was startled to see the following entry for November 26: "Give thanks for Louis and Susan Bauer, who are completing their teaching ministry at Paulinum Seminary in Namibia, but will be starting a new call in Ghana at Good News Theological College and Seminary."

Nine months earlier, Harold, DGM's Director for International Personnel, had asked us to consider accepting those calls to Ghana. Although the positions had been tempting, we believed that we needed to return to the States for a while to reconnect with our family and culture, and establish a home base. So we declined—twice—once in January and again when Harold approached us in May. Apparently, word had not reached all units at DGM. Or was Harold trying to tell us something? Now we were wondering if we had made the wrong decision. Perhaps there was another way to think about our future. We might be able to return to the States for a year or so, spend some time with our family and pick up some temporary work, and later go to Ghana, if the positions were still available. We sent Harold an e-mail, outlining our thoughts.

The following morning, two men from the shipping company came to our flat and picked up our twenty-three boxes. We had arranged to have them shipped to a church in North Carolina, from which we would collect them and transport them to our mountain cottage in Virginia. How barren our flat looked without the colorful African art, piles of books, and happy clutter with which we'd lived for over five years.

That evening we took Bishop Diergardt and his wife out to dinner. I remembered the first time we'd met Bishop Diergardt, seven years earlier, when he had introduced himself to us with his apology for forgetting to pick us up from the airport. Since then, we had attended the wedding of his son and the funeral of one of his daughters, and been his sympathetic listeners when Johan van Wyk had filed a vindictive lawsuit against the Southern Church. Now, over our dinner of grilled ostrich steaks, Mrs. Diergardt said that in their retirement she and the bishop were raising five grandchildren. "They all live with us, you know. My husband spends all his time driving them to and from their different schools."

When the waitress brought our desserts, the bishop told us the Church had stopped providing medical insurance for all of its current and retired pastors, so he and his wife could no longer afford to buy the blood pressure medication they needed. "Last year, when we visited the United

States, some people in companion synods in New Jersey and Iowa promised to help us out financially with monthly contributions. So far, they have not done so."

"Are you able to send e-mail from your home?" asked Lou.

"No, we don't have a computer in our home, and I don't really think I can do this from the church headquarters. People in that office are very…curious, and I wouldn't want them to know."

"Come to our flat tomorrow morning," said Lou. "We still have our computer and our Internet connection, so I can help you send e-mails to those people."

When the bishop came to the flat, we also gave him the money that we had left in our discretionary fund. As he was leaving, a fierce wind slammed our front door shut. An unusual cold front had arrived from Antarctica, and that night the temperature dipped into the mid-forties. Since we were usually complaining about the heat at this time of the year, I had packed our sweaters in the cartons that were on their way to the States. Lou and I wrapped blankets around our shoulders and stepped out onto the balcony to look at the stars. I glanced at the bottlebrush tree in the large clay pot in the corner of the balcony. Two baby birds, one blue and the other brown, their downy feathers fluffed, were sleeping on the same branch. Their tiny heads were tucked under their wings. They must have been happy to find a bedroom perch away from the cold wind, and they didn't seem bothered about being from different tribes. They didn't move while we stood there watching them. We tiptoed back through the balcony door into the living room. Neither of us felt sleepy, so I boiled water for tea and we picked up the threads of the conversation we had been having for the past few months.

"I'm wondering if we made a big mistake when we declined that invitation to go to Ghana directly from Namibia," said Lou. "I had no idea leaving Africa would feel as painful as this. Sure, it's relinquishing the missionary identity, but it's also the feeling that there's really nothing back in the States to look forward to. Other than seeing the kids, of course."

"I doubt we would be a big part of their lives, anyway, especially with Jason in Denver and us in North Carolina or Virginia. Who knows where Megan will decide to live once she's finished nursing school?" I brought two steaming mugs of tea into the living room. "You're right about not having anything to look forward to," I continued. "Do you know what really bothers me the most? The thought of having to return to some sort of boring desk job after having experienced all this."

"Or just knowing that when things get rough we won't be able to take off for a few days and rent a bungalow in Etosha. Some of the happiest times I've had in Namibia have been spent watching the elephants and the zebras at a waterhole, or taking a game drive in the late afternoon."

"Or going to guest lodges like Schonfeld, or visiting people like the Amaambos at their homesteads. And then there were those incredible vacations in Cape Town and Durban and KwaZulu Natal. I almost feel guilty about our adventures."

Lou didn't say anything, so I continued, "I know that a lot of other missionaries live in much more primitive situations than ours. How many of them have telephones and a microwave and computers with Internet access right in their homes? Sometimes I have felt guilty about that."

"You shouldn't," said Lou. "I'm sure many of our colleagues in Japan, and Eastern Europe and even other African countries have the same amenities. We have both worked hard here. Think about how much you have given of yourself. Think about how simple a life we have led. We've learned that we can happily live with a fraction of the stuff we had back in the States."

My tea was getting cold. "There's something else, Lou. I'm ashamed to say this, but I have enjoyed feeling, well, special. I like telling people we meet back home that I live in Africa. It feels exotic and adventurous, and I guess I like that. I have loved living as an expatriate in a foreign country. When I was in college, I used to think how marvelous it would be to have the opportunity to live and work in another culture. I feel so very blessed to have had that experience. I guess my motivations for wanting to stay in Africa aren't very pure, are they?"

"Do you think you are the only missionary who feels that way?"

I shrugged.

"Of course you aren't. I don't think there's anything wrong in enjoying our special status. It's the same thing I mean when I talk about missionary identity. This has not been an easy journey, and it's not going to be an easy departure. Now, let's check our e-mails and go to bed."

Although it was bedtime in Namibia, people were still at their desks in Chicago. When we connected to the Internet, we saw that Harold had sent us an e-mail while we'd been sipping tea: "I have told the seminary in Ghana about you, and they are very excited to have you. I want you to go there as soon as we get your paperwork in order. You will teach practical theology, Lou. Susan, you will teach English." Harold said that DGM would keep us on the payroll during the next three months back in the United States. At the conclusion of our home leave we would travel to Ghana, and stay there for two years. He explained that Good News was an African Independent Church (AIC) seminary. "You will love Ghana," he concluded. "The people are the friendliest of any in Africa. Try to let me know your decision before you leave Namibia, so we can get to work on your visa applications."

"Well," laughed Lou, "Harold seems to have made up our minds for us. I guess we'll have a chance to test our 'missionary identity,' won't we?"

He was right. Ghana would be a far less developed country than Namibia. We already knew that the seminary in Accra did not have telephone lines. Would the campus even have reliable electricity and plumbing? I remembered learning that Ghana had been the first African country to gain its independence—in 1957. Namibia had been the last. How fitting to conclude our missionary work where our adventures had begun ten years ago: in West Africa.

Our Air Namibia jet taxied down the runway. I pressed my nose against the window and tried to imprint the purple mountains upon my memory. I imagined Matheus driving back to the campus from the airport, and I wondered if he was remembering all the previous times he'd taken us to the airport and picked us up, all the conversations and adventures we'd shared. I knew he would miss us as much as we would him. The plane banked and turned northeast, toward Johannesburg. The sun glinted off the wing, and I leaned back and closed my eyes.

I pondered the vocational choices we had made. Perhaps stepping into the vast unknown territory of an African missionary vocation did require a measure of bravery. Although I had never considered myself a person of great courage, I realized I had very few misgivings about the choice. Perhaps, after all, I didn't choose this vocation. Maybe it chose me. I remembered Paul Muha's drummer. The one who disappeared into the Kapende Tree. I knew that I had heard that drummer after all. I knew that he was calling me back to Africa.